TOWARDS A SPATIAL SOCIAL POLICY

Bridging the Gap Between Geography and Social Policy

Edited by Adam Whitworth

P

First published in Great Britain in 2019 by

Policy Press
University of Bristol
1-9 Old Park Hill
Bristol
BS2 8BB
UK
t: +44 (0)117 954 5940
pp-info@bristol.ac.uk
www.policypress.co.uk

North America office:
Policy Press
c/o The University of Chicago Press
1427 East 60th Street
Chicago, IL 60637, USA
t: +1 773 702 7700
f: +1 773-702-9756
sales@press.uchicago.edu
www.press.uchicago.edu

© Policy Press 2019

British Library Cataloguing in Publication Data
A catalogue record for this book is available from the British Library

Library of Congress Cataloging-in-Publication Data
A catalog record for this book has been requested

978-1-4473-3790-4 hardback
978-1-4473-3791-1 paperback
978-1-4473-3792-8 ePdf
978-1-4473-3793-5 ePub

The right of Adam Whitworth to be identified as editor of this work has been asserted by him in accordance with the Copyright, Designs and Patents Act 1988.

Cover design by Clifford Hayes
Front cover image: iStock

Contents

List of figures and tables

Figures

Tables

Notes on contributors

Adam Whitworth is a senior lecturer at the University of Sheffield, UK. Situated in a geography department and with a background in social policy, his research into employment policy and public service integration spans the disciplinary divide through its focus, amongst other priorities, on illuminating the myriad nature and implications of the frequently neglected and misunderstood spatialities of social policy scholarship and practice.

Martin Jones is Deputy Vice-Chancellor of Staffordshire University, UK. A geographer by background, he is an interdisciplinary researcher working in the broad area of society and space and specifically on the interface between economic and political geography.

Chris Philo, University of Glasgow, UK, conducts research focusing on the historical, cultural and rural geographies of mental ill-health as well as across a range of cognate interest around Foucauldian studies, children's geographies and historical and contemporary figurations of public space.

Anna Minton is a reader in architecture at the University of East London, UK, and an expert in contemporary housing studies. A regular media commentator, her books include *Ground Control* and, most recently, *Big Capital* (London: Penguin).

Jay Wiggan is a lecturer in the School of Social and Political Sciences at the University of Edinburgh, UK. His research concentrates on the politics and governance of active labour market policy including the temporal and spatial variability of the 'activation' turn in public policy and its manifestation in policy discourse.

Jessica Pykett is a senior lecturer in the School of Geography, Earth and Environmental Sciences at the University of Birmingham, UK. She is a social and political geographer with research interests in citizenship, governance and political subjectivities. Her research focuses on affective and emotional techniques of governance, the influence of neuroscience and behavioural science on public policy and economic theory, and political geographies of emotional regulation.

Richard Harris is a social geographer by training and is Professor of Quantitative Social Geography at the University of Bristol, UK. His research encompasses spatial statistical analyses of geographies of education and learning, socio-spatial segregation and ethnic polarisation, and supporting quantitative and statistical literacy amongst geographers and undergraduate social scientists. His research has a particular focus on the application of spatial statistics and geodemographics in public policy and urban geography.

Scott Orford is a professor in the School of Geography and Planning at Cardiff University, UK. His research interests are in GIS and quantitative human geography, particularly modelling socioeconomic processes using techniques that are sensitive to spatial context.

Brian Webb is Senior Lecturer in Spatial Planning at Cardiff University, UK, with research interests in the spatial analysis of urban and regional environments and comparative intergovernmental policy analysis. Through his research he seeks to understand multi-scalar interactions and how space is conceptualised, lived and developed depending on the scale of analysis from the neighbourhood to the national level and beyond.

John Clarke is Emeritus Professor in Social Policy and Criminology at the Open University, UK. His research focuses on the ways in which welfare states have been transformed since the late twentieth century, with a particular interest in how the relationships between welfare, state and nation have been reconstructed. A continuing focus of his research has been explorations of what the 'social' in social policy means, and how its meanings are constructed and contested, particularly in relation to dominant political and managerial conceptions of the public and the public interest.

1

Introduction

Adam Whitworth

Like much of today's economy, modern-day academia is, for many good reasons, driven by specialisation. Structured into a strikingly standardised set of disciplinary labels and departmental units internationally, this specialisation affords individual scholars the ability to become leading experts in their particular fields, driving forward ideas and understandings within their specific disciplines and sub-disciplines. That progress is evident in the escalation in the volume of specialist sub-disciplinary academic journals and published journal articles.

The intellectual contributions that have flowed in terms of new ideas, theories, methods and empirical understandings have been considerable. So too have been the wider social, economic, cultural and technological gains from this intellectual specialisation. The instrumentalisation (both attempted and actual) of higher education by national governments towards these wider non-academic (and especially economic) objectives in recent years continues to be a source of debate (Jazeel, 2010; Phillips, 2010; Pain et al., 2011; Williams, 2012), with academics rightly determined both to retain their intellectual freedom and to maximise the value and benefits of their expertise in the wider world. And the contributions of academia's intellectual specialisation are considerable. Within the UK, for instance, the recent evaluations of 'impact' within the university system's Research Excellence Framework (REF) exercise testifies to a vibrant array of significant benefits to the UK's wider social, cultural, economic and political world generated through and from its higher education research expertise (REF, 2014). The upcoming update in REF2021 looks set to show a similarly rich set of research contributions to life beyond the academy and, indeed, will represent a notably larger weighting for UK universities in the measurement of their overall research quality within this assessment exercise. Indeed, it has recently been claimed by a US scholar that academic research has been key to 40% of top inventions since the 1950s (Times Higher Education, 2017).

Therefore, although in many ways highly productive, the risk of this linked structural and intellectual specialisation within modern academia is the inevitable tendency to look inwards within one's own disciplinary and, narrower still, sub-disciplinary boundaries rather than connecting to the wider range of distinct yet often fertile related agenda and ideas beyond those intellectual walls. Whilst affecting all fields of intellectual study, these concerns have been particularly keenly recognised and discussed within social science scholarship. This is understandable given the nature of the social sciences, as virtually all of the specialist research areas under study interact with and are informed by wider perspectives within and beyond those particular disciplinary interests. The growing chorus for the types of interdisciplinary social science scholarship that recognise the multifaceted nature of today's social, political and economic grand challenges are welcome and important. At the same time, however, such calls act only as a limited counterweight to the prevailing underlying pressures, trends and logics towards specialisation that exist across academia as both a sector and scholarship practice.

Rooted in this current context of social science scholarship, the motivation of this edited collection is to shine a light on the fertile, multifaceted yet largely unexplored links between the concepts, perspectives, knowledges and methodological approaches of human geography and their contributions to what remains a largely aspatial social policy discipline and set of applied policy practices across the public, private and third sectors – despite the myriad spatial natures, influences and impacts of that social policy scholarship and policy practice, as the chapters illustrate.

By making explicit these neglected crossovers between human geography and social policy thinking the chapters in this edited collected seek to unlock richer layers of conceptual, empirical, methodological and policy understanding in both academic social policy scholarship and professional policy practice. The hope more broadly is also to encourage others to similarly continue those interdisciplinary explorations in their own thinking, scholarship and policy activities.

Why though the need? In what ways are the concepts, perspectives, knowledges and methods of human geography unhelpfully divorced from social policy scholarship and practice, and what is the value-added of their richer connection? And in what ways can this richer pull-through of human geography's unique perspectives into applied policy scholarship and practice help to enrich and strengthen human geography as an academic discipline?

Spatially blinkered social policy

Though the practice of social policy has in some form always been a feature of human societies it was not until the mid-twentieth century that social policy was recognised as an independent scholarly discipline, even if it was at that time with a particular lens towards public administration and primarily in the Anglo-Saxon of the UK and US. Social policy today is radically transformed from those humble beginnings, even if the concerns of social justice and well-being remain important themes within its far wider canvas. Although social policy scholarship remains dominated by the advanced economies, it is as an academic discipline increasingly global in its reach. Its range of concerns and perspectives have also widened significantly since its origins. In terms of thematic foci social policy has expanded far beyond public administration, and where public administration is under study its scope has evolved beyond the historic focus on the management of state delivery into a multifaceted study of myriad governance and delivery arrangements across increasingly complex mixed economies of welfare over the state, private, voluntary and informal sectors. In terms of its thematic reach and styles of scholarship too, modern social policy scholarship has been transformed, with a wide range of normative, conceptual, comparative and empirical analyses that were not at its original core now key to modern social policy scholarship. This is all to the good in creating what is today a rich, vibrant and relevant intellectual discipline and community of research scholarship.

Indeed, partly as a consequence of its breadth and depth, social policy as an academic discipline is notoriously difficult to define (Alcock et al., 2012; Spicker, 2014), fuzzy at its edges and slipping imperceptibly into a range of aligned disciplines such as politics, sociology, economics, education, criminology, urban studies, housing studies and – our focus in this edited collection – human geography.

For social policies are inevitably made, implemented and felt in spatial contexts – national government offices, regional and local governments, frontline provider sites, service users travelling to and from their families and communities between different welfare services, and the spatially embedded lives, relationships and identities shaped and situated geographically by the ways in which social policies define and treat differently positioned citizens.

And the research which focuses on those and other social policy topics is equally infused with spatial relevance and the corresponding geographic potential to enrich understanding of those topics. Yet social policy as an academic discipline routinely neglects these spatial dimensions in its thinking and analysis. Rather, geography flows through discrete debates and particular sub-disciplinary fields of social policy enquiry.

Global and comparative social policy research, for example, provides vibrant sub-disciplinary fields of enquiry. Indeed, comparative social policy might be understood more fully as a conceptual, methodological and empirical approach and mode of thinking rather than a mere sub-disciplinary field. These comparisons of policy systems and approaches help analysts to draw out deeper understandings about policy options, choices, dependencies and implications, enabling scholars to more fully reflect back on particular national policy approaches. An entire social policy sub-literature has emerged in this vein around welfare typologies, with geography at its heart via the comparative assessment and subsequent categorisation of typically national policy systems (Esping-Andersen, 1990; Arts and Gelissen, 2002; Danforth, 2014; Powell and Barrientos, 2015).

Geography flows similarly through social policy debates around governance and policy processes where issues of de/recentralisation and multi-scalar policy governance are frequently key (Birrell, 2009; Greer, 2009; van Berkel et al., 2011). A comparative perspective again helps to highlight the alternative trajectories that different countries take and the implications for service user experiences and social and spatial outcomes. In single national contexts such scholarship highlights that these trajectories are often complex, path dependent and contested politically as policy actors at local, regional and central tiers of government act and react iteratively to layer up always evolving policy systems that resemble complex, oscillating and often contested and conflicting multi-scalar policy patchworks. In the UK context, for instance, the geographical nature of those social policy debates are clear in relation to the devolution of key and increasing social policy powers from Westminster to the Scottish Parliament, where a visibly more progressive alternative social policy trajectory to the rest of the UK is gradually being carved out. Within England, similar political and policy debates are circling around a series of the key urban city-region Mayoral Combined Authorities pushing for more powers in order to deliver better tailored and integrated social policies across their differing local areas.

And moving down to the level of communities and service users, geography can again be seen to flow through these social policy debates and scholarship. Area-based research perspectives and policy approaches help to illuminate that key social policy concerns around outcomes and equity take on powerful spatial dimensions as well as the more commonly analysed social dimensions across different types of people. And though there remains uncertainty around whether people-based or place-based policy interventions are more effective in tackling disadvantage (Griggs et al., 2008), specifically area-based policy interventions are frequently implemented to seek to tackle geographical concentrations of particular target policy outcomes – employment, crime and housing deprivation for example. Naturally, however, even where social policies do not have an explicitly geographical focus (as most social policies do not), and indeed where geography may not even be in the minds of policy makers and analysts, social policies almost always have indirect spatial impacts that further or weaken existing spatial inequalities in systemic ways through their varying effects on different types of individuals distributed in patterned ways across space.

Area-based research perspectives also help to highlight the ways in which those spatial concentrations and community characteristics interact with individuals and families and affect their opportunities and outcomes. Poverty research, for example, has been enriched by the growing attentiveness to individuals' lived experiences and to the importance of the particular embedded and varying nature of the wider spatial contexts in which individuals live those experiences (Patrick, 2014; McKenzie, 2015). Childcare (Skinner, 2005) and criminological (Wiles and Costello, 2000) research has in differing ways similarly brought important new insights to bear on social policy understandings and practices through greater awareness and understanding of the importance of routine travel patterns and spatial rhythms to key social policy outcomes (in these cases childcare utilisation, female employment, gender equality, crime) as well as to the effectiveness of policy interventions to affect them.

However, a key motivation and rationale for the chapters that follow is a recognition that the distinct conceptual, methodological and empirical insights and contributions that human geography has to offer social policy scholarship and applied practice have an uncertain place in, and relationship with, modern social policy scholarship – at once both present and absent, core and partial.

Whilst geography does flow through particular debates in social policy scholarship and does appear within social policy practice, its treatment is highly limited in both its reach and its depth. For in academic social policy scholarship space features only in a particular minority of sub-disciplinary debates and predominantly only in a particular absolute Cartesian understanding of what space is and can be, neglecting the fuller insights and contributions that a richer understanding of geography has the potential to offer social policy scholarship and practice. In this way the conceptual, empirical and methodological potentials of human geography thinking to social policy scholarship and practice is highly partial and with considerable potential left unexplored and untapped.

And there is much potential to explore at the interface of human geography and social policy both as scholarship and professional practice. As an academic discipline human geography is replete with alternative conceptualisations of space that are multidimensional, diverse, subtle, complex and dynamic (Crang and Thrift, 2000; Hubbard et al., 2002; Cresswell, 2004; Hubbard and Kitchin, 2011). As several of the following chapters explore in different ways, this conceptual spatial richness offers the potential to bring new dimensions and layers to the understanding of social policy issues and responses. Methodologically, as well as sharing core quantitative and qualitative research methods with social policy scholarship, human geography uniquely brings new methodological possibilities through spatial statistics and quantitative geographic information systems (GIS) as well as increasing innovations around qualitative GIS. Illuminating these unique disciplinary potentials from human geography scholarship for key social policy debates are key motivations for the chapters that follow.

Policy geographies: missed opportunities and ongoing debates

And for human geography? Looking at the same policy–geography intersection from the other direction, the extent of human geography's connection with applied policy concerns, and the realisation of its potential to inform those policy concerns, have been an ongoing and at times somewhat explosive topic of debate within its scholarly community. At a time of such complexity and discord in the world around us it is now more than ever important that human geography as an intellectual discipline shares its unique perspectives and potentials as we seek to tackle the grand challenges that face us nationally and globally.

In a repeat of the discipline's similar existential debate in the 1970s (Coppock, 1974), the early-to-mid 2000s was a period of intense debate within the discipline of human geography about the relevance of its academic scholarship and external non-academic contributions. At heart the debate reflected a shared concern by many human geography scholars of a 'growing dealignment' (Peck, 1999: 132) from, and 'missing agenda' (Ward, 2005: 311) of, spatially relevant policy engagement and influence. If Peck's balanced interventions in many ways launched and framed the debate (Peck, 1999, 2000), the key message was, as Massey (2001: 12) put it, that 'we may be underplaying our hand' as a discipline.

The losses were considered intellectual, disciplinary and applied: lost critical incisiveness that richer policy insights might bring (Philo and Miller, 2014); concerns that academic geography was via its claimed detachment and insularity becoming less highly regarded inside and outside the academy and less critically incisive (Peck, 1999; Martin, 2001; Massey, 2001); and a waste of the discipline's undoubted critical and empirical insights and potential contributions to policy and society as well as a neglect of the significant spatial impacts of policy (whether aspatial or explicitly spatial in their focus) (Peck, 1999; Martin, 2001; Massey, 2001).

For some more applied geographers the issue was the abstracted content and style of much modern human geography scholarship (Hamnett, 1997; Markusen, 1999: 880; Anderson and Smith, 2001: 7; Martin, 2001: 189). Martin (2001: 189) argued unequivocally that 'much contemporary social and economic geography research renders it of little practical relevance for policy, in some cases of little social relevance at all'. More critically oriented scholars rightly highlighted the potentially disruptive nature of critical geographical thinking and the importance of retaining intellectual autonomy (Fuller and Kitchin, 2004; Imrie, 2004; Mitchell, 2004). At a time of increasing instrumentalisation of academic knowledge within the growing and problematically operationalised 'impact' agenda such cautions are important to note (Pain et al., 2011). Somewhat ironically, for some 'critical scholars' the depiction of policy work slipped frequently into crude accusations of uncritical, atheoretical empirical work that responded blindly to the whims and questions of policy makers (Fuller and Kitchin, 2004; Imrie, 2004; Burawoy, 2005). Ideas of servile contractual and consultancy-based relationships around already narrowly predefined analyses and evaluations were common targets, mirroring the crude caricatures of critical geographies painted by some more applied colleagues.

For those in the centre ground seeking to argue in a balanced way that human geographers could do more to inform social policy scholarship and practice within their distinctive spatial thinking it was Massey and Peck who made the case most clearly and most deeply (Peck, 1999; Massey, 2001). Focusing on ideas of 'space, and the possibilities for its reimagination' (Massey, 2001: 14) with respect to policies to tackle spatial poverty and inequality, Massey argues that the problem with policy thinking in this context is one of 'spatial fetishism' (Massey, 2001: 16) – a misplaced obsession with geographical scales, surfaces and boundaries when the causal processes of persistent geographical poverty and inequality rest instead on a relational view of space rooted in the power-infused webs of social relations across and between places and people. Yet beyond that spatial misspecification in policy debates Massey (2001: 7–8) expressed 'gloom not so much at the regional inequality itself as at the whole conceptual framing of the question … [yet] the import of [human geography's] philosophical and conceptual arguments was nowhere to be seen'.

The (mis)reading of 'policy' was a key implicit source of disagreement within the policy geographies debate of the 2000s. On the one hand, a more conceptual, disruptive and reframing 'deep' view of spatial policy scholarship is evident upstream in the policy process focusing around reframing questions, ideas and foundation of applied policy work (Peck, 1999, 2000). On the other hand, an alternative view from more critical scholars unnecessarily and unhelpfully boxed spatial policy research as being narrower, more technically oriented and policy-directed, if not co-opted (Harvey, 1974; Mitchell, 2004). An important distinction between the two is that those upstream phases of the policy process relate to the human geographer's role in understanding, (re) conceptualising and (re)framing the later phases of the policy process whilst those 'downstream' phases focus more specifically on the implementation and evaluation of particular policies.

Central to Massey and Peck's interest in this debate – and to the interest of this edited collection – is in exploring those currently neglected deep upstream philosophical and conceptual linkages between human geography and social policy to better enable human geography to utilise its unique theoretical, methodological and empirical spatial insights to more fully reconceptualise policy agendas – their issues, nature, problematisation and possible solutions (Peck, 1999, 2000; Massey, 2001). Language, ideas, understandings of issues and their causes – and the distinctively geographical dimensions to these conceptualisations across many fields of policy activity – in these ways become central to what policy geographies can and should be: '[G]eographical imaginations … are not simply mirrors; they are *in some sense* constitutive figurations; *in some sense* they "produce" the world in which we live and within which they are themselves constructed' (Massey, 2001: 10).

Structure of the book

Situated within and motivated by these disciplinary concerns, joint needs and missing connections, the following chapters of this edited collection focus in different ways on a variety of currently untapped issues at this interface between human geography and social policy scholarship. Taken together its chapters draw out and develop a range of new conceptual, methodological, empirical and policy insights for the richer understanding of the themes that they examine. In doing so the collection highlights the fertile intellectual terrain that exists at this disciplinary intersection and offers encouragement for others to continue to explore this social policy–geography interface in their own research and policy activities.

The potential points of productive connection at the interface of the two disciplines is recognised to be multidimensional in nature cutting across conceptual, methodological and empirical domains. The chapters speak to each of these key dimensions structured across its three main sections – *Concepts*, *Themes* and *Methods*. A final *Retrospective* looks back across the contributions to crystallise their key messages as well as looking forward to future implications and research agenda.

In the first section the focus is on drawing out alternative theoretical ideas within human geography scholarship around the multiple possible understandings of space and demonstrating their potentials to inform social policy scholarship and practice. In these ways the chapters draw attention to the body of often neglected conceptual spatial thinking and illustrate ways in which their recognition and incorporation into social policy is able to add new perspectives and layers to frequently aspatial policy thinking.

Jones's work looks instead at the evolving discourses, natures and contradictions of recent phases in decentred state making in the UK, giving voice to what Jones describes as their 'somewhat silent space making'. In particular, Jones argues that localities must be understood not only in terms of absolute spaces on maps but also as relative and relational dynamic entities immersed with connections, nodes, flows and emotionally embodied meshes and networks. The implications of these perspectives are striking. Not only do boundaries become fuzzy, variable and permeable but the nature of localities themselves become critical objects of enquiry and identification in ways that are able to incorporate the inherent interactions between their linked material and imagined identities. Such insights tease out critical inconsistencies and contradictions in localised economic policy strategies in the UK that adopt a discourse of universal localised prosperity alongside a spatial policy reality of extended spatial poverty and inequality underpinned by inbuilt failures in the UK's systems of regional economic governance.

Instead, Philo's chapter focuses on Foucault's vast and rich body of scholarship, concentrating in particular on the role of space within Foucault's writing on power, discipline and governmentalities. As such, the chapter positions these elements of Foucault's oeuvre as offering a conceptually rich spatial history of social policy.

As noted, the relevance of geography to social policy scholarship is frequently restricted to a partial set of explicitly scalar debates – 'global' social policy, 'national' welfare regimes', 'regional' devolution, 'community' regeneration, and so on. This both rests on a limited understanding of the conceptual, thematic and methodological richness of human geography scholarship and unhelpfully restricts the intellectual contact points between the two disciplines to an unduly narrow set of sub-debates, both of which serve to artificially undercut the potential layers, types and range of synergies and contributions between them. The central *Themes* section aims instead to highlight the relevance of exploring the interface between geography and policy scholarship across mainstream policy debates and, in so doing, to encourage others to do similarly in their policy scholarship. Four chapters from Minton, Whitworth, Wiggan and Pykett respectively take interdisciplinary spatial policy perspectives on key issues and debates across both disciples.

Situated within her wider research programme around urban justice and spatial neoliberalism, Minton's chapter takes as its focus the Grenfell Tower fire of 2017 and in particular the broader housing context within which that tragic fire must, she argues, be understood. In particular, the chapter explores ways in which place and housing have in the UK been structured, narrated and framed not as spaces for individuals, families and communities to coexist and flourish but instead as commodified assets to be sold and resold to the highest bidder through various positively spun 'placemaking' strategies. Whilst the ultra-wealthy gain a housing playground to enjoy, the consequences for ordinary individuals and communities is argued to be systemic housing insecurity that underpins not only social cleansing and vulnerability to landlord exploitation but also normalised housing-led mental health harms.

Picking up on ideas elaborated within Jones's chapter on alternative conceptualisations of space in UK localism, Whitworth explores the ways in which the distinct absolute, relative and relational conceptualisations of space can be interwoven with Hägerstrand's classic spatial diorama in order to add new layers of understanding to our analytical and policy understandings of welfare-to-work policies. With a focus on service user perspectives, the chapter draws out new perspectives and insights from across these alternative spatial perspectives that can help to make activation policies not only more effective but also a better experience for service users and the frontline practitioners tasked with supporting their range of whole-person needs.

Echoing some of Peck's work on fast policy transfer (Peck, 2015), Wiggan looks at the transnational flows of financialised logics and approaches to social policy thinking and design. The chapter focuses specifically on the recent experimentation in social investment bonds (SIBs) as a new financial vehicle to structure the financing, payment and incentive structures of a growing array of social policy interventions. In doing so the chapter understands SIBs as the latest iteration of the ongoing neoliberal search for spatio-temporal fixes to inherent contradictions within the processes of capitalist accumulation, extending and deepening the reach of neoliberal capitalist policy approaches in response to crises of its own creation. Taking the area of youth employability policy as its empirical case study, Wiggan sets out ways in which this marks a distinct process of extensive financialisation that takes finance capital into the new spatial scale of person-centred policy interventions. In doing so this process is argued to create new financial chains of value (Sokol, 2015) that transform geographically rooted ('problem') populations and welfare delivery into spatially detached investable products that reflect a reallocation in the capture of value creation between capital(s) as well as between capital and state.

Pykett's chapter zooms in on the scale of the individual and, indeed, further still, into the ways in which 'nudge' policy interventions based on behavioural economics and the (re)framing of subject's choice architectures are carving out new neurological spatial scales at which social policies are increasingly targeted. Recognising that individuals do not behave according to the neoliberal maxims of economic rationality, Pykett argues that there has been a shift in emphasis from structural, through individuated and towards neuro-molecular scales of explanation for social problems. In response the chapter outlines a critical neuro-geography to highlight the strategic but typically overlooked importance of spatialities – including sites and milieux, scalar claims and distributed assemblages of policies and power – to these new and growing forms of governance targeted at the brain, behaviour and soul.

In the third section of the book the focus shifts to the value-added to be gained for social policy scholarship and practice from greater awareness both of the relevance of the often neglected spatial dimension to empirical policy analysis as well as to the use of some of the spatial methodological perspectives and techniques specific to human geography as a discipline. Two chapters from Harris and from Orford and Webb reflect on recent innovations in spatial methodologies and their implications in terms of the additional insights that these types of spatial methods can offer typically aspatial policy analysis.

Statistical regression analysis is a staple quantitative technique of social policy evaluation and analysis, yet, as Harris's chapter discusses, it is applied almost universally without regard for the geographical nature of the social and economic phenomena that those social policies interact with and act upon. As Harris discusses, this spatial neglect not only routinely violates technical assumptions of independence within such statistical methods but, and more powerfully, neglects in a substantive sense the systemic spatial patterns, processes and policy implications that spatially sensitive statistical approaches are able to reveal. In response, the chapter walks through a series of key spatial statistical techniques and accompanying insights that can be brought to bear on standard quantitative policy research in order to support richer understandings of these key, commonplace yet frequently neglected geographical dimensions to social policy research and practice.

Geographic information systems – the (now usually digital) spatial analysis of geographically referenced data – is a powerful methodological approach distinct to the discipline of geography. GIS is separate from the traditional dichotomy of aspatial quantitative and qualitative methods that dominates the social sciences and social policy analysis, but also overlapping with and complementary to those approaches. Inclusive in its reach, the chapter by Orford and Webb provides a brief history and overview of GIS methods before moving through a curation of visually narrated methodological case study examples of qualitative as well as quantitative GIS analyses that inform richer analysis and understanding of their policy case studies. In doing so the chapter offers a grounded and holistic overview of the (currently often untapped) potential of GIS techniques for social policy analysis as well as a reflection on likely future trends and developments in what is a fast-evolving methodological field.

A final chapter by Clarke looks back across the contributions in the *Concepts*, *Themes* and *Methods* sections. It steps out to reflect on the overarching messages for scholarship and applied policy practice from their differing perspectives on this shared focus on the often neglected social policy–geography interface. Although its chapters illuminate the potential theoretical, methodological, empirical and policy contributions that a new attention to this interface can bring, given the vastness of each discipline and of the connective space between them this edited collection can inevitably do little more than scratch the surface of this potential. One motivation of the collection is to offer motivation, guidance and encouragement for others to follow to continue to explore this fertile interdisciplinary terrain in their own scholarly research and policy activities. To this end, the *Retrospective* therefore also looks forward to offer reflections and encouragement to others on the next steps and key areas for focus as we together advance the continued study and application of a newly spatialised social policy.

References

Alcock, P., May, M. and Wright, S. (eds) (2012) *The Student's Companion to Social Policy*. Chichester: Wiley-Blackwell.

Anderson, K. and Smith, S. (2001) Editorial: Emotional geographies. *Transactions of the Institute of British Geographers* 26: 7–10.

Arts, W. and Gelissen, J. (2002) Three worlds of welfare capitalism or more? A state-of-the-art report. *Journal of European Social Policy* 12(2): 137–158.

Birrell, D. (2009) *The Impact of Devolution on Social Policy*. Bristol: Policy Press.

Burawoy, R. (2005) 2004 American Sociological Association presidential address: for public sociology. *The British Journal of Sociology* 56(2): 259–294.

Coppock, J. (1974) Geography and public policy: challenges, opportunities and implications. *Transactions of the Institute of British Geographers* 63: 1–16.

Crang, M. and Thrift, N. (2000) *Thinking Space*. London: Routledge.

Cresswell, T. (2004) *Place: A Short Introduction*. Oxford: Blackwell.

Danforth, B. (2014) Worlds of welfare in time: A historical reassessment of the three-world typology. *Journal or European Social Policy* 24(2): 164–182.

Esping-Andersen, G. (1990) *The Three Worlds of Welfare Capitalism*. Princeton, NJ: Princeton University Press.

Fuller, D. and Kitchin, R. (2004) Radical theory/critical praxis: Academic geography beyond the academy? In Fuller, D. and Kitchin, R. (eds) *Radical Theory/Critical Praxis: Making a Difference beyond the Academy?* Vernon and Victoria, BC: Praxis (e)Press, 1–20.

Greer, S. (2009) *Devolution and Social Citizenship in the UK*. Bristol: Policy Press.

Griggs, J., Whitworth, A., Walker, R., McLennan, D. and Noble, M. (2008) *Person or Place-Based Policies to Tackle Disadvantage? Not Knowing What Works*. York: Joseph Rowntree Foundation.

Hamnett, C. (1997) The sleep of reason? *Environment and Planning D: Society and Space* 156: 127–128.

Harvey, D. (1974) What kind of geography for what kind of public policy? *Transactions of the Institute of British Geographers* 63: 18–24.

Hubbard, P. and Kitchin, R. (eds) (2011) *Key Thinkers on Space and Place*. London: Sage.

Hubbard, P., Kitchin, R., Bartley, B. and Fuller, D (2002) *Thinking Geographically: Space, Theory and Contemporary Human Geography*. London: Continuuum.

Imrie, R. (2004) Urban geography, relevance, and resistance to the 'policy turn'. *Urban Geography* 25(8): 697–708.

Jazeel, T. (2010) Impact: an introduction. *Social Text Periscope* 27(August).

Markusen, A. (1999) Fuzzy concepts, scanty evidence, policy distance: the case for rigour and policy relevance in critical regional studies. *Regional Studies* 33(9): 869–884.

Martin, R. (2001) Geography and public policy: the case of the missing agenda. *Progress in Human Geography* 25(2): 189–210.

Massey, D. (2001) Geography on the agenda. *Progress in Human Geography* 25(1): 5–17.

McKenzie, L (2015) *Getting By: Estates, Class and Culture in Austerity Britain*. Bristol: Policy Press.

Mitchell, D. (2004) Radical scholarship: a polemic on making a difference outside the academy. In Fuller, D. and Kitchin, R. (eds) *Radical Theory/Critical Praxis: Making a Difference beyond the Academy?* Vernon and Victoria, BC: Praxis (e)Press, 21–31.

Pain, R., Kesby, M. and Askins, K. (2011) Geographies of impact: power, participation and potential. *Area* 43(2): 183–188.

Patrick, R. (2014) Working on welfare: findings from a qualitative longitudinal study into the lived experiences of welfare reform in the UK. *Journal of Social Policy* 43(4): 705–725.

Peck, J. (1999) Editorial: grey geography? *Transactions of the Institute of British Geographers* 24: 131–135.

Peck, J. (2000) Jumping in, joining up and getting on. *Transactions of the Institute of British Geographers* 25: 255–258.

Peck, J. (2015) Political economies of scale: fast policy, interscalar relations, and neoliberal workfare. *Economic Geography* 78(3): 331–360.

Phillips, R. (2010) The impact agenda and geographies of curiosity. *Transactions of the Institute of British Geographers* 35: 447–452.

Philo, C. and Miller, D. (eds) (2014) *Market Killing: What the Free Market Does and What Social Scientists Should Do About It*. London: Routledge.

Powell, M and Barrientos, A (2015) Introduction: twenty five years of the welfare modelling business. *Social Policy and Society* 14(2): 241–245.

Research Excellence Framework (REF) (2014) *REF 2014 Impact Case Studies*. https://impact.ref.ac.uk/casestudies/Results.aspx?val=Show%20All

Skinner, C. (2005) Co-ordination points: a hidden factor in reconciling work and family life. *Journal of Social Policy* 34(1): 99–119.

Sokol, M. (2015) Financialisation, financial chains and uneven geographical development: towards a research agenda. *Research in International Business and Finance* 39: 678–685.

Spicker, P. (2014) *Social Policy: Theory and Practice*. Bristol: Policy Press.

Times Higher Education (2017) University researchers key 'in 40% of top inventions since 1950s', 21 May.

Van Berkel, R., de Graaf, W. and Sirovatka, T. (eds) (2011) *The Governance of Active Welfare States in Europe*. Basingstoke: Palgrave Macmillan.

Ward, K. (2005) Geography and public policy: a recent history of 'policy relevance'. *Progress in Human Geography* 29(3): 310–319.

Wiles, P. and Costello, A. (2000) *The Road to Nowhere: The Evidence for Travelling Criminals*. London: Home Office, Research Study No. 207.

Williams, G. (2012) The disciplining effects of impact evaluation practices: negotiating the pressures of impact within an ESRC-DFID project. *Transactions of the Institute of British Geographers* 37: 489–495.

PART I:

Concepts

2

Spaces of welfare localism: geographies of locality making

Martin Jones

Introduction

> Responsibility for the development and oversight of social security policy in Great Britain (GB) has for many years been strongly centralised ... In recent years, however, the assumptions underpinning these arrangements have been challenged: the idea that 'one size fits all' is no longer accepted; hoped for economies of scale are contrasted with the need to flex both policy and delivery to local circumstances; and there is increased demand for devolution to Scotland, Wales and Northern Ireland and for the potential role that local government can play. (Social Security Advisory Committee, 2015: 5)

The last 20 years have certainly witnessed a creeping 'welfare localism' in advanced capitalism across the globe (compare Whitworth, 2016; King and Le Gales, 2017; Flint, 2019; Jessop, 2018). In short, national states have actively sought to reduce commitments to integrated welfare entitlements and redistributive urban and regional policies in favour of supply-side neoliberal initiatives intended to promote technological innovation, labour market flexibility, lean management and endogenous growth. The quotation above is taken from the Social Security Advisory Committee's insightful review into the localisation of social security policy in Great Britain. This documents a creeping localisation agenda over a period of 20 years, covering the areas of decentralisation, de-concentration, devolution and subsidiarity. The Social Security Advisory Committee (2015: 8, emphasis added) sees 'localism and localisation as general terms that relate to those policies, schemes or funds that are developed and/or delivered via local institutions or agencies, to meet the needs of citizens *living in a particular locality*'. Underpinning GB government policy has been the argument that previous attempts at promoting social development had been too centralised and there is a need to curtail top-down initiatives that had ignored the varying needs of different areas.

Indicate of this, the Coalition Government of 2010–15, and the Conservative Government from May 2015 to 2017, has purported to offer a radically different approach to economic and social development policy. To give one example, the rollout of Universal Credit (UC) involving merging benefits and a tapering system linked to in-work benefits and wages designed to 'make work pay' involves a more disciplinary and conditional welfare system through a tougher claimant regime in which sanctions are an integral feature. Furthermore, in-work conditionality is a central feature of UC in terms of 'making work pay', with the requirement for claimants to attain an 'earning threshold' set at the level of effort it is reasonable for an individual to undertake. This act of welfare reform is geographically significant and this chapter discusses ways of conceptualising developments such as this.

I suggest that the localisation of welfare is a national state project for transferring aspects of social policy from the (collective) public to the (individualised) private sphere, articulated locally through the changing internal structures of the state and acts of space-making.

This chapter offers a contextual framework to explore some of the somewhat silent space-making geographies of what I have previously called the 'new new localism' (Jones and Jessop, 2010). In doing so, the chapter seeks to offer theoretical insights into the rhetoric of decentralist discourses and the geographical complexities and contradictions of state remaking on-the-ground.

Localism is an old concept (see Peck, 1995) – and one that will doubtless recur (see Jones, 2019). The latest variant of (new new) localist thinking draws extensively on some key antecedents. According to the 'Big Society' guru, Jesse Norman MP, localism 'is a coherent and logistical expression of a conservative tradition which goes back to the 18th century' (Norman, 2011: 201). Edmund Burke's 'little platoons' pepper this literature and are presented as progressive enablers for a democratic form of civil society-centred economic and social policy (Willetts, 1994). The reanimation of civil society is in turn viewed as a means of stimulating localist economic development (Beel et al., 2017). In the words of Jesse Norman (2011: 197) again, the Conservative's new localism stresses a 'three way relationship between individuals, institutions and the state. It is when this relationship is functioning well that societies flourish. This requires each element in the triad to be active and energised in its own right ... Societies should be thought of as ecosystems'. The chapter explores the conceptual significance of this notion of 'ecosystems' (Whitworth and Carter, 2017) for geography and beyond.

It is suggested here that there is considerable mileage in the notion of 'locality' to advance critical social policy analysis. During the mid-to-late 1980s, 'locality' was *the* spatial metaphor deployed to describe and explain the shifting world of regional studies (Cooke, 2006). Building on previous research (Jones, 2011, 2017; Jones and Woods, 2013; Jones et al., 2015), it is argued below that the resulting 'localities debate' saw a potentially important concept prematurely abandoned. I urge a 'return to locality' to enlighten studies of social policy. Three new readings of locality are offered, which, when taken together, constitute the basis for thinking about geography through the lens of *new localities*. I suggest that, first, locality can be seen as bounded territorial space, recognised politically and administratively for the discharge and conduct of public services, and for the collection and analysis of statistical data. Second, locality represents a ways of undertaking comparative research analysis, linked to processes occurring within and outside localities and also connecting them. Third, locality can be used to read spaces of flows for numerous policy fields, which in turn exhibit spatial variations due to interaction effects. Additionally, it is suggested that for locality to have analytical value it must also have both an imagined and material coherence. Last, the chapter draws on these constructs to argue that combined and uneven development ought not to be neglected when thinking about the new localism and the paternalism of people and place.

Locality and the rise and fall of spatial metaphors

'Locality' was the buzz-word of the mid-1980s, even a 'new geography' (Cochrane, 1987), used to frame research on economic geography. It filled the pages of human geography journals and, I would argue, contributed to the intellectual development of regional studies (see also Cooke, 1990). For Duncan (1989), locality was being employed as a misleading catch-all term, an 'infuriating idea' used imprecisely to describe the local autonomy of areas, case study areas, spatially affected processes (social, political, economic, cultural), spaces of production and consumption, the local state, and so on.

Massey's (1984) text *Spatial Divisions of Labour* was pivotal to starting what became the locality debate. This was written during an era of intense economic restructuring and challenged how geographers thought about 'the local' in an increasingly internationalising and globalising world in which Fordist and Keynesian certitudes were perceptibly unravelling. The tangible impact of all this was an acceleration of uneven development, with acute job loss in some areas juxtaposed with accelerating growth in others, as distinctive localities began to emerge in the context of globalisation and economic restructuring (see also Lovering, 1989; Werner et al., 2018).

The intellectual goal in this was to tease out the dialectic between space and place by looking at how localities were being positioned within, and could themselves help to reposition, the changing national and international division of labour. For Massey (1991), 'the local in the global' was not simply an area around which a line can be drawn; instead, localities were defined in terms of sets of social relations or processes under consideration. This highly influential 'new regional concept of localities' (Jonas, 1988) influenced two government-sponsored research initiatives in the UK, delivered through the Economic and Social Research Council – the Social Change and Economic Life programme and the Changing Urban and Regional Systems (CURS) programme. Both were given substantial funding and remits to uncover the effects of international and global economic restructuring on local areas, exploring why different responses and impacts were reported in different places. Locality research, independent of these programmes, was already taking place at Lancaster University (Murgatroyd et al., 1985) and Sussex University (Duncan, 1989), which fuelled an interest in this important topic – although, as Barnes (1996) notes, notions of 'locality' differ across all these interventions and focusing on the CURS programme is most helpful to get behind the meaning of locality.

In seeking to put 'the local' into 'the global', the CURS initiative set out to undertake theoretically informed empirical research in seven localities between 1985 and 1987. The goal was to examine the extent to which localities themselves could shape their own transformation and destiny as agents and not be passive containers for processes passed down from above. Two edited books documented the fortunes of a series of mainly metropolitan deindustrialising towns/regions and rural areas, tracking the impacts of globalisation and economic restructuring on 'the local' and considering the complex and variable local–global interplay that conditioned locality experiences (Cooke 1989a; Harloe et al., 1990).

Particularly worthy of note here was the work of Hudson and Beynon (see Beynon et al., 1989), whose research closely followed Massey's theoretical and interpretative framework. Their account of economic change in Teesside seemed to demonstrate a 'locality effect' of local particularities in global times: the different ways in which 'rounds of investment' can impinge on the local economic landscape, how local politics played a role in international investment decisions, and in turn how attempts to cope with deindustrialisation (by either building a service-based economy or using state-sponsored local economic initiatives to create employment opportunities) were expressed on the ground.

As argued by Gregson (1987), Duncan and Savage (1991) and Barnes (1996), there is a fundamental difference between locality research (the CURS findings) and the resulting 'locality debate' across human geography and the social sciences. The latter was fuelled by a desire to rethink the theorisation of socio-spatial relations across disciplines, within the context of a broader transition from Marxist to poststructuralist research enquiry. The localities debate was also informed by shifting research methodologies and practices, such as the rise and fall of critical realism (see Pratt, 2004). In this febrile intellectual context, the journal *Antipode*, between 1987 and 1991, published a series of often heated exchanges on the conceptual and empirical value of localities (for summaries, compare Pratt 2004; Cooke 2006). The initial assault came from North America by Smith (1987), who bemoaned the perceived shift away from (Marxist) theory to a critical realist-inspired regional world of empirics, worthy of nothing more than a 'morass of statistical data'. Smith's memorable dismissal of localities research had it that 'like the blind man with a python in one hand and an elephant's trunk in the other, the researchers are treating all seven localities as the same animal' (p. 63). This was supported, to a differing degree, by Harvey (1987), who saw these projects as refusing to engage in any theoretical or conceptual adventures. The consequences, for Scott (1991: 256–257), was to encourage 'a form of story-telling that focuses on dense historical and geographical sequences of events, but where in the absence of a strong interpretative apparatus, the overall meaning of these events for those who live and work in other places is obscure'.

Duncan (1989) offered a more sympathetic critique, which saw locality – in the wrong hands – as a form of reified uniqueness and 'spatial fetishism': in what sense can localities act, or is it the social forces within these spaces that have this capacity? In two influential papers with Savage, Duncan made the first serious interventions on the relationships between spatial scales (Duncan and Savage, 1990; Savage and Duncan, 1990). Duncan concluded with some thoughts on three ways forward for research on locality: considerations of spatially contingent effects (processes contained in places); propositions on local causal process (locally derived forces of change); and the notion of locality effects (the combination of the previous two, affording a capacity to localities to act). Warde (1989) recognised the value of locality for empirical research but also argued that the scale of locality changes according to the object of analysis under question. Cooke (1987, 1989b), the Director of CURS, took a more defensive and ultimately pragmatic line, arguing that CURS was about seeking to make some general claims from multi-site case study research, even if this was about nothing more than local labour markets and its boundaries. The CURS findings were, therefore, empirical and not empiricist (see Cooke, 2006).

A special issue of *Environment and Planning A* offered further critique and extension, and contended that locality was still a valuable concept to be grappled with. For Jackson (1991), the danger was that cultural change and political change were overly attributed to economic factors, at odds with a reality in which each was embedded in the other. Pratt (1991) took a similar line and suggested a need to look at the discursive construction of localities and their material effects. Paasi (1991), much inspired by the 'new regional geography' material that the locality debate uncovered and which helped rekindle interest in regions, encouraged scholars to take 'geohistory' more seriously and offered the idea of 'generation' to distinguish between the concepts of locality, place and region. Duncan and Savage (1989, 1991) pushed what they saw as the missing agenda of place formation and class formation and the interconnections of these within and between localities. Cox and Mair (1991; see also Cox, 1993) offered an agenda-setting account of localities in the United States as arenas for economic development coalitions, and as ways of fixing and scaling socio-spatial relations. Their research took the debate forward and brought agency and scale to the fore through notions of 'local dependency', the 'scale division of labour' and the 'scale division of the state' – concepts that highlighted the location and mobility of actors at different times. Cox and Mair claimed this avoided 'spatial fetishism' (a criticism levelled by Sayer, 1991) as locality is seen not in physical terms but as a 'localised social structure'. Finally, Massey's (1991, 1994) interventions offered some sensible qualifiers on what CURS had initially set out to achieve, shifting the scale of debate from locality to 'senses of place'.

As Cooke's (2006) subsequent retrospective commentary notes, because CURS and the locality debate became so quickly mired in these debates, the potentially useful notion of locality was jettisoned somewhat prematurely. Debates moved on and during the mid-1990s economic geographers became preoccupied not so much with localities per se but with the links between space and place as a way of looking at the 'local in the global'. Massey (1994) argued that globalisation is happening but that the extent of time–space compression is socially and spatially uneven due to the variable mobility potential of people in place. 'Power geometries', a metaphor for capturing geographies of power, exist and therefore constrain some and enable others. This makes generalisations about the powerlessness of 'the local' in a globalising world unwise (cf. Harvey, 1989). The argument here was that localities need to be understood in terms of 'global senses of place' – as interconnected nodes in spaces of flows, stretching back and forth, ebbing and flowing according to how they are positioned by, and positioning, socio-spatial relations. Two distinctions are then made to get a handle on 'the local in the global'. The first is a 'regressive sense of place', based on rejection of the potentials of globalisation and the embrace instead of heritage and other forms of 'romanticised escapism'. The second is a more 'progressive sense of place', based on harnessing and making the most of difference and diversity through those stretched-out connections. Massey discusses this through her own experiences of living in Kilburn (a cosmopolitan area of North London) and her approach has no truck with locality perspectives that stick to administrative boundaries or tightly drawn labour market areas. Localities as 'global senses of place' are *relational* in the sense of seeing the local as an unbounded mosaic of different elements always in a process of interaction and being made. In short, one cannot explain locality or place by only looking inside it, or outside it; the 'out there' and 'in here' matter *together* and are dialectically intertwined (see Massey, 2005, 2007).

Bringing localities back: towards 'new localities'

In the early 1990s, 'region' replaced locality as the spatial descriptor around which economic and political geography cohered. Academic trends tend to closely mirror political and policy events (see Cooke and Morgan, 1998) and economic geographers began increasingly to focus on the perceived re-emergence of regional economies and new spaces of economic governance across the globe. These spaces had been initially flagged by writers talking about post-Fordism and the geographies of flexible accumulation. From these initial efforts came wider attempts to delimit the contours of a 'regional world' (Storper, 1997). Scott, for instance, in the text *New Industrial Spaces* (1988), offered a new way of looking at agglomeration and the development of distinct local territorial production complexes or industrial districts. Whereas Fordist accumulation was favoured by and grew in accordance with economies of scale and vertical integration, economic development after Fordism was seen to be linked to spatially specific economies of scope resulting from the vertical disintegration of production and the development, amongst other things, of flexible working practices and shared support mechanisms. The geographical extent of this phenomenon and its reproducibility and sustainability was discussed at length in various edited collections (see Storper and Scott, 1992). Inspired by this, debates gradually shifted throughout the 1990s to examine the governance of local economies in global contexts through a 'new regionalist' perspective – as part of a broader 'institutional turn' in economic geography. A parallel set of debates, also drawing on 'new regionalist' thinking, took place in political science on 'multilevel governance', driven by the so-called hollowing out of the national state and the 'Europe of the Regions' thesis (Keating, 1998; Scott, 2001). For Cooke this was important for locality studies:

> Probably the longest-lasting legacy of locality studies has been the rise of so-called 'new regionalism'. Already spotted around the time of his return from Australia by Nigel Thrift (1983) this theorised regional political economy analysis was gaining ground rapidly as we have seen, in the new times of 'global localisation'. The locality studies themselves and the comparative methodology that allowed spatial variety to be explained within a coherent and satisfying theoretical framework furthered this impulse. (Cooke, 2006: 10)

This orthodoxy and alleged theoretical coherence referred to above by Cooke has, of course, been subjected to piercing academic critique. In a similar manner to some of the critiques of locality, philosophically (via critical realism), the new regionalism is deemed guilty of 'bad abstraction' in that it ignores the role of multiple and contingent factors (both economic and non-economic) that produce regions. For this reason Lovering (1999) argues that the region is becoming a 'chaotic conception'; generalised claims are being made based on selective empirical evidence to support the centrality of this scale for stimulating economic growth. Consequently, he argues, this approach is a theory led by selective empirical developments and recent public policy initiatives. It is 'a set of stories about how *parts* of a regional economy *might* work, placed next to a set of policy ideas which *might* just be useful in *some* cases' (Lovering, 1999: 384, emphasis original). These arguments have been developed and extended by others (see MacLeod, 2001; Hadjimichalis, 2006, 2018; Painter, 2008; Harrison, 2010).

New regionalist thinking has been, in turn, challenged by relational approaches to space, where – building on the work of Massey (1994) – geographies are made through unbounded relations influenced by global flows and local nodal interactions. Space here is a reflection of networked, nodal and open place-based relationships, rather than merely a container or independent backdrop for existence. This argument, of course, has been clearly articulated by those advocating that space is a relational concept (Amin, 2004, 2007; see also Marston et al., 2005). 'Unbounded' or 'relational' regions need not be territorially coherent or contiguous. 'Alternative regional geographies' involve spatial configurations and boundaries that are no longer necessarily or purposively territorial or scalar, since social, economic, political and cultural processes are constituted through actor networks which are becoming increasingly dynamic and varied in spatial constitution (Amin, 2004; Massey, 2007: 89; Massey, 2011; Amin and Thrift, 2013, 2016).

Radical open-ended politics and economics of *place* are proposed, in opposition to frameworks of so-called bounded territorial economic development, to create spaces of opportunity for localities under globalisation. This perspective is evidenced in the text *Cities: Reimagining the Urban*, where Amin and Thrift (2002) view localities as unbounded, fuzzy, fluid, complex and mixed entities, formed through recurring practices, movements and experiences. They claim this has implications for developing successful economies in a context of economic globalisation, building institutional and policy frameworks for economic governance, nurturing civic participation and delivering radical democracy (cf. Massey, 2007). Putting 'the local into the global' has 'far less to do with territorial properties (such as localized linkage, local identity and identification, scalar politics, and governance) than with *the effects of spatial and temporal exposure and connectivity* (such as continual and open-ended change, juxtaposition of difference, overlap of networks of different global connections)' (Amin, 2002: 391, emphasis added).

This is a perspective that stretches the imagination of economic geography but those working within state theoretic frameworks and more grounded approaches to economic geography have taken issue with the *realpolitik* of 'the local' grappling with the challenges of globalisation. For example, it is important to consider the ways in which cities and regions can be categorised as problematic by the state and those seeking to direct resources to different geographical areas. It is also important not to lose sight of the ways in which contentious politics are being played out across the globe. One instance of this in recent years has seen campaigns for devolved government and cultural rights linked to territorially articulated spaces (see Jones and MacLeod, 2004; Keating, 2013). For Tomaney (2007, 2013), localities, then, are more than the local articulation of global flows, and concerns with territorialised culture need not necessarily be atavistic, archaic or regressive.

Commentators on the territorial-relational debate suggest several ways forward. Jonas (2012) suggests that the distinction between territorial and relational can be 'registered obsolete' if critical attention is paid to matters of territory and the nature of territorial politics, both of which are products of bounded and unbounded forces. Moreover, he argues, the form this takes is contingent, and requires empirical investigation. The way forward, then, is 'further examples of both relational thinking about territorial politics and of territorial thinking about relational processes' (Jonas, 2012: 270; see also Allen and Cochrane, 2014).

Rolling space forward: a 'new localities' research agenda

Some 25 years on, in the wake of long-running debates about the new regionalism and glocalisation and about relational and bounded territoriality, how useful is the concept of locality? Can it be energised by these debates and developed in order to begin to answer the challenges thrown up by Jonas (2012)? In this respect, it is worth revisiting Duncan's (1989) claim:

> Localities in the sense of autonomous subnational social units rarely exist, and in any case their existence needs to be demonstrated. But it is also misleading to use locality as a synonym for place or spatial variation. This is because the term locality inevitably smuggles in notions of social autonomy and spatial determinism, and this smuggling in excludes examination of these assumptions. *It is surely better to use terms like town, village, local authority area, local labour market or, for more general uses, place, area or spatial variation.* These very useable terms do not rely so heavily on conceptual assumptions about space vis-à-vis society. (Duncan, 1989: 247, emphasis added)

Counter to this analysis, I would suggest that locality has the capacity to capture those spatial categories deemed by Duncan (1989) to be more useful units of analysis. It is exactly those 'conceptual assumptions' which render locality free of charges of 'spatial determinism'. Locality is a meaningful term (Meegan, 2017). This stance, however, requires some hard thinking and the introduction of a new conception of locality: that of 'new locality'.

Savage et al. (1987: 30) argue that '[g]reater clarification of the concept "locality" should start with an analysis of the significance of space in general'. In response, three readings of 'new locality' can be formulated from the three commonly understood notions of space used in the physical and social sciences – absolute, relative and relational – which, as Harvey (1969) has highlighted, can coexist.

This coexistence can be illustrated in relation to the conceptual treatment of local areas in a global context. In *absolute* understanding of space, the local is treated independently; locality is a discrete space around which a line can be drawn and where a loose spatial determinism has some purchase. Concerns with *relative space*, by contrast, lead us to consider the relationship between localities in an increasingly internationalising world of processes and patterns. The notion of *relational space*, by way of further contrast, is a truly radical attempt to collapse analysis into networked concerns such that there is no global and local to talk about, only unbounded and networked geographies of 'jostling' (Massey, 2007), 'throwntogetherness' (Massey, 2005) and conjunctural becoming (Woods, 2007). Sites become the sources of analysis, but how they relate to each other is not clear, such that research needs to pay attention to power and policy relations flowing in and through localities. These three notions of space therefore inform different ways of identifying localities as objects of research, each of which can be found employed in the social science literature, namely:

- From the perspective of *absolute space*, localities can be presented as bounded territories, such as local authority areas, which are recognised politically and administratively for reasons of electoral accountability, for the discharge and conduct of public services, and for the collection and analysis of statistical data. They are not naturally occurring entities (though some may be contiguous with natural features such as islands), but they do have a stable and precisely delimited materiality that can form the focus for traditional, single place-based or comparative case study research (Bennett and McCoshan, 1993).
- From the perspective of *relative space*, localities can be seen as connected containers for spatial analysis. Here localities are identified by their cores, not their edges, and are not necessarily consistent

with formal administrative geographies. In this perspective, the boundaries of localities are relative, fuzzy and sometimes indeterminate, contingent on the processes and phenomena being observed, and shaped by dynamics within, outside and between localities. Such a notion of locality forms the basis for research sensitive to connective forms of enquiry, including for example work on city regions and nested hierarchies (Etherington and Jones, 2009, 2016, 2018).

• From the perspective of *relational space*, localities are nodes or entanglements within networks of interaction and spaces of flow. They are not bounded in any conventional understanding of the term, but have a topography that is described by lines of connectivity and convergence. Localities transgress inscribed territories and are not necessarily discrete, sharing points of coexistence. Such a conceptualisation of locality lends itself to counter-topographical research (Katz, 2001; see also Heley and Jones, 2012), or the practice of a 'global ethnography' (Burawoy, 2000).

Unlike earlier locality debates, the 'new localities' approach does not seek to adjudicate between these different representations of locality, but rather recognises that all are valid ways of 'talking about locality', and each captures a different expression of locality. New localities are, therefore, multifaceted and multidimensional. They are 'shape-shifters' whose form changes with the angle from which they are observed. As such, the identification of localities for research can be freed from the constraints of the rigid territoriality of administrative geography and should move beyond the reification of the local authority scale that was implicit in many previous locality studies. Warde's comments of 20-plus years ago on this remain critical:

> Deciding on an appropriate spatial scale depends initially on the research problem. If we want to know about foreign policy we might choose states; if voting behaviour, constituencies; if material life, perhaps the labour market; if everyday experience, maybe the neighbourhood. Greater difficulty arises if we want to know about the intersection of several of these, the burden of the restructuring thesis. Concepts with substantive spatial properties ought to be theoretical predicates. Conscripting the concepts of locality requires that a theoretical decision be made. (Warde, 1989: 277)

In recognising the contingency and impermanence of localities, and acknowledging Warde's (1989) plea for notions of 'intersection', the new localities approach also focuses attention on processes of 'locality-making', or the ways in which stable and popularly recognised representations of locality are brought into being through the moulding, manipulation and sedimentation of space within ongoing social, economic and political struggles (see Pierce et al., 2011; Jonas, 2012). Indeed, it is in these acts of locality-making that localities are transformed from mere points of location (a description of where research was conducted) to socioeconomic–political creations that provide an analytical framework for research. For the concept of locality to have analytical value, it must be possible to attribute observed processes and outcomes to social, economic and political formations that are configured in a given locality, and this, it can be argued, requires a locality to possess both material and imagined coherence.

Material coherence refers to the particular social, economic and political structures and practices that are configured around a place. Thus, material coherence may be provided by the territorial ambit of a local authority, by the geographical coverage of an economic development initiative, by the catchment area of a school or hospital, by a travel-to-work area, by the reach of a supermarket or shopping centre, or by any combination of the above and other similar structures and practices. Material coherence hence alludes to the institutional structures that hold a locality together and provide vehicles for collective action.

Imagined coherence relates to collective resident consciousness and the sense of shared identity and affinity with a place, resulting in a perceived community with shared patterns of behaviour and common geographical reference points. Imagined coherence therefore makes a locality meaningful as a space of collective action. There are territorial units that exhibit material coherence but lack a strong imagined coherence (such as artificially amalgamated local authority areas) and there are territories with an imagined coherence but only a weak material coherence (for example, where institutional boundaries bisect contiguous urban areas or where areas with strongly developed popular consciousness exist within much larger institutional units). Areas falling into either of these categories could not be considered coherent functioning localities.

Both material coherence and imagined coherence are also important in fixing (through multiple intersections) the scale at which localities can be identified (Jones and Woods, 2013). The imagined coherence of a locality is framed around perceived shared forms of behaviour, whether linked to common patterns of collective consumption, shared affinity with sporting or cultural institutions, or common geographical/ historical reference points. However, this imagined coherence is not founded on direct interpersonal connection between residents (cf. Anderson, 1991). In this sense it differs from the social coherence of a neighbourhood – which may share some of the aforementioned attributes but is framed around the probability of direct interaction between members. It also differs from the imagined coherence of a region – which is a looser affiliation that draws more on perceived cultural and political identities and economic interests.

Similarly, the material coherence of a locality should be denser and more complex than that found at a neighbourhood or regional scale. The material coherence of a neighbourhood will be restricted by its situation within a larger geographical area for employment, administrative and many service provision functions, while the material coherence of a region could be fragmented by the inclusion of several different labour markets, local authority areas, sub-regional shopping centres and so on. Savage's (2009) work on 'granular space' is illustrative of these concerns:

> People do not usually see places in terms of their nested or relational qualities: town against country: region against nation, etc. but compare different places with each other without a strong sense of any hierarchical ordering. I further argue that the culturally privileged groups are highly 'vested' in place, able to articulate intense feelings of belonging to specific fixed locations, in ways where abstract and specific renderings of place co-mingle. Less powerful groups, by contrast, have a different cultural geography, which hives off fantasy spaces from mundane spaces. (Savage, 2009: 3)

The attributes of localities outlined above do not easily translate into discrete territorial units with fixed boundaries. Labour market areas overlap, as do shopping catchment areas; residents may consider themselves to be part of multiple localities for different purposes and at different times; the reach of a town as an education centre may be different to its reach as an employment centre; and so on. The boundaries that might be ascribed to a locality will vary depending on the issue in question (Warde, 1989).

All this has a bearing on how localities are identified, defined and constructed for case study research. The argument of Beauregard

(1988) on the 'absence of practice' in locality research is important here, in calling for both methodological and political interventions. The application of the approach discussed logically leads us to start by identifying localities by their cores – whether these be towns or cities or geographical areas – rather than as bounded territories, and working outwards to establish an understanding of their material and imagined coherence. This process will necessarily require mixed methods, combining cartographic and quantitative data on material geographies with qualitative evidence of imagined coherence and performed patterns and relations. This is more than just an exercise in boundary-drawing. Whilst it may be possible to identify fixed territorial limits for the reach of a locality with respect to certain governmental competences or policy fields, applying proxy boundaries to imagined localities must necessarily assume a degree of permeability, and that localities may be configured differently depending on the object of inquiry.

Conclusion: localism and uneven development

This chapter has proposed a new approach to thinking about localities in the context of welfare localism in the UK. This recognises that localities do not only exist in absolute space as bounded territories but have expression in relative and relational space where boundaries are at best 'fuzzy' and permeable. Whilst each representation may be legitimately employed to frame localities in particular contexts, taken together they point to a new understanding of localities as multifaceted, dynamic and contingent entities that change shape depending on the viewpoint adopted. Constructing localities as frames for the analysis of social, economic or political phenomena, therefore, requires investigation of both their imagined and material coherence, which in combination make a locality meaningful and create a capacity for action.

This chapter has proposed that the 'new localities' approach has at least three implications for case study-oriented geographical research. Firstly, it provides a revised model for understanding locality effects that does not take localities as a given bounded spatial unit, but instead emphasises the contingency and relationality of localities. Secondly, the new localities approach therefore requires identification and description of the locality to be incorporated as an intrinsic part of the research process, rather than treating locality as a taken-for-granted backdrop. This approach further recognises that the shape, reach and orientation of a locality might differ according to the research questions being examined. Thirdly, the new localities notion consequently demands a new body of research concerned with establishing the material and imagined coherences of localities, employing mixed-method strategies. Through these mechanisms, 'locality' can be reclaimed as a meaningful and useful concept in social and economic research. In its resurrected guise, 'locality' can be freed from the shackles of fixed boundaries. As such, whilst locality research can be spatially focused, it should not be spatially constrained, and needs to be prepared to follow networks and relations across scales and spaces in order to reveal the full panoply of forces and actors engaged in the constitution of a locality (Jones and Woods, 2013).

All of this raises the issue of relationships within and between localities, constituted in and as the landscapes of combined and uneven development. On the one hand, there are statements from the UK Government such as:

> We think that the best means of strengthening society is not for central government to try and seize all the power and responsibility for itself. It is to help people and their locally elected representatives to achieve their own ambitions. This is the essence of the Big Society ... The Localism Act sets out a series of measures with the potential to achieve a substantial and lasting shift in power away from central government and towards local people. (Greg Clark MP, Minister of State for Decentralisation, Foreword, *A Plain English Guide to the Localism Act*, DCLG, November 2011)

> *The policy implications of theories of agglomeration is that enabling people and firms to benefit from proximity to centres of activity, bring beneficial economic outcomes* ... This implies empowering and incentivising local government, firms and people across economic centres and natural economic geographies [cities] to promote growth and correct the market and government failures which are acting as barriers to economic development. (BIS, 2010: 25, emphasis added)

Such sentiments, though, explicitly ignore the complex and contradictory relationships within and between places and regions. Expressed simply, everywhere cannot win, everywhere cannot raise performance above the average (because it is the average), and everywhere cannot mobilise the so-called local agglomeration forces into temporary permanent fixes for economic success, social cohesion and democratic renewal (cf. Bond, 2010; Cheshire et al., 2014). The landscape of England's localities is a story of competition hot-spots and not-spots; a tapestry of some places developing out of control, boom to bust, and other places stagnating and witnessing little in the way of sustained economic development (see McCann, 2016; Waite and Morgan, 2018; Jones, 2019). Drawing parallels with literature in development studies, it remains the case that 'by focusing so heavily on "the local" … manifestations tend to underplay both local inequalities and power relations as well as national and transnational economic and political forces' (Mohan and Stokke, 2000: 247). The institutions of economic governance simply lack the *regulatory capacity* to correct market or governance failure. The current debate on the rollout of Universal Credit and its shortcomings are certainly indicative of this (see National Audit Office, 2018), where 'reductions in benefit entitlements have left people on the lowest incomes more vulnerable to short-term financial crises' (House of Commons Work and Pensions Committee, 2016). In the closing words of Meegan (2017: 1292), 'locality research rides again'.

References

Allen, J. and Cochrane, A. (2014) The urban unbound: London's politics and the 2012 Olympic games. *International Journal of Urban and Regional Research* 38: 1609–1624.

Amin, A. (2002) Spatialities of globalisation. *Environment and Planning A* 34: 385–399.

Amin, A. (2004) Regions unbound: towards a new politics of place. *Geografiska Annaler* 86B: 33–44.

Amin, A. (2007) Rethinking the urban social. *City* 11: 100–114.

Amin, A. and Thrift, N. (2002) *Cities: Reimagining the Urban.* Cambridge: Polity.

Amin, A. and Thrift, N. (2013) *Arts of the Political: New Openings for the Left.* Cambridge: Polity.

Amin, A. and Thrift, N. (2016) *Seeing Like a City.* Cambridge: Polity.

Anderson, B. (1991) *Imagined Communities: Reflections on the Origin and Spread of Nationalism.* London: Verso.

Barnes, T. (1996) *Logics of Dislocation: Models, Metaphors, and Meanings of Economic Space.* New York: Guildford.

Beauregard, R.A. (1988) In the absence of practice: the locality research debate. *Antipode* 20: 52–59.

Beel, D., Jones, M., Jones, I.R. and Escadale, W. (2017) Connected growth: developing a framework to drive inclusive growth across a city-region. *Local Economy* 32: 565–575.

Bennett, R.J. and McCoshan, A. (1993) *Enterprise and Human Resource Development: Local Capacity Building*. London: Paul Chapman.

Beynon, H., Hudson, R., Lewis, J., Sadler, D. and Townsend, A. (1989) 'It's all falling apart here': coming to terms with the future in Teesside. In Cooke, P. (ed) *Localities: The Changing Face of Urban Britain*. London: Unwin Hyman.

BIS (2010) *Understanding Local Growth: BIS Economics Paper 7*. London: Department for Business, Innovation and Skills.

Bond, P. (2010) *Red Tory: How Left and Right Have Broken Britain and How We Can Fix It*. London: Faber and Faber.

Burawoy, M. (2000) *Global Ethnography*. Berkeley: University of California Press.

Cheshire, P.C., Nathan, M. and Overman, H.G. (2014) *Urban Economics and Urban Policy: Challenging Conventional Policy Wisdom*. Cheltenham: Elgar.

Cochrane, A. (1987) What a difference the place makes: the new structuralism of locality. *Antipode* 19: 354–363.

Cooke, P. (1987) Clinical inference and geographical theory. *Antipode* 19: 69–78.

Cooke, P. (ed) (1989a) *Localities: The Changing Face of Urban Britain*. London: Unwin Hyman.

Cooke, P. (1989b) Locality-theory and the poverty of 'spatial variation'. *Antipode* 21: 261–273.

Cooke, P. (1990) *Back to the Future: Modernity, Postmodernity and Locality*. London: Unwin Hyman.

Cooke, P. (2006) *Locality Debates*. Mimeograph, Centre for Advanced Urban Studies, Cardiff University, Cardiff, Wales.

Cooke, P. and Morgan, K. (1998) *The Associational Economy: Firms, Regions, and Innovation*. Oxford: Oxford University Press.

Cox, K. (1993) The local and the global in the new urban politics: a critical view. *Environment and Planning D: Society and Space* 11: 433–448.

Cox, K. and Mair, A. (1991) From localised social structures to localities as agents. *Environment and Planning A* 23: 197–213.

DCLG (2011) *A Plain English Guide to the Localism Act*. London: Department for Communities and Local Government.

Duncan, S. (1989) What is locality. In Peet, R. and Thrift, N. (eds) *New Models in Geography: Volume Two*. London: Unwin Hyman.

Duncan, S. and Savage, M. (1989) Space, scale and locality. *Antipode* 21: 179–206.

Duncan, S. and Savage, M. (1990) Space, scale and locality: a reply to Cooke and Ward. *Antipode* 22: 67–72.

Duncan, S. and Savage, M. (1991) New perspectives on the locality debate. *Environment and Planning A* 23: 155–164.

Etherington, D. and Jones, M. (2009) City-regions: new geographies of uneven development and inequality. *Regional Studies* 43: 247–265.

Etherington, D. and Jones, M. (2016) The city-region chimera: the political economy of metagovernance failure in Britain. *Cambridge Journal of Regions, Economy and Society* 9: 371–389.

Etherington, D. and Jones, M. (2018) Restating the post-political: depoliticisation, social inequalities, and city-region growth. *Environment and Planning A* 50: 51–72.

Flint, J. (2019) Encounters with the centaur state: advanced urban marginality and the practices and ethics of welfare sanction regimes. *Urban Studies* 56: 249–265.

Gregson, N. (1987) The CURS initiative: some further comments. *Antipode* 19: 364–370.

Hadjimichalis, C. (2006) Non-economic factors in economic geography and in 'new regionalism': a sympathetic critique. *International Journal of Urban and Regional Research* 30: 690–704.

Hadjimichalis, C. (2018) *Crisis Spaces: Structures, Struggles and Solidarity in Southern Europe.* London: Routledge.

Harloe, M., Pickvance, C. and Urry, J. (eds) (1990) *Place, Policy and Politics: Do Localities Matter?* London: Unwin Hyman.

Harrison, J. (2010) Networks of connectivity, territorial fragmentation, uneven development: the new politics of city-regionalism. *Political Geography* 29: 17–27.

Harvey, D. (1969) *Explanation in Geography.* London: Arnold.

Harvey, D. (1987) Three myths in search of a reality in urban studies. *Environment and Planning D: Society and Space* 5: 367–376.

Harvey, D. (1989) *The Condition of Postmodernity: An Enquiry into the Origins of Cultural Change.* Oxford: Blackwell.

Heley, J. and Jones, L. (2012) Relational rurals: some thoughts and relating things and theory in rural studies. *Journal of Rural Studies* 28: 208–217.

House of Commons Work and Pensions Committee (2016) *The Local Welfare Safety Net: Fifth Report of Session 2015–16, HC 373.* London: The Stationery Office.

Jackson, P. (1991) Mapping meanings: a cultural critique of locality studies. *Environment and Planning A* 23: 215–228.

Jessop, B. (2018) Neoliberalism and the welfare state: Schumpterian or Ricardian. In Cahill, D., Cooper, M., Konings, M. and Primrose, D. (eds) *The Sage Handbook of Neoliberalism.* London: Sage.

Jonas, A. (1988) A new regional concept of localities. *Area* 20: 101–110.

Jonas, A. (2012) Region and place: regionalism in question. *Progress in Human Geography* 36: 263–272.

Jones, M. (2011) The local in the global., in Leyshon, A., Lee, R., McDowell, L. and Sunley, P. (eds) *The Sage Handbook of Economic Geography*. London: Sage.

Jones, M. (2017) New localism, new localities... In Deas, I. and Hincks, S. (eds) *Territorial Policy and Governance: Alternative Paths*. London: Routledge.

Jones, M. (2019) *Cities and Regions in Crisis: The Political Economy of Subnational Economic Development*. Cheltenham: Edward Elgar.

Jones, M. and Jessop, B. (2010) Thinking state/space incompossibly. *Antipode* 42: 1119–1149.

Jones, M. and MacLeod, G. (2004) Regional spaces, spaces of regionalism: territory, insurgent politics and the English question. *Transactions of the Institute of British Geographers* 29: 433–452.

Jones, M. and Woods, M. (2013) 'New localities', *Regional Studies* 47: 29–42.

Jones, M., Orford, S. and Macfarlane, V. (eds (2015) *People, Places and Policy: Knowing Contemporary Wales Through New Localities*. London: Routledge.

Katz, C. (2001) On the grounds of globalization: a topography for feminist political engagement. *Signs* 26: 1213–1234.

Keating, M. (1998) *The New Regionalism in Western Europe*. Cheltenham: Elgar.

Keating, M. (2013) *Rescaling the European State: The Making of Territory and the Rise of the Meso*. Oxford: Oxford University Press.

King, D. and Le Gales, P. (eds) (2017) *Reconfiguring European States in Crisis*. Oxford: Oxford University Press.

Lovering, J. (1989) The restructuring approach. In Peet, R. and Thrift, N. (eds) *New Models in Geography: Volume One*. London: Unwin Hyman.

Lovering, J. (1999) Theory led by policy: the inadequacies of the 'new regionalism' (illustrated from the case of Wales). *International Journal of Urban and Regional Research* 23: 379–395.

MacLeod, G. (2001) New regionalism reconsidered: globalization, regulation, and the recasting of political economic space. *International Journal of Urban and Regional Research* 25: 804–829.

Marston, S.A., Jones, J.P. III and Woodward, K. (2005) Human geography without scale. *Transactions of the Institute of British Geographers* 30: 416–432.

Massey, D. (1984) *Spatial Divisions of Labour: Social Structures and the Geography of Production*. Basingstoke: Macmillan.

Massey, D. (1991) The political place of locality studies. *Environment and Planning A* 23: 267–281.

Massey, D. (1994) *Space, Place and Gender*. Cambridge: Polity.

Massey, D. (2005) *For Space*. London: Sage.

Massey, D. (2007) *World City*. Cambridge: Polity.

Massey, D. (2011) A counterhegemonic relationality of place. In McCann, E. and Ward, K. (eds) *Mobile Urbanism: Cities and Policy-making in the Global Age*. Minneapolis: University of Minnesota Press.

McCann, P. (2016) *The UK Regional-National Economic Problem: Geography, Globalisation and Governance*. London: Routledge.

Meegan, R. (2017) Doreen Massey (1944–2016): a geographer who really mattered. *Regional Studies* 51, 1285–1296.

Mohan, G. and Stokke, K. (2000) Participatory development and empowerment: the dangers of localism. *Third World Quarterly* 21: 247–268.

Murgatroyd, L., Savage, M., Shapiro, D., Urry, J., Walby, S., Warde, A. and Mark-Lawson, J. (1985) *Localities, Class, and Gender*. London: Pion.

National Audit Office (2018) *Rolling Out Universal Credit*. London: Stationery Office.

Norman, J. (2011) *The Big Society*. Buckingham: The University of Buckingham Press.

Paasi, A. (1991) Deconstructing regions: notes on the scales of spatial life. *Environment and Planning A* 23: 239–256.

Painter, J. (2008) Cartographic anxiety and the search for regionality. *Environment and Planning A* 40: 342–361.

Peck, J. (1995) Moving and shaking: business elites, state localism and urban privatism. *Progress in Human Geography* 19: 16–46.

Pierce, J., Martin, D.G. and Murphy, J.T. (2011) Relational place-making: the networked politics of place. *Transactions of the Institute of British Geographers* 36: 54–70.

Pratt, A.C. (1991) Discourses of locality. *Environment and Planning A* 23: 257–266.

Pratt, A.C. (2004) Andrew Sayer. In Hubbard, P., Kitchin, R. and Valentine, G. (eds) *Key Thinkers on Space and Place*. London: Sage.

Savage, M. (2009) *Townscapes and Landscapes*. Mimeograph, Department of Sociology, University of York, York, England.

Savage, M. and Duncan, S. (1990) Space, scale and locality: a reply to Cooke and Ward. *Antipode* 22: 67–72.

Savage, M., Barlow, J., Duncan, S. and Saunders, P. (1987) Locality research: the Sussex programme on economic restructuring, social change and the locality. *Quarterly Journal of Social Affairs* 3: 27–51.

Sayer, A. (1991) Behind the locality debate: deconstructing geography's dualisms. *Environment and Planning A* 23: 283–308.

Scott, A.J. (1988) *New Industrial Spaces: Flexible Production Organisation and Regional Development in North America and Western Europe.* London: Pion.

Scott, A.J. (2001) Globalization and the rise of city-regions. *European Planning Studies* 9: 813–826.

Smith, N. (1987) Dangers of the empirical turn: some comments on the CURS initiative. *Antipode* 19: 59–68.

Social Security Advisory Committee (2015) *Localisation and Social Security: A Review.* SSAC, Occasional Paper 14, London.

Storper, M. (1997) *The Regional World: Territorial Development in a Global Economy.* New York: Guilford Press.

Storper, M. and Scott, A.J. (eds) (1992) *Pathways to Industrialization and Regional Development.* London: Routledge.

Tomaney, J. (2007) Keep a beat in the dark: narratives of regional identity in Basil Bunting's Briggflatts. *Environment and Planning D: Society and Space* 25: 355–375.

Tomaney, J. (2013) Parochialism: a defence. *Progress in Human Geography* 37: 658–672.

Waite, A. and Morgan, K. (2018) City deals in the polycentric state: the space and politics of metrophilia in the UK. *European Urban and Regional Research.* doi: 10.1177/0969776418798678.

Warde, A. (1989) A recipe for a pudding: a comment on locality. *Antipode* 21: 274–281.

Werner, M., Peck, J., Lave, R. and Christophers, B. (eds) (2018) *Doreen Massey: Critical Dialogues.* Newcastle upon Tyne: Agenda Publishing.

Whitworth, A. (2016) Neoliberal paternalism and paradoxical subjects: confusion and contradiction in UK activation policy. *Critical Social Policy* 36: 1–20.

Whitworth, A. and Carter, E. (2017) Rescaling employment support accountability: from negative national neoliberalism to positively charged integrated city-region ecosystems. *Environment and Planning C: Government and Policy* 36: 274–289.

Willetts, D. (1994) *Civic Conservatism.* London: Social Market Foundation.

Woods, M. (2007) Engaging the global countryside: globalization, hybridity and the reconstitution of rural place. *Progress in Human Geography* 31: 485–507.

3

Doing space and star power: Foucault, exclusion–inclusion and the spatial history of social policy

Chris Philo

Foucault as spatial historian of social policy

Heeding the central purpose of the present collection, I position Michel Foucault (1926–84), the French intellectual, as a spatial historian of social policy. Casting Foucault as a researcher of social policy is not necessarily how many see him, but, if 'social policy' refers to how different agencies – including formal state institutions and other civic bodies – operate upon 'the social' to shape, order or control it, then he can surely be so characterised. In this connection, it is instructive to recall Titmuss' description of social policies as 'concerned with the right ordering of the network of relationships between men and women who live together in societies' (Titmuss, 1974: 28).

Foucault was particularly concerned with 'the mad, the sad and the bad' (Philo, 2011a: 166), loosely mapping on to the fates of people with mental or psychiatric illnesses (for example Foucault, 1965, 2006a, 2006b), with physical sicknesses or conditions (Foucault, 1973), or who are malefactors from the broadly misbehaved to the perpetrators of serious crimes (Foucault, 1976, 2015). He asked searching questions about the social policies – or, more narrowly, the psychiatric, medical and judicial regimes – framing the problems that such people seemingly pose *for* wider society, probing both the specific institutions confronting them (the asylum, the hospital and the prison) and the specialist knowledges or discourses produced about such people, problems and institutions. His lens widened to take in the economic, political, cultural and 'moral' relations – increasingly conceived as power relations – spun around diverse representations of and practices directed at these problematic mind-bodies, all the while attending to multiple mechanisms meeting the injunction that, as Foucault (2003b) suggested, 'society must be defended'. He thereby initiated a *critical* account of social policy interrogating the manifold ways in which this 'defence of society' takes place, exploring theoretically and empirically how society's defensive mechanisms become thought, enacted and, on occasion, resisted.

While his political energies often turned to the contemporary state of psychiatry or penal policy (Elden, 2017), his substantive inquiries always proceeded historically, informed by detailed engagements with diverse archival sources. For this reason, I champion him as an historian of social policy, notwithstanding objections about the extent and quality of his historical scholarship, most obviously perhaps around his earlier work on the history of madness (Philo, 2013). His historical inquiries can be critiqued, to be sure, but it is mistaken to deny his commitment 'to the fundamental words, phrases and propositions' – indeed, 'the severe poetry of what is said' (Deleuze, 1988: 17, 18) – found on the yellowing pages of archival documents. Deleuze (1988: 1 and chapter 1) positions Foucault as '[a] new archivist' and Badiou (2016: 119) celebrates him as '[a] scholar, in the excellence of that term', unflinching in knowing that '[he] would need to examine a collection of archives comprising official orders, statutes, hospital or prison records, court proceedings and so on' (Foucault, 1969, in Rabinow, 1997: 6). For Foucault, the words from old texts were never merely windows on some truer extra-discursive past, but rather were always 'operative within it; … part of the dramaturgy of the real' (Foucault, 2002: 160), running alongside and sometimes flaking off into the more material dimensions of historical reality, programming it (in the words of powerful agencies), resisting it (in those of dissidents) or routinely enacting it (in those of the rest of 'us') (McGeachan and Philo, 2014). In this sense, Foucault was arguably *more* attentive to the archive, to its multiple accretions and subsequent organisation (Foucault, 1972), than are many empiricist historians who otherwise denounce what he located there in his labours as the critical historian of madness, badness, sadness, sexuality, self-care and more besides. In capsule definition, Foucault was *the* historian of social policy who brought to life an explosively provocative *critical* approach to understanding the articulation of institutions, discourses and power in a generalised will to achieve Titmuss' 'right ordering' of the social.

In my opening assertion, there is an additional term, 'spatial', inserted before 'historian', that is the hinge of everything to follow. It is not uncommon to find Foucault identified as a 'spatial historian', not least since Elden's (2001) impressive elucidation of what he termed Foucault's role, coupled with Heidegger, in 'the project of a spatial history'. Elden underlines Foucault's highly spatialised language, peppered with terms (in English translation) such as 'space', 'place', 'geography', 'environment', 'terrain', 'territory', 'site' and more, stating that 'what is important about Foucault's use of overtly spatialised language is that it enables him to free his histories from the teleological basis of alternative accounts' (Elden, 2001: 94; also Soja, 1989, chapter 1). In his 1976 'Questions on geography' exchange with the *Hérodote* interviewers, Foucault (1980a: 69) acknowledged his 'spatial obsessions', before making his well-known claim about how intellectuals have practised 'a devaluation of space' *contra* an overvaluation of time: '[s]pace was treated as the dead, the fixed, the undialectical, the immobile. Time, on the contrary, was richness, fecundity, life, dialectic' (Foucault, 1980a: 70). Instead, Foucault argued that 'the use of spatial, strategic metaphors enables one to grasp precisely the points at which discourses are transformed in, through and on the basis of relations of power' (Foucault, 1980a: 70), thereby cracking open such relations which risk being obscured – smoothed out – by the fetishisation of history, temporality, narrative and determination. There is more to say about the lineaments of 'Foucault's geography' (Philo, 1992; also Crampton and Elden, 2007), but for present purposes it can suffice to recall Foucault's oft-cited declaration in a 1977 interview that '[a] whole history remains to be written of *spaces* – which would at the same time be the history of *powers* (both these terms in the plural) – from the great strategies of geopolitics to the little tactics of the habitat' (Foucault, 1980b: 149, original emphases).

This statement was followed in the 1977 interview by a reference to 'institutional architecture from the classroom to the design of hospitals' (Foucault, 1980b: 149), all set within discussion about 'the eye of power' comprised by Jeremy Bentham's infamous later eighteenth century Panopticon prison-house design. I will return to the Panopticon later – it is unavoidable in any account of Foucault, history and social policy – but the key consideration here is simply to clarify that, for Foucault, addressing the history of social policy necessarily meant thinking spatially. Moreover, such a spatialisation at the heart of historical social policy analysis has now become familiar to many studies in this broad field, with historical geographers – meaning scholars who would self-identify as such – leading the way in creating an impressive corpus of inquiries into the spatial histories of prisons, reformatories, workhouses, lunatic asylums, idiot asylums, hospitals, sanatoria, prostitution, urban sanitation, racial governmentality, and much more (for example Driver, 1993; Robinson, 1996; Ogborn, 1998; Craddock, 2000; Hannah, 2000;

Philo, 2001, 2004; Kearns, 2007; Legg, 2007; Howell, 2009). In his pioneering 1993 monograph on the historical geography of the nineteenth century English workhouse system, Driver offers the following thumbnail account of social policy:

> The concept of social policy assumes the existence of discrete social spaces, bounded in some way by recognisable territorial limits, containing populations which are the objects of 'policy'. Social policy also requires there to be some notion of what is to be policed, and therefore some idea of norms, patterns of conduct, health and welfare. This in turn implies the desire to collect information about the population, on the one hand, and the capacity to issue regulations, on the other; particular forms of knowledge (statistics, the science of states) coupled with particular mechanisms of regulation. (Driver, 1993: 6–7)

References to policing, norms, knowledge and regulation resound with Foucauldian echoes, as too does the prominence of 'power' in the monograph's title, while references to 'social spaces' and 'territorial limits' immediately accent matters of geography. Following this quote, Driver elaborates on both the broader sense of 'police' and the specific concern for 'disciplinary spaces' (Driver, 1993: 10) such as Bentham's Panopticon – here an influence on English workhouse design and function – that contour his substantive inquiries, advancing the impression of a Foucauldian spatial history of social policy. Authored more recently *without* even referencing Foucault, Beckingham's monograph on *Regulating Drink in Liverpool, 1830–1920* nonetheless circles in the same orbit. 'This is not so much an account of Liverpool's history of drinking', writes Beckingham when distinguishing his approach from orthodox local histories, 'as one of the relationship of reputation [images and knowledges of Liverpool] to the municipal regulation of social problems' (Beckingham, 2017: 1). Historical geographies of social and moral regulation are centralised in a journal special issue section (Legg and Brown, 2013), again with scant explicit reference to Foucault, but here too 'we may return … to the Foucauldian emphasis on the link between self-reformation and governmental practices and processes' (Howell, 2013: 199) as now set alongside questions about nation, state, empire, colony, transnationalism and scale. A spatial history of social policy, of how spaces are implicated in the 'right ordering' of the social, is hence alive, kicking and still owing much to its Foucauldian inheritance.

Exclusion to inclusion I: a big shift in Foucault's histories of social policy

My contribution now in this chapter is to rehearse a significant manoeuvre – a shift or break even – in Foucault's thinking as a spatial historian of social policy. This manoeuvre is one that takes him from a spatial imagination centred on exclusion, most obviously featuring in his early work on the landscapes of reason and madness, towards one where certain orders of exclusion remain pertinent but where space – its design, function, organisation and imbrication within the machinations of (what Foucault will term) 'disciplinary power' – acquires a more dissembled and dispersed materiality. The historical geographers of social policy (and their fellow-travellers in other disciplines) are aware, if not of this shift per se, then of the more nuanced rendering of space at which Foucault arrives. Indeed, it is this rendering of space that runs throughout *Discipline and Punish* (Foucault, 1976), arguably his best-known book and the one that has, for good reason, become the go-to reference for anyone aiming to be a spatial historian of social policy. There is nonetheless much to learn from retracing this shift in Foucault's spatial conceptualisations, arguably returning us to certain primitives of what it means to take space seriously in studies of social policy, historically or today. Moreover, an original move for the present chapter will be to anatomise precisely this shift occurring in his translated series of lectures given in 1972–73, published as *The Punitive Society* (Foucault, 2015),[1] as yet little discussed in any context, which foreshadow much (but by no means all) of what appears in *Discipline and Punish*. Before dipping into these lectures, though, I will first chronicle how Foucault effectively changed his mind on space between the early 1960s and the mid-1970s.

Exclusionary geographies

It has been said that *Madness and Civilization* (Foucault, 1965) pivots around what Serres once termed 'a "geometry of negativities"' (in Major-Poetzl, 1983: 120), perhaps most graphically captured in the following passage:

> Between labour and idleness in the classical world ran a line of demarcation that replaced the exclusion of leprosy. The asylum was substituted for the lazar house, in the geography of haunted places as in the landscape of the moral universe. The old rites of excommunication were revived, but in the

world of production and commerce. It was in these places of doomed and despised idleness, in this space ... which had derived an ethical transcendence from the law of work, that madness would appear and soon expand until it had annexed them. A day was to come when it could possess these sterile reaches of idleness by a sort of very old and very dim right of inheritance. The nineteenth century would consent, would even insist that to the mad and to them alone be transferred these lands on which, a hundred and fifty years before, men [*sic*] had sought to pen the poor, the vagabond, the unemployed. (Foucault, 1965: 157)

Foucault hence crafts[2] a spatial narrative of how European societies – with France as the prime referent – have passed through phases in which different cohorts of troubled and troubling individuals have been subject to exclusionary pressures, essentially those of banishment whereby such cohorts get banished to 'marginal', 'sterile', largely 'uninhabitable' reaches stretching beyond 'the gates of cities' (paraphrasing the first sentence of the first chapter in Foucault, 1965: 3). In this 'geography of haunted places', it was the lepers, regarded as physically and morally polluting, who were cast out by medieval Europeans; then it was the idle, meaning all those who could or would not labour, that were cast out by the early modern Europeans; and then it was the mad who were cast out by the modern Europeans, consigned to the same barren tracts set apart from the normal scenes of human encounter and exchange. '[A]ll these forms of unreason which had replaced leprosy in the geography of evil, and which had been banished into the remotest social distance, now became a visible leprosy' (Foucault, 1965: 205); thereby positioning leprosy and 'unreason' (all that constitutes what is reckoned 'unreasoning' and 'unreasonable') as equivalent states of non-being successively swept away into the 'social distance'.

In part this big-picture story is metaphorical, a dramatic device that conjures Foucault's account of how an unbridgeable chasm opens up and indeed widens between Reason and Unreason, and more specifically Madness, from medieval times through to the present (with the capitalised first letters implying the sense of these world-historical forces marching down the ages, increasingly at loggerheads). In the original preface to *Madness and Civilization*, Foucault speaks of wanting to reconstruct how 'Reason and Madness [become pushed] to one side or the other ... as things henceforth external, deaf to all exchange, and as though dead to one another' (Foucault, 1965: ix). He aims to trace the processes through which representatives of madness – the mentally unwell, whether manic or melancholic – have been progressively silenced, forced to communicate not in their own mad 'murmurings' (Philo, 2013) but in 'the merciless language of non-madness' (Foucault, 1965: ix) increasingly comprised by the technical lexicons of medicine, psychiatry and even psychoanalysis. Yet, accepting the metaphorics of the text, Foucault consistently tethers his account to material spaces, so that the bricks and mortar of leper-houses, houses of industry and lunatic asylums – or the mud and foliage of rural retreats – really matter to the arguments being unfolded: they are much more than incidental stage sets to the overall drama (Philo, 2004: 38–42). My own 2004 monograph comprises a sustained attempt to evidence such a Foucauldian real-world historical geography of madness – and of the 'secure places' supposed to contain, sustain, shelter and possibly 'cure' mad people, often sited in rural districts, from medieval times to the 1860s – drawing upon the archival record in England and Wales. A broadly similar *longue durée* historical geography can also be tracked in the Scottish case from two unpublished PhD theses (Donoho, 2012; Ross, 2014).

Inclusionary geographies

Foucault's account contains a tension of sorts, however, because the big-picture presentation tends to centre on banishment or exile, on the troublesome being chased away to forests, wastes, rivers and seas, whereas the narrower focus – particularly as the text progresses – tends to concentrate on the troublesome being captured and detained: in effect, therefore, being *excluded* from wider society, but only by being *included* in more or less secure spaces from which they cannot easily re-emerge. Dimly aware of this tension in my own monograph, I deployed an early medieval 'life' of Merlin (Clarke, 1975) – who goes mad and flees into the woods, but on occasion returns to the royal court and is detained – to reflect upon differences between exclusion as exile (voluntary or enforced) and exclusion as confinement (in chains or kindly treated) (Philo, 2004: 75–85). Acknowledging this tension also highlights deficiencies in overstating a strict binary between different categories of people and their attributes: in supposing a rigid demarcation, imagined and materialised, between the sane and the insane (or, more broadly, between those accepted as 'normal', like 'us' or 'the Same' and those dismissed as 'abnormal', unlike 'us' or 'the Other'[3]). I would argue that, in the grain of its empirical detail and theoretical nuance, *Madness and Civilization* always keeps this binary in check, never supposing that it tells the whole story; but I have also stressed the need to supplement the 'geometry' (of inside and outside) integral to this work – and to other of Foucault's writings – with a heightened alertness to place-based differences that commonly muddy any simplified portrayal of universal spatial separation (see Philo, 1992, 2004: 42–44). What is apparent, however, is that Foucault himself began to have second thoughts about whether his 1961 epic was remiss in its treatment of exclusion, and whether there might be other geographies that should be more explicitly inspected here (and elsewhere).

Derrida's fierce critique of *Madness and Civilization* in a lecture of 1963 (Derrida, 1981) may have been a factor, since on philosophical grounds Derrida '[r]efus[ed] the model of exclusion, that is, of an expulsion that produces an outside' (Penfield, 2016: 11), objecting that Foucault's 'typical gesture consists in hardening into an opposition a more complicated play of differences' (Derrida, 2004, in Nealon, 2016: 254). While Foucault's tardy response to Derrida, appearing in 1972 (Foucault, 1974), objects to Derrida's philosophical elitism, he still suppressed the original preface (which most starkly spoke of the great schism between reason and madness) in subsequent editions of the book. He also ends up repositioning 'the most essential part of the work' as 'the analysis of these events, these bodies of knowledge, and those systematic forms that link discourses, institutions and practices' (Foucault, 2006a: 578 – a republication of Foucault, 1974), sidestepping any portrayal of *Madness and Civilization* in terms of a grand binary set within an overarching 'geography of evil'. Tellingly, when he returned to the themes of his first major book during his lectures of 1973–74 published as *Psychiatric Power* (Foucault, 2006b), consulting a wealth of new archival and library sources, the approach taken was quite different and more akin to the book, *Discipline and Punish* (Foucault, 1976), which he was then in the process of completing. Entirely shorn of the latter's big-picture historical sweep, and with nothing like its philosophical-phenomenological undertow, these lectures offer instead a claustrophobic 'scenography' (Philo, 2007a) of countless tiny scenes, enacted in asylums across nineteenth century Europe, wherein alienists were striving to exert power over their mad inmates. The practices deployed in these scenes, including a 'Panopticon'-like diffusion of the 'body' of the asylum's medical superintendent into every corner of asylum space, fuelled a mushrooming technology of disciplinary control that doubled as a pseudo-knowledge (the embryonic 'psy'-disciplines) of mental and, increasingly, nervous diseases.[4] This change in emphasis holds profound spatial ramifications – it encompasses precisely the broader shift in Foucault's spatial history of social policy that I outlined – but the task of scrutinising them in detail will be reserved for the next section of this chapter, when I consider the lecture series delivered by Foucault a year earlier, 1972–73, *The Punitive Society*, as introduced overleaf.

For the moment, however, I wish to jump ahead to the lecture series delivered a year later, 1974–75, published as *Abnormal* (Foucault, 2003a). The focus here is on how nineteenth century European societies created a cast of human characters increasingly identified as 'abnormal' – including the moral 'monster' or (potentially) 'dangerous' individual, the incorrigible person and the child masturbator (Philo, 2011b) – whose cases, biographies and bodies should become the subject of intense knowledge creation and diverse interventions (by families, experts and the state; in and out of institutional settings; all unarguably 'social policies').[5] Undergirding these lectures is a distancing from 'this model of the exclusion of lepers' (Foucault, 2003a: 44), the prime spatial organising principle of *Madness and Civilization*, complete with its 'entire arsenal of negative concepts or mechanisms of exclusion' (Foucault, 2003a: 44).

He accepts its applicability in certain times and places, but he now specifies 'another model of control that seems to me to have enjoyed a much wider and longer success,' framed as 'the model of the inclusion of plague victims' (Foucault, 2003a: 44). Describing the meticulous, micro-territorial planning of the post-seventeenth century 'plague town' under quarantine – 'a territory that was the object of a fine and detailed analysis, of a meticulous spatial partitioning (*quadrillage*)' – and the conjoint 'surveillance [that] had to be exercised uninterruptedly', Foucault begins to specify a fleet of inclusionary, rather than exclusionary, geographies:

> You can see that this kind of organisation is in fact absolutely antithetical to, or at any rate different from, all the practices concerning lepers. It is not exclusion but quarantine. It is not a question of driving out individuals but rather of establishing and fixing them, of giving them their own place, of assigning places and of defining presences and subdivided presences. Not rejection but inclusion. (Foucault, 2003a: 46)

In parallel, Foucault characterises the form of control afforded through these spatial fixities, ones permitting the constant inspection, examination and registration of peoples and districts for the appearance of plague, as a novel and specific modality of how authorities exercise power over subject populations:

> The moment of the plague is one of an exhaustive sectioning (*quadrillage*) of the population by political power, the capillary ramifications of which constantly reach the grain of individuals themselves, their time, habitat, localisation, and bodies. ... [P]lague ... brings the political dream of an exhaustive, unobstructed power that is completely transparent to its object and exercised to the full. (Foucault, 2003a: 47)

The upshot was 'the invention of positive technologies of power', and '[w]e pass from a technology of power that drives out, excludes, banishes, marginalises, and represses, to a fundamentally positive power that fashions, observes, knows and multiplies itself on the basis of its own effects' (Foucault, 2003a: 48).[6] For the spatial analyst of social policy, there is so much to learn here from the *explicit* manner whereby Foucault contrasts exclusionary and inclusionary spatialities of how society may respond to socially problematic peoples, places and pathologies.

Anyone familiar with *Discipline and Punish* will recognise what is occurring in these *Abnormal* lecture notes: namely, a mash-up of decisive moves taken in the former, specifically the discussion of plague, quarantine and space that introduces the chapter on 'Panopticism' (Foucault, 1976: Part 3.3), but more broadly the exposition of modern 'disciplinary power' as a bundle of 'technologies' conceived not as 'repressive' – as in negative, preventative, curtailing, exclusionary – but as 'productive' – as in positive, enabling, generative, inclusionary.[7] I will assume that readers appreciate the core concerns of *Discipline and Punish*: in baldest outline, the transition circa the later eighteenth century from the 'sovereign power' of the European *ancien régime*, predicated on the bloody spectacle of violence against the body of the criminal, to the quieter, gentler, anonymous 'disciplinary power' exerted over prisoners, miscreants and (eventually) a wider lower-class populous, designed less to break them physically and more to reorientate them towards being 'docile bodies' able to (re)take their place as productive and responsible citizens. Foucault captures this transition in various ways, but of particular note is his suggestion that the 'birth certificate' of the modern way of power was issued in 1827 when Julius, Professor of Criminal Law in Berlin, distinguished between antiquity's 'society of the spectacle', with public life regularly punctuated by festivals and rituals where so often 'blood flowed', and modernity's 'society of surveillance', demanding '"ever more profound intervention in all the details and all the relations of social life"' (Foucault, 1976: 216–217, quoting Julius). If 'the architecture of temples, theatres and circuses' accompanied the former, then the latter elicited '"the building and distribution of buildings intended to observe a great multitude of men [*sic*] at the same time"' (Foucault, 1976: 216, 217, latterly quoting Julius).

As already hinted and as this borrowing from Julius confirms, *Discipline and Punish* is the spatial historian's dream: it is pockmarked throughout by an acute spatial sensibility, most obviously when discussing 'the art of distributions' – '[i]n the first instance, discipline proceeds from the distribution of individuals in space' (Foucault, 1976: 141), distinguished in terms of 'enclosure', 'partitioning', 'functional sites' and 'rank' (Foucault, 1976: 141–149) – and when diving deeply into the spaces of 'panopticism' through the example of the aforementioned plague town (Foucault, 1976: 195–198), the schema of Bentham's Panopticon (Foucault, 1976: 200–204), the design of 'complete and austere institutions' (Foucault, 1976: Part 4.1), and the example of the Mettray reformatory for delinquents as perhaps the most non-prisonlike institution still holding family resemblance to Bentham's Inspection-House (Foucault, 1976: 293–296).

Too often, though, the message of *Discipline and Punish* is reduced to the Panopticon – as Elden (2001: 135–136) objects – whereas Foucault himself stresses how the machinations of 'disciplinary power' 'have a tendency to become "de-institutionalised", to emerge from the closed fortresses in which they once functioned and to circulate in a "free" state' (Foucault, 1976: 211). Via the likes of Mettray, Christian schools and other semi-institutional spaces, he envisages a 'swarming' of the disciplines – as conjoint practices and knowledges – out into '[t]he carceral city, with its imaginary "geo-politics"', devoid of any 'centre of power' (no 'sovereign'), but rather constituted by 'a multiple network of diverse elements – walls, space, institution, rules, discourse' as 'a strategic distribution of elements of different natures and levels' (Foucault, 1976: 307). Such is Foucault's vision of modern power, a diffuse and (in intention at least) ever-present 'policing' of the social order, predicated less on a singular logic of exclusion and more on a dizzying spatiality of multiplicity (Plotnisky, 2016) that hoovers up – includes, identifies, fixes, observes, records – just about everything imaginable as grist 'to an indefinitely generalisable mechanism of "panopticism"' (Foucault, 1976: 216). Such is what the spatial historian of social policy must grasp and with which they must grapple.

Exclusion to inclusion II: social policy, penal policy and *The Punitive Society*

The final substantive part of this chapter will now return to the lecture course called *The Punitive Society*, delivered in 1973 (but administratively credited to academic year 1972–73). My purpose is to dig deeper into the spatial problematic gradually unfolded overleaf: namely, the shift from exclusionary to inclusionary geographies, where 'inclusion' is primarily (but not only) configured as the more or less enforced 'inclusion' of certain human cohorts – ones that are difficult or in difficulties – within bounded, visible spaces. 'The most obvious way to read the course is as an early draft of *Discipline and Punish*', writes Elden, before qualifying that 'Foucault discusses a number of themes [in the course] which do not appear in the book, and puts a different emphasis on much that does' (Elden, 2017: 83–84). Garland (2016: 4), meanwhile, casts the course as 'for the most part a work of historical sociology', in contrast to *Discipline and Punish* as 'a more philosophical work'. The lectures have a stuttering feel, as Foucault repeats, elaborates and even contradicts prior claims, groping towards 'his mature view of power' as displayed in the later book, completed August 1974 and published (in French) in February 1975, and 'beginning to sketch the broad contrast between sovereign power and a type of power he ... calls disciplinary power' (Elden, 2017: 102). It is perhaps surprising how *little* is said in these lectures about the Panopticon: just one mention of Bentham's model as 'the architectural matrix for European prisons' (Foucault, 2015: 64), one mention in the course summary (Foucault, 2015: 258) and stray references in the accompanying notes for the course. This relative absence supports warnings not to over-state the importance of the Panopticon to *Discipline and Punish*, although the term 'panopticism' appears occasionally in the accompanying notes to the lectures, rendered on one occasion as 'social panopticism' (Foucault, 2015: 219), while the course summary boldly asserts that '[t]he nineteenth century founded the age of panopticism' (Foucault, 2015: 258; also Elden, 2017: 94).

These remarks run ahead of what we need to explore in rounding off this chapter, however, and so I must backtrack to demonstrate how *The Punitive Society* meshes tightly with the debate staged above about Foucault's shift from assuming exclusionary to analysing inclusionary geographies of social policy. Indeed, the central task for the lecture course could be cast as critiquing a predominant focus on exclusion in the spatial history of social policy, and more particularly as addressing the status, meaning and implications of exclusion as confinement, as a form of incorporation rather than banishment. It furnishes the conceptual (and, to an extent, empirical) throat-clearing that precedes what occurs in *Discipline and Punish*, as well as what becomes further clarified in those claims previously noted from the *Abnormal* course. The lectures hence open with Foucault wondering how to conceive 'the fate [that societies] reserve for those of the living whom they wish to be rid of', by which he refers 'to delinquents, to ethnic, religious and sexual minorities, to the mentally ill, and to individuals who fall outside the circuits of production or consumption, in short to all those who may be regarded as abnormal or deviant' (Foucault, 2015: 2, 3). Here he anticipates his later emphasis on the 'abnormal' as well as encapsulating many aspects of his own overall *oeuvre*, including later interests in matters of sexuality and its regulation (Foucault, 1979, 1985, 1986). He turns for guidance to anthropology, specifically Lévi-Strauss, for a distinction – with alimentary allusions – drawn between, on the one hand, societies that 'vomit' out their troublesome individuals, ejecting and isolating them from everyday social life, and, on the other, societies that 'absorb' (we might say 'ingest') these individuals, assimilating and thereby neutralising them (paraphrasing Foucault, 2015: 2). The notion of exclusion has often been wielded 'rather vaguely' to convey both of these possibilities, he reflects, confessing that 'I myself have used, and maybe abused it' (Foucault, 2015: 2), likely an allusion to his own approach in *Madness and Civilization*.

Instead, he insists, there is a need to be more exacting, arguing that exclusion remains 'the general effect in representation of a number of strategies and tactics of power that the very notion of exclusion itself is unable to get at' (Foucault, 2015: 3). Such a 'composite and artificial' notion 'does not take into account ... or analyse the [struggles], relations, and specific operations of power on the basis of which, precisely, exclusion takes place' (Foucault, 2015: 2, 3). Exclusion in a psychiatric hospital is not the same as expulsion to the forest, since the latter entails abandonment – ceasing all involvement with the individuals concerned – whereas the former potentially entails their subjection to a welter of practices (diagnoses, prognoses, treatments, new regimes in the realms of diet, exercise and occupation) designed to manage, even to cure, them as 'patients'. At the same time, the inhabitants of asylum space are subjected to surveillance, reporting and recording, informing the discourses of the physicians, and are thereby caught up in the relations of what Foucauldians will subsequently call 'power/knowledge'. Foucault (2015: 4–5) himself elaborates this 'psychiatric power' example, cementing the sense that *The Punitive*

Society doubles as a critical reflection upon *Madness and Civilization*, but the wider point is to disclose how, in their exclusion from routine social life, individuals may not be left alone, forsaken, but rather actively engaged for definable reasons.

Foucault then catalogues the 'four major forms of punitive tactics' (Foucault, 2015: 6) to which proven wrongdoers might be subjected, two of which are 'compensation', as in financial or labour penalties imposed on a malefactor to recompense the victims of their wrongdoing, and 'marking', chiefly the scarring, amputation and dismembering of 'the tortured body' that is emblematic of (what he will later term) 'sovereign power' (Foucault, 2015: 8). The other two forms are more obviously spatial: 'exclusion', 'in the strict sense of driving, forcing out' (Foucault, 2015: 6), and 'confinement', '[t]he tactic we [modern societies] practice', which suppresses an individual's 'right of residence' by 'forcing him to look elsewhere for a place in the sun' (Foucault, 2015: 8, 9).[8] By this token, confinement prevents someone from residing where they wish to reside, forcing them to stay in some other residence, most likely one with walls, bars and locks from which they cannot escape to reclaim their preferred 'place in the sun'.

Foucault thereby returns to first principles about exactly what confinement – and, more precisely, prison – achieves, its deepest rationales, as a thoroughly spatialised species of punishment. He deconstructs what 'we' moderns tend to take for granted as a certain keystone of an overall policy towards 'the social' – namely, that punishing wrongdoers means depriving them of their liberty via imprisonment – and in so doing he repeatedly emphasises the relative *newness* of imprisonment: not for 'holding' either dangerous people to neutralise their risk or debtors while they accrue funds to pay their dues, which were older uses of prison, but as punishment. 'A new tactic, prison, despite appearance, is in fact not a very old punishment whose fortune has grown continuously over the centuries', Foucault declares, for '[u]ntil the end of the eighteenth century it was never really a punishment within the penal system' (Foucault, 2015: 63). 'The birth of the prison', the subtitle of *Discipline and Punish*, duly becomes the focus; and, drawing from a variety of archival sources, many passages in *The Punitive Society* trace how imprisonment entered late eighteenth and nineteenth century penal codes – mainly but not exclusively French – as *the* punishment for proven infractions against the law.

Furthermore, many passages explain how the prison punishment form *cannot* be derived from contemporary penal theory (theory of penalties to be imposed on wrongdoers) or judicial practice (how courts decide on crimes and consequences), but rather must be understood contextually, set within the run of early modern social and labour history. More than half of *The Punitive Society* is devoted to such a history, confirming Garland's description of it as 'historical sociology', and to how it intersects with the deepening of confinement as punishment for those on the distaff side of the powerful. It is in this connection that Foucault talks of a 'civil war', not some Hobbesian 'war of all against all', but instead a war of collectivities, social classes included, which hinges on criminals (outlaws, law-breakers) becoming regarded less as threats to individual well-being and more as part of a generalised 'social enemy': 'a war of rich against poor, of owners against those who have nothing, of bosses against proletarians' (Foucault, 2015: 13, 22, 36). What Foucault calls 'the criminal-social enemy' (for example Foucault, 2015: 63, 65) comprised two constituencies: a determined element of hardened criminals – occupying 'this geography peculiar to crime', hiding in 'extra-social sites: convents, castles, underground passages, a mountain hollowed out like a fortress' (Foucault, 2015: 55) – and, increasingly once into the nineteenth century, those lower-class full-time or occasional wage labourers indulging in petty 'illegalisms' or 'dissipating' their labour-power – occupying 'a whole coherent, underground and parasitic [realm of] economic activity' (Foucault, 2015: 147) found in ports, factories, forests and wherever workers, industrial or agricultural, were proximate to, but legally dispossessed from, the 'things' or resources of capital value.[9] If the former reflected a fear of those waging a war against society, possessions and property, provoking a will to 'control … marginal, dubious, restless, wandering elements' (Foucault, 2015: 106), the latter responded to a sense of conjoint economic and moral war being mounted against capital and civility.

Foucault stresses the appearance, notably in eighteenth century England, of Christian (notably Quaker and Methodist) organisations seeking to (re)moralise the criminal-social enemy, 'explicitly adopting the aim of supervision, control, and punishment' (Foucault, 2015: 102). He also argues that 'the State', notably in nineteenth century France, progressively responded to criminality, depredations and sheer 'laziness' with the recognition that 'the working class must be "regenerated", "moralised"' (Foucault, 2015: 149, 187–189) in such a manner that 'recidivism', the loss of moral self-control, was countered. There are many aspects to how Foucault draws these connections, but crucial is what he claims about the invention of 'the penitentiary', with Quaker roots, as an institutional space where wayward individuals –

left alone as much as possible with their inner thoughts – would be forced to reflect, to be penitent, to forsake their old bad ways (for example Foucault, 2015: 88–89; also Bender, 1987).[10] As religious and state apparatuses fused, so 'the bourgeoisie respond[ed] with a gigantic operation of penal and penitentiary encirclement of lower-class illegalism in general' (Foucault, 2015: 161–162). The penal, the penitentiary and diverse physical structures hence coalesced, called forth by the blossoming social-criminal enemy, the consequence being – in the first instance at least – a geography of confinement[11] that was not solely exclusionary, as in throwing away the key and abandoning the wrong-headed in caged darkness, but rather inclusionary, as in operating what might be termed the earliest versions of 'disciplinary power' (finally named as such almost at the close of the final lecture in the course: Foucault, 2015: 237).

From different angles, Foucault elaborates how imprisonment became calibrated, at least in theory, to create equivalence between crime and punishment: between the time that convicted individuals had effectively denied to capitalism by their being unproductive – being slovenly working bodies (perhaps due to the effects of drink), by pilferage (siphoning off the labour time invested in the value of commodities by other workers) and even by violence (rendering other workers unproductive due to injury or death) – and the time that these individuals were to be deprived of their liberty behind bars. In like manner, he relates the 'prison-form' and the 'wage-form': 'just as the wage is given for a period of labour, so a period of liberty is taken as the price of an infraction', meaning that 'the prison-form and the wage-form are historically twin forms' (Foucault, 2015: 71). The will to make malefactors perform 'free labour' in prison only adds to this twinning, as too, if more subtly, does the project of seeking to reform prisoners, to convert them into potentially productive workers able to turn their bodies and time back to the great task of capital accumulation: '[h]ence the tendency to organise the prison like a factory' (Foucault, 2015: 71). At issue, then, is 'the introduction of the quantity of time as measure, and not only as economic measure in the capitalist system, but also as moral measure', leading to stark claims about 'a real extraction of time' and 'the introduction of *time* into the capitalist system of power and into the system of penality' (Foucault, 2015: 83, 72, original emphasis).[12]

Shadowing this logic of prisons as punitive instruments for 'doing time' in concert with the project of disciplining and moralising inmates, there emerged a parallel logic of what might be dubbed 'doing space'; and this doing of space, as explored at various moments in *The Punitive Society*, must now – in bringing this section to a close – be more fully explored. A caveat is that at one moment Foucault stresses the importance of time *over* space: 'the problem of capitalist society is not so much to tie individuals down locally, as to capture them in a temporal mesh that ensures that their life is effectively subjected to the time of production and profit' (Foucault, 2015: 211). The implication is that controlling 'a mass of time' is more significant than the controlling of space, but my own reading is that, in practice, Foucault has no doubt about 'fixing locally' and 'local confinement' (Foucault, 2015: 210, 211, footnote) as necessities for the exertion of disciplinary power (both inside institutions and beyond).[13] Indeed, Foucault makes plain that doing space is about more than just the flint-hard boundaries of confinement, meaning the exterior walls of prisons, the walls of cells, the gates, doors, keys and locks. It is also about how spaces are configured inside institutions, inhabitants grouped and moved, individuals fixed and collectivities dispersed, attendants deployed and, of course, the whole landscape of a prison – all corners, objects, persons and activities – brought under surveillance.

Early in the lecture course, Foucault introduces the Julius distinction between societies of spectacle and surveillance, using much the same words that recur in *Discipline and Power* (Foucault, 2015: 22–23), before appending the following:

> this is precisely what takes place in the modern epoch: this inversion of the spectacle into surveillance. We are in the process of inventing, Julius says, not just an architecture, an urbanism, but a whole mental disposition in general, such that, henceforth, men [*sic*] will be offered as a spectacle for a small number of people, even for a single individual charged with keeping watch over (*surveiller*) of them. The spectacle is turned round into surveillance; the circle of citizens around a spectacle is reversed. We have a completely different structure in which individuals who are set out alongside each other in a flat space are watched from above by someone who is a kind of universal eye. (Foucault, 2015: 23)

Bentham's Panopticon remains unmentioned, but, as indicated, a concern for institutional structures that ensure a 'panopticism' of occupants pervades many lecture passages, notably when alluding to the 'architecture of the inverted theatre, where the aim is to ensure that the maximum number of people come under the gaze and supervision of the smallest number of people' (Foucault, 2015: 204).

Most clearly, though, in his concluding lecture Foucault – hailing Julius again – brings together much that he has presented about the diverse spatial features of the emerging prison, this engine of 'disciplinary power':

> There is a certain spatial form of the prison: that of the star, with a centre that is the point of constant and universal surveillance, in every direction and at every moment; around the centre are wings in which the life, the work of the prisoners take place; and, constructed on the central point, a tower, which is the heart of the edifice in which authority is established, from which orders are transmitted and to which information flows in from the whole. This is an exact diagram of order as command and regularity; the architectural problems of the theatre, but reversed: showing everything, to a single individual; of the fortress, but reversed: for the latter defined a place that shields you and allows you to see everything happening outside, whereas with the prison it is a case of seeing everything taking place inside without being able to see in from the outside, and, at the same time, of the holder of power inside the prison being shielded from the very one he [sic] sees. (Foucault, 2015: 226–227)

At this juncture, Foucault's manuscript includes a reference to 'Bentham → Petite Roquette' (Foucault, 2015: 226, footnote),[14] revealing that the Panopticon was in his mind, although it must be acknowledged that the Panopticon was formally a circle, not a star, and that the (popular) radiating 'wings' prison design was actually a sizeable departure from Bentham's ideal (Evans, 1978: 4; also Grünhut, 1948 and see Figure 3.1).[15] Nonetheless, this remarkable and comprehensive summation of institutional 'star power' is arguably the 'eureka' passage from the whole lecture course, the culmination of Foucault's journey in this lecture course from a singular spatiality of exclusionary, unproductive exile to a multiplex one of inclusionary, productive confinement.[16]

Figure 3.1: Contrasting the circular Panopticon and the cross-shaped Ray System (the simplest form of the 'star' system)

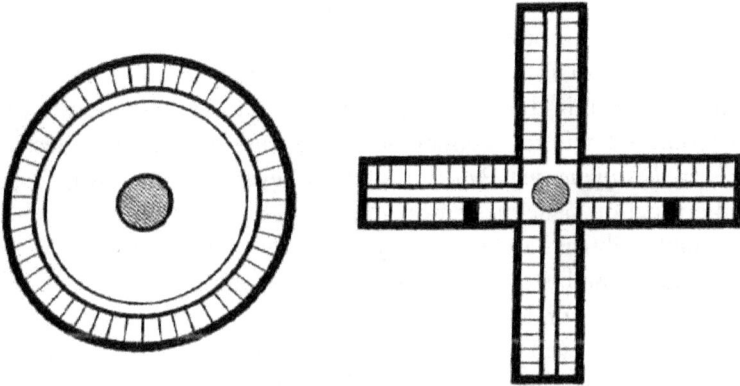

FIG. I   FIG. II

FIG. I
Bentham's Panopticon.
Western Penitentiary, Pittsburgh, 1818.

FIG. II
Havilland's Ray System.
Eastern Penitentiary, Cherry Hill, 1829.   Pentonville, 1842.
New Jersey State Prison, Trenton, 1833.   Bruchsal, 1848.
Moabit, 1849.

Source: Grünhut, 1948: 47

Conclusion: why Foucault's spatial history of social policy matters

This chapter has not really touched on the work of the so-called 'later' Foucault (Elden, 2016). Neglected are the arguments towards the end of the *'Society Must be Defended'* course (Foucault, 2003b) about a 'race war', running alongside the aforementioned 'civil war', whereby mainstream Western societies turn on their imagined 'biological' enemies – especially physically, mentally and behaviourally 'defective' representatives of the idealised national state species – to the point of consigning such unfortunates to the likes of Nazi death camps. Also neglected are claims about 'biopower' and 'biopolitics' in the *Security, Territory, Population* and *The Birth of Biopolitics* courses (Foucault, 2008a, 2008b) wherein discursive constructions of, and interventions in, the social worlds of economic life – entailing careful calibration of 'risk' and the overall 'metabolic' functioning of settlements and states – have commanded attention. Neglected too are diverse 'technologies of the self' and versions of 'pastoral power', traced by Foucault from Victorian Europe back into the fog of Greco-Roman antiquity and medieval Christian Europe, as tackled in his final books (Foucault,

1979, 1985, 1986) and courses (Foucault, 2005, 2010a, 2010b, 2014) which treat in part – but hardly in sum – the fields of sexual health, conduct and regulation. All this material is and should be a fecund hunting ground for the spatial historian of social policy. The chapter has also skated over the works of Foucault that *have* been consulted, even in the dissection of *The Punitive Society* course, since I have omitted here to elaborate how Foucault's optic in these lectures – as in *Discipline and Punish* – widens beyond institutional forms: '[t]he function of sequestration should be located not only in those geographically and architecturally isolated establishments, but also in all those diffuse instances that assure control around them or in place of them' (Foucault, 2015: 208).[17]

It is hoped, even so, that enough has been said to demonstrate Foucault's status as a premier spatial analyst of social policy, and more narrowly to track what I regard as a highly significant mutation in his thinking about space: from a blunt sense of space as physical distance used to put problematic persons well away from the normal round of societal functioning, to a more nuanced sense of space as a portfolio of relations, arrangements, distributions and more – a layering of geometries; a maze of intersecting lines, locations, shapes and surfaces – all enlisted in the disciplining (and potential re-moralising) of society's damaged and damaging populations. As emphasised, the shift is from a clunky view of exclusion as exile, little more than a hounding into the wilderness, to a more complex view in which exclusion still figures, but now more as a means to include – to keep individuals relatively close by, if behind high fences and bolted gates – and then to experiment with the possibility of eventually *re*-including such individuals, once more healthy, capable and responsible, into everyday social scenes. This more complex view addresses the question of how to act with and upon space to promote the 'right ordering of the social', by setting apart those who disrupt that order but still operating upon them with the goal of their later restoration as re-programmed agents of ordering (not disordering). To put matters another way, it is to insist that critical work on the spatial dimensions of social policy should always keep in mind the following headline consideration: the need to be forensically alert to distinctions between social policies that deploy space as barrier/distance (for excluding, setting aside, abandoning) and ones that deploy space as a more complex resource (for including, assimilating, rehabilitating).

Although the narrative thrust of my chapter suggests the superiority of Foucault's revised take on space, my final twist would be to propose that there is still much to learn from taking seriously exclusion as exile, echoing Foucault (2015: 3) when stating: 'I do not think that this notion has been useless'. Indeed, in many times and places certain peoples have been subject to the most brutal forms of exclusion, including banishment, abandonment and death, while such a highly negative orientation towards difficult others – destructive, not immediately productive – arguably *still* retains salience as an exclusionary impulse lurking behind the 'inclusionary' machinations of confinement. It might even be understood as the dark, emotional and even psychodynamic imperative[18] that remains at the heart of the lighter, more rational and discursively reasoned strategies central to programmes of confinement, imprisonment, the penitentiary and (modern) 'disciplinary power'. The spatial historian of social policy would be well advised not to forget this dark heart, and hence always to recognise *both* these spatial models – the nuanced inclusionary *and* the stark exclusionary – as they thread their way throughout Foucault's remarkable corpus.

Acknowledgements

Huge thanks to Adam Whitworth for getting me involved in this project, for his patience and for his helpful guidance. Thanks as well to Stuart Elden and Dan Clayton for supportive remarks.

Notes

[1]   Alongside Foucault's published books, shorter pieces and interviews, his Collège de France lecture courses from 1970–71 through to 1983–84 (he died in 1984) – based on recordings and supplemented by manuscript notes – have been gradually appearing since the late 1990s, first in French and then in English. These lectures, designed as reports from Foucault's frontline research, open a tantalising window on his thought processes – his constant reworking of both ideas and empirics – and much can now be better understood about trajectories, including apparent breaks, highways and byways, in his evolving scholarship (Elden, 2016, 2017). It can be argued that 'a new Foucault' (Philo, 2012) surfaces in the process, one demanding renewed attention from readers who may feel that they already 'know' their Foucault.

[2]   When conducting close textual exegesis of Foucault's own words, I will deliberately deploy the present tense (for example 'Foucault says' not 'Foucault said').

[3]   In *The Order of Things*, originally published in 1966, Foucault (1970: xxiv) elucidates what a given culture conceives as 'the Same' (its core intellectual statements – its *oeuvre* – alongside those humans who create, represent or broadly conform to the letter of what is effectively a societal self-idealisation conveyed by these statements) in contradistinction to 'the Other' (its unreason or madness –maybe its counter-*oeuvre* – alongside those who fall under the umbrella of this designated 'othered' status). As Foucault explains, *The Order of Things* reconstructs a history of 'the Same', whereas *Madness and Civilization* tells a history of 'the Other'.

[4] Ross (2014) provides a rare instance of a scholar drawing in detail upon the *Psychiatric Power* lectures to inform a substantive inquiry in psychiatric history (specifically here the spatialities of Scottish district asylums).

[5] Donoho (2012) provides a rare instance of a scholar drawing in detail upon the *Abnormal* lectures to inform a substantive inquiry into the history of psychiatric history (specifically the practices of Scottish Highlanders in seeking 'public' assistance, through the Poor Law or emerging district asylums, for their mentally 'abnormal' dependants).

[6] Foucault cites his one-time teacher Canguilhem (1973), writing about the complex entanglings of 'the normal and the pathological', as a pivotal influence on his rethinking of exclusion here as something less binary, more negotiated and negotiable, and subject to variability dependent on local *milieu*. For a commentary on what might be termed 'Canguilhem's geography', see Philo (2007b).

[7] Which is not to say that these inclusionary moves were necessarily all that pleasant for those on the receiving end of them: they were not, and would often, if not always, have been individually experienced as 'repressive'. The thesis of power as 'productive' rather than 'repressive' is a key motif of *Discipline and Punish*: it is very well known, and I will not elaborate it here.

[8] Foucault adopts both wider and narrower definitions of exclusion: sometimes it includes all forms of setting apart problematic populations, whether through exile or confinement, but sometimes it narrows solely to exile, set in contrast to confinement (as a form of what might be termed inclusionary exclusion).

[9] Central to his argument is a claim about how 'wealth, in its materiality, is spatialised in new forms and runs the risk of being attacked frontally by a lower-class illegalism … [clashing] with its goods themselves in their material existence' (Foucault, 2015: 156). Growing urban centres, and notably the concentrations of wealth as goods around docks and warehouses, are considered at some length (for example Foucault, 2015: 104), but so too is the restructuring of the countryside under capitalism, with the loss of common 'heaths', 'enclosures' and increased exploitation of forest resources (for example Foucault, 2015: 157–158).

[10] Quakers provided 'an external control, inasmuch as there was the question of providing for the needs of all the equivocal, shifting elements that could circulate on the fringes of groups: the unemployed, destitute, disabled, mad (we may recall that the first clinic in England was opened near York by the Society of Friends)' (Foucault, 2015: 102). The reference in parentheses is to the York Retreat, a charitable lunatic hospital opened by Quakers near York in the 1790s, which practised a 'moral treatment' of mentally unwell 'Friends'. A pivotal institution in psychiatric history, Foucault had already examined its brand of moral control in *Madness and Civilization* (Foucault, 1965: chapter IX; also Philo, 2004: 480–490).

[11] 'In the first half of the nineteenth century there was a whole enterprise of confinement, of lodging the working class in barracks and, apart from the whole apparatus of production, in a whole series of non-productive [economically] institutions such as, for example, pedagogical institutions: crèches, schools, orphanages; correctional institutions: agricultural colonies, reformatories, prisons; therapeutic institutions: homes, asylums' (Foucault, 2015: 203). Foucault gives various examples, such as 'the institutionalisation of the factory-barracks-convent' of a silk mill at Jujurieux in the Ain in 1840, the precise disciplinary regime of which, its minute control over time-space, he portrays in some detail (Foucault, 2015: 201–202).

¹² The Marxist cast of Foucault's argument here is unavoidable: it is deeply rooted in the labour theory of value, particularly in the sense of how waged labour-time instils capital value into commodities. Interestingly, though, the lectures effectively stage a subterranean exchange between different varieties of Marxism: notably between Thompson's humanistic labour class struggle variety and Althusser's structuralist 'State apparatus' variety (Althusser, 1969, 1971; Thompson, 1963, 1978) (both authors evidently influencing different parts of Foucault's reasoning). It might be said that Foucault occupies a not entirely dissimilar middle ground, complete with its attention to the complex spatialities of capital and class, as located by Gregory (1982) when authoring a critical historical geography of the Yorkshire woollen industry.

¹³ Foucault explains that capitalist employers wished 'to fix the working class to an apparatus of production, to avoid worker nomadism, and [so] it fixed the working class in space by fixing it in time' (Foucault, 2015: 228–229). Wage labouring demanded that workers be available every morning to work, fit and ready, which also necessitated their residential proximity and sufficient savings – not squandered on the likes of drink – to 'keep house' and family in a proper manner (to avoid dissipation). Imprisonment equally fixed them in time–space as punishment for breaking the time–space demands of wage labouring, and hence the close ties that Foucault detects between the 'wage-form' and the 'prison-form'.

¹⁴ 'Petite Roquette' was a Parisian prison for young offenders apparently 'based on plans inspired by Bentham's Panopticon' (Foucault, 2015: 242, note 2).

¹⁵ 'The surveillance that was such a strong forming agency of the [radiating wing plan as at Pentonville, London] was not surveillance of the inmates as it has been in the Panopticon and in certain American penitentiaries; it was surveillance of the silent space [the corridors] that separated them' (Evans, 1978: 4). This simple spatial distinction is often lost in secondary commentaries that describe all such institutions – circular, cross-shaped or stars – as 'Panopticons': there are similar logics at work, to be sure, but the precise spatial configurations and sight-lines are significantly different (see Figure 3.1).

¹⁶ Space precludes me from fuller remarks on the implications of my excursion into *The Punitive Society* for debates within the rapidly emerging sub-field of 'carceral geographies', wherein questions about exactly what produces and then comprises 'the carceral' – including about the extent to which it pivots around exclusionary confinement or other radiating relays or 'circuits' of control – are foundational (for example Gill et al., 2018; Moran et al., 2018).

¹⁷ 'Sequestration', for Foucault, is a catch-all term that includes physical exclusion – isolation in an institution – but also 'that kind of arbitral authority that seizes something, withdraws it from free circulation, and keeps it at a certain point, for a certain time, until the court's decision' (Foucault, 2015: 208–209). He speaks about 'instruments of sequestration' as adjunct to 'the State', as 'apparatuses' more or less loosely affiliated to 'the State': 'they are all little States that are made to function inside the State' (Foucault, 2015: 209). More could be said about the debate engaged here with Althusser, and also about links through to Foucault's later claims about 'governmentality' (Foucault, 2008a, 2008b).

¹⁸ There are diverse theories concerning the psychodynamics of 'othering', distancing, rejection, abjection, disgust and reactions to 'the uncanny', all of which have salient spatial dimensions: personally, I remain heavily influenced by Sibley (1981, 1995).

References

Althusser, L. (1969) *For Marx*. London: Allen Lane.

Althusser, L. (1971) Ideology and ideological state apparatuses. In *Althusser, Lenin and Philosophy and Other Essays*. London: New Left Books, 121–176.

Badiou, A. (2016) *Pocket Pantheon: Figures of Postwar Philosophy*. London: Verso.

Beckingham, D. (2017) *The Licensed City: Regulating Drink in Liverpool, 1830–1920*. Liverpool: Liverpool University Press.

Bender, J. (1987) *Imagining the Penitentiary: Fiction and the Architecture of Mind in Eighteenth-Century England*. Chicago: University of Chicago Press.

Canguilhem, G. (1973) *On the Normal and the Pathological*. Dordrecht: D. Reidel Publishing Co.

Clarke, B. (1975) *Mental Disorder in Earlier Britain*. Cardiff: University of Wales Press.

Craddock, S. (2000) *City of Plagues: Diseases, Poverty and Deviance in San Francisco*. Minneapolis: University of Minnesota Press.

Crampton, J.W. and Elden, S. (eds) (2007) *Space, Knowledge and Power: Foucault and Geography*. Aldershot: Ashgate, 67–82.

Deleuze, G. (1988) *Foucault*. Minneapolis: University of Minnesota Press.

Derrida, J. (1981) Cogito and the history of madness. In Derrida, J., *Writing and Difference*. London: Routledge, 31–63.

Donoho, E. (2012) *Appeasing the Saint in the Loch and the Physician in the Asylum: The Historical Geography of Insanity in the Scottish Highlands, from the Early Modern to Victorian Eras*. Unpublished PhD thesis, University of Glasgow (available at: http://theses.gla.ac.uk/5320/)

Driver, F. (1993) *Power and Pauperism: The Workhouse System, 1834–1884*. Cambridge: Cambridge University Press.

Elden, S. (2001) *Mapping the Present: Heidegger, Foucault and the Project of a Spatial History*. London: Continuum.

Elden, S. (2016) *Foucault's Last Decade*. Cambridge: Polity Press.

Elden, S. (2017) *Foucault: The Birth of Power*. Cambridge: Polity Press.

Evans, R. (1978) *The Fabrication of Virtue: English Prison Architecture, 1750–1840*. Cambridge: Cambridge University Press.

Foucault, M. (1965) *Madness and Civilization: A History of Insanity in the Age of Reason* (abridged English edition). New York: Pantheon.

Foucault, M. (1970) *The Order of Things: An Archaeology of the Human Sciences*. London: Tavistock.

Foucault, M. (1972) *The Archaeology of Knowledge*. London: Tavistock.

Foucault, M. (1973) *The Birth of the Clinic: An Archaeology of Medical Perception*. London: Tavistock.

Foucault, M. (1974) 'My body, this paper, this fire'. *Oxford Literary Review* 4: 9–28.

Foucault, M. (1976) *Discipline and Punish: The Birth of the Prison*. London: Penguin Books.

Foucault, M. (1979) *History of Sexuality, Volume 1: The Will to Knowledge*. London: Penguin Books.

Foucault, M. (1980a) Questions on geography. In Gordon, C. (ed) *Michel Foucault – Power/Knowledge: Selected Interviews and Other Writings, 1972–1977, by Michel Foucault*. Brighton: Harvester Press, 63–77.

Foucault, M. (1980b) The eye of power. In C. Gordon (ed) *Michel Foucault – Power/Knowledge: Selected Interviews and Other Writings, 1972–1977, by Michel Foucault*. Brighton: Harvester Press, 146–165.

Foucault, M. (1985) *History of Sexuality, Volume 2: The Use of Pleasure*. London: Penguin Books.

Foucault, M. (1986) *History of Sexuality, Volume 3: The Care of the Self*. London: Penguin Books.

Foucault, M. (2002) Lives of infamous men. In Faubion, J.D. (ed.) *Michel Foucault: Essential Works of Foucault, 1954-1984, Vol. 3: Power*. London: Penguin, 157–175.

Foucault, M. (2003a) *Abnormal: Lectures at the Collège de France, 1974–1975*. London: Verso.

Foucault, M. (2003b) *'Society Must be Defended': Lectures at the Collège de France, 1975–1976*. New York: Picador.

Foucault, M. (2005) *The Hermeneutics of the Subject: Lectures at the Collège de France, 1981–1982*. New York: Picador.

Foucault, M. (2006a) *History of Madness* (unabridged English edition). London: Routledge.

Foucault, M. (2006b) *Psychiatric Power: Lectures at the Collège de France, 1973–1974*. Palgrave Macmillan: Hampshire.

Foucault, M. (2008a) *Security, Territory, Population: Lectures at the Collège de France, 1977–1978*. London: Palgrave Macmillan.

Foucault, M. (2008b) *The Birth of Biopolitics: Lectures at the Collège de France, 1978–1979*. London: Palgrave Macmillan.

Foucault, M. (2010a) *The Government of Self and Others: Lectures at the Collège de France, 1982–1983*. London: Palgrave Macmillan.

Foucault, M. (2010b) *The Courage of Truth (The Government of Self and Others II): Lectures at the Collège de France, 1983–1984*. London: Palgrave Macmillan.

Foucault, M. (2014) *On the Government of the Living: Lectures at the Collège de France, 1979–1980*. London: Palgrave Macmillan.

Foucault, M. (2015) *The Punitive Society: Lectures at the Collège de France, 1972–1973*. London: Palgrave Macmillan.

Garland, D. (2016) Bars and stripes: the thinking and rethinking that led Michel Foucault to write his finest book. *Times Literary Supplement* 5887(January): 3–4.

Gill, N., Conlon, D., Moran, D. and Burridge, A. (2018) Carceral circuitry: new directions in carceral geography. *Progress in Human Geography* 42: 183–204.

Gregory, D. (1982) *Regional Transformation and Industrial Revolution: A Geography of the Yorkshire Woollen Industry*. London: Macmillan.

Grünhut, M. (1948) *Penal Reform: A Comparative System*. Oxford: Clarendon Press.

Hannah, M. (2000) *Governmentality and the Mastery of Territory in Nineteenth-Century America*. Cambridge: Cambridge University Press.

Howell, P. (2009) *Geographies of Regulation: Policing Prostitution in Nineteenth-Century Britain and the Empire*. Cambridge: Cambridge University Press.

Howell, P. (2013) Afterword: remapping the terrain of moral regulation. *Journal of Historical Geography* 42: 193–202.

Kearns, G. (2007) The history of medical geography after Foucault. In Crampton, J.W. and Elden, S. (eds) *Space, Knowledge and Power: Foucault and Geography*. Aldershot: Ashgate, 205–222.

Legg, S. (2007) *Spaces of Colonialism: Delhi's Urban Governmentalities*. Oxford: Wiley-Blackwell.

Legg, S. and Brown, M. (eds) (2013) Special Issue section: geographies of moral regulation. *Journal of Historical Geography* 42: 134–202.

Major-Poetzl, P. (1983) *Michel Foucault's Archaeology of the Western Culture: Towards a New Science of History*. Chapel Hill, NC: University of North Carolina Press.

McGeachan, C. and Philo, C. (2014) Words. In Lee, R., Castree, N., Kitchin, R., Lawson, V., Paasi, A., Philo, C., Radcliffe, S., Roberts, S.M. and Withers, C. (eds) *The SAGE Handbook of Human Geography*. London: Sage, 545–570.

Moran, D., Turner, J. and Schliehe, A.K. (2018) Conceptualising the carceral in carceral geography. *Progress in Human Geography* 42: 666–686.

Nealon, J.T. (2016) Living and dying with Foucault and Derrida: the question of biopower. In Aryal, Y., Cisney, V.W., Morar, N. and Penfield, C. (eds) *Between Foucault and Derrida*. Edinburgh: Edinburgh University Press, 237–250.

Ogborn, M. (1998) *Spaces of Modernity: London's Geographies, 1680–1780*. New York: Guilford.

Penfield, C. (2016) Introduction: between Foucault and Derrida. In Aryal, Y., Cisney, V.W., Morar, N. and Penfield, C. (eds) *Between Foucault and Derrida*. Edinburgh: Edinburgh University Press, 1–26.

Philo, C. (1992) Foucault's geography. *Environment and Planning D: Society and Space* 10: 137–161.

Philo, C. (2001) Accumulating populations: bodies, institutions and space. *International Journal of Population Geography* 7: 473–490.

Philo, C. (2004) *A Geographical History of Institutional Provision for the Insane from Medieval Times to the 1860s in England and Wales: 'The Space Reserved for Insanity'*. Lewiston: Edwin Mellen Press.

Philo, C. (2007a) Review essay: Michel Foucault, *Psychiatric Power: Lectures at the Collège de France, 1973–1974*. *Foucault Studies* 4: 149–163.

Philo, C. (2007b) A vitally human medical geography? Introducing Georges Canguilhem to geographers. *New Zealand Geographer* 63: 82–96.

Philo, C. (2011a) Foucault's children. In Holt, L. (ed) *International Perspectives on Geographies of Children, Youth and Families: Exploring Young People in their Socio-Spatial Contexts*. London: Routledge, 27–54.

Philo, C. (2011b) Michel Foucault. In Hubbard, P. and Kitchin, R. (eds) *Key Thinkers on Space and Place*, 2nd edition. London: Sage, 162–170.

Philo, C. (2012) A 'new Foucault' with lively implications – or 'the crawfish advances sideways'. *Transactions of the Institute of British Geographers* 37: 496–514.

Philo, C. (2013) 'A great space of murmurings': madness, romance and geography. *Progress in Human Geography* 37: 167–194.

Plotnitsky, A. (2016) The folded unthought and the irreducibly unthinkable: singularity, multiplicity and materiality, in and between Foucault and Derrida. In Aryal, Y., Cisney, V.W., Morar, N. and Penfield, C. (eds) *Between Foucault and Derrida*. Edinburgh: Edinburgh University Press, 169–185.

Rabinow, P. (ed) (1997) *Essential Works of Michel Foucault, 1954–1984, Volume 1: Ethics, Subjectivity and Truth*. New York: New Press.

Robinson, J. (1996) *Power of Apartheid: Territoriality and Government in South African Cities*. London: Butterworth-Heinemann.

Ross, K. (2014) *The Locational History of Scotland's District Asylums, 1857–1913*. Unpublished PhD thesis, University of Glasgow (available at: http://theses.gla.ac.uk/3315/)

Sibley, D. (1981) *Outsiders in Urban Societies*. Oxford: Blackwell.

Sibley, D. (1995) *Geographies of Exclusion: Society and Difference in the West*. London: Routledge.

Soja, E.W. (1989) *Postmodern Geographies: The Reassertion of Space in Social Theory*. London: Verso.

Thompson, E.P. (1963) *The Making of the English Working Class*. London: Victor Gollancz.

Thompson, E.P. (1978) *The Poverty of Theory and Other Essays*. London: Monthly Review Press.

Titmuss, R.M. (1974) *Introduction to Social Policy*. London: Routledge.

PART II:

Themes

4

Grenfell and the place of housing in modern life

Anna Minton

Grenfell

On the morning of 14 June 2017, I woke to find an email from the *Evening Standard* in my inbox, asking if I would write a piece on the Grenfell Tower fire. The email was timed 7.40 am and they wanted an article by 9.30 am on 'the housing apartheid in London, how London's poor end up living in death trap towers'. My instinct was to decline the commission, not least because the limited time ensured I would be unlikely to do a good job. The reference to 'death trap towers' also raised alarm bells, given the planned demolition of so many of London's housing estates, which was at the centre of heavily contested debates around housing at the time. Against my better judgement I wrote the piece, basing it around a horrifyingly prescient and now defining blog post entitled 'Playing with Fire' by a local campaign group, the Grenfell Action Group. The blog stated that: 'It is a truly terrifying thought but the Grenfell Action Group firmly believe that only a catastrophic event will expose the ineptitude and incompetence of our landlord' (Grenfell Action Group, 2016). My article focused on repeated failures of management and accountability on the part of the Arms Length Management Organisation in charge of the 10,000 homes in Kensington & Chelsea, which had ignored Grenfell residents' complaints about safety standards again and again (Minton, 2017). Their concerns were later confirmed by the expert report submitted to the Grenfell Inquiry by fire safety engineer Professor Barbara Lane, which found the cladding, doors, ventilation system, fire lifts and the building's 'dry fire main system' were all non-compliant with recommended fire performance criteria. 'The number of non-compliances signify a culture of non-compliance at Grenfell Tower', the report said (Lane, 2018).

I was angered but not entirely surprised when the *Evening Standard* emailed to say that they wouldn't use the piece as it 'wasn't the right fit', although later in the day the *Guardian* ran it instead (Minton, 2017b).

It seemed clear to me that the *Evening Standard* wished to publish a piece about the conditions faced by poor people forced to live in ghetto conditions. The reality which later emerged was the more nuanced picture of a mixed community which had been ignored in raising safety concerns by an unaccountable property management company – which took over management as part of the 'stealth privatisation' (Watt and Minton, 2016) of housing which will be discussed later in this chapter.

This anecdote serves to illustrate the role played by media narratives in creating and reinforcing spatial narratives around social housing. These spatial narratives, which rely on stereotypical depictions of 'death trap towers' and ghettoes of deprivation, interact with policy making to further undermine the place of social housing within the spatial social policy picture.

The *Evening Standard* was not alone in promoting this spatial narrative, which many housing campaigners suspected was being cynically deployed by a number of politicians in the aftermath of the Grenfell fire to boost estate demolition and regeneration programmes. Writing in the *Observer* the weekend after Grenfell, London Mayor Sadiq Khan sparked condemnation when he said: 'Nowadays, we would not dream of building towers to the standards of the 1970s, but their inhabitants still have to live with that legacy. It may well be the defining outcome of this tragedy that the worst mistakes of the 1960s and 1970s are systematically torn down' (Khan, 2017). Again, a more nuanced picture swiftly emerged; rather than spatial segregation and the construction of the building, the Grenfell Inquiry expert reports focused on the poor regulation regarding fire safety standards and the retrofitted flammable cladding surrounding the tower.

The widespread coverage of the agony of residents losing everything, including their loved ones and much-loved homes, and the mounting protests against many estate regeneration schemes, ensured that the tower block demolition agenda did not take off. Nonetheless, it is instructive to see how easily social housing is shoehorned into stigmatised media and therefore spatial narratives, regardless of the evidence. Contrast that with 1960s portrayals of homelessness when public awareness of the issue shot to prominence with the broadcast of the seminal BBC film *Cathy Come Home*, and subsequent efforts by housing charity Shelter to highlight housing problems (Watt and Minton, 2016). Today, Cathy's equivalents are more likely to feature in 'poverty porn' reality TV programmes such as Channel 5's execrable

'Can't Pay? We'll Take it Away!', where bailiffs are filmed evicting people from their homes.

Alongside 'poverty porn' are the numerous 'property porn' programmes that have defined broadcasting schedules over the last 15 years; in 2017 alone Channel 4 screened 18 property shows, from 'Millionaires' Mansions' to 'Location, Location, Location', which with bulging property supplements and adulatory media coverage of rising house prices present an aspirational image of homeownership as the ideal state. These media narratives interact with spatial policy making around the commodification and financialisation of housing, with the promotion of estate regeneration in 'opportunity areas' throughout London boroughs, which reinforce the importance of homeownership and foreign investment, alongside the managed decline, stigmatisation and demolition of social housing. This chapter will investigate the causes and consequences of what is termed the 'housing crisis', drawing conclusions on the place of housing in modern life, with an emphasis on the precarity and displacement forced upon those at the sharp end, who are displaced from their homes to make way for investment properties in luxury schemes. It will focus on the UK, but the themes discussed are equally relevant to housing and property markets in Atlanticist economies in particular and to a large extent throughout North America and Europe.

The 'housing crisis'

> Our broken housing market is one of the greatest barriers to progress in Britain today.
> Theresa May, Prime Minister (DCLG, 2017: 5)

> The so-called housing shortage, which plays such a great role in the press nowadays, does not consist in the fact that the working class generally lives in bad, overcrowded or unhealthy dwellings. This shortage is not something peculiar to the present; it is not even one of the sufferings peculiar to the modern proletariat in contradistinction to all earlier oppressed classes. On the contrary all oppressed classes in all periods suffered more or less uniformly from it.
> Friedrich Engels (Madden and Marcuse, 2016: 9-10)

As Engels famously highlighted in *The Housing Question* (Engels, 1936 [1872]), the housing crisis is nothing new. Although politicians and policy makers routinely talk of a housing crisis (Healey, 2018), progressive commentators argue that the UK does not have a housing crisis (Harper, 2016). Rather, the situation should be seen as the direct result of housing policies that favour financialised, market-based solutions for every type of housing. This spans homeownership (which includes 'low-cost homeownership' in the shape of 'starter homes' and 'shared equity'), the private rented sector (which now takes in new sub-divisions such as 'pocket living' and 'guardianship'), student accommodation and the market in housing benefit.

Prime Minister Theresa May's comments about the 'broken housing market' are taken from the Foreword to the Government's Housing White Paper which focused on 'affordable housing' in the shape of 'starter homes' to buy, but did not mention the term 'social housing' once.

While the parallels between Engel's observations and the present day are striking, it is equally notable that the generation of post-war 'baby boomers' did not experience the soaring house prices and rents that currently define housing in the UK. Nor do citizens of many other European countries today; in Germany for example house price inflation has been relatively stable for the last 40 years (Minton, 2017a). In 1979, when Margaret Thatcher came to power in the UK, there was no housing shortage or housing crisis and one-third of the population, the majority of whom were in work, lived in council housing, as social housing was then known. As council housing catered to such a large proportion of people, its precipitous decline is the single biggest cause of the UK's housing shortage.

Nonetheless, although housing as a policy issue has appeared to be in almost continuous crisis for the last generation, it was not until 2010 that the situation entered the acute phase it remains in to this day. This followed the 2008 financial crash and the election of the Conservative-led government in the UK in 2010, which embarked on a series of austerity policies that included sharp cuts in housing benefits alongside an emphasis on homeownership and foreign investment in the housing market. It is the acute phase of the crisis which has brought housing to national attention as the middle classes are priced out of homeownership and in cities such as London routinely forced to pay more than half of their income on soaring rents (Minton, 2017a).

For almost 40 years, social housing has been subject to neoliberal reforms under the twin lodestars of Conservative-led 'privatisation' and New Labour-engineered 'modernisation' (Watt and Minton, 2016). These processes can be described as 'rollback' Thatcherite and 'roll-out' New Labour neoliberalism (Peck and Tickell, 2002); Conservative governments in the 1980s were driven to roll back the state, while New

Labour embedded and rolled out Conservative-inspired privatisation and de-municipalisation, in the guise of 'modernisation'.

The UK's single most important housing policy, and arguably the most important privatisation of the last 40 years, has been Right to Buy, introduced by Margaret Thatcher in 1981 and continued in England to this day. Designed to transfer wealth to the less well-off through the provision of substantial discounts enabling council tenants to buy their own homes, the flagship policy was justifiably popular. For Conservatives, it also served to create an electoral base of homeowners who they believed would continue to vote Conservative. As shadow environment secretary during the 1970s, the responsibility for formulating the party's housing policy fell to a policy group under the leadership of Margaret Thatcher, which reported that Right to Buy was an 'imaginative' policy which might win over a million voters (Davies, 2013), a view echoed by a later generation of Tories; former Deputy Prime Minister and Liberal Democrat leader Nick Clegg recounted how former Chancellor George Osborne and former Prime Minister David Cameron blocked plans to build more social housing because 'it just creates Labour voters' (Stone, 2016).

Creating an electoral base, growing markets and undercutting local authorities underpinned the policy, with councils, in the process of being stripped of a raft of responsibilities, not allowed to use the proceeds from council house sales to build new homes. The result was that close to 2 million homes were sold but not replaced whilst valuable rental income sources for local authorities to maintain housing stock were cut.

While councils sold their homes and lost their ability to build new ones, the role of housing associations grew exponentially, with New Labour for example aiming to transfer up to 200,000 homes a year from councils to housing associations through its 'stock transfer' programme. This became the main 'option' for implementing New Labour's 'Decent Homes' programme to ensure that all social tenants would live in a 'decent home' that met minimum standards. The other two 'options' councils had for meeting Decent Homes targets were the Private Finance Initiative (PFI) and Arms Length Management Organisations (ALMOs) – all options that ensured marketisation either directly or indirectly, by ruling out direct public investment by councils in their stock (Watt and Minton, 2016). While housing associations did upgrade many of the homes transferred, they never came close to making up for the decimation of the social housing stock, as shown by the graph in Figure 4.1. As for the Private Finance Initiative, schemes have been accompanied by the same ballooning

Figure 4.1: Permanent dwellings completed in England by tenure, 1946 to 2015

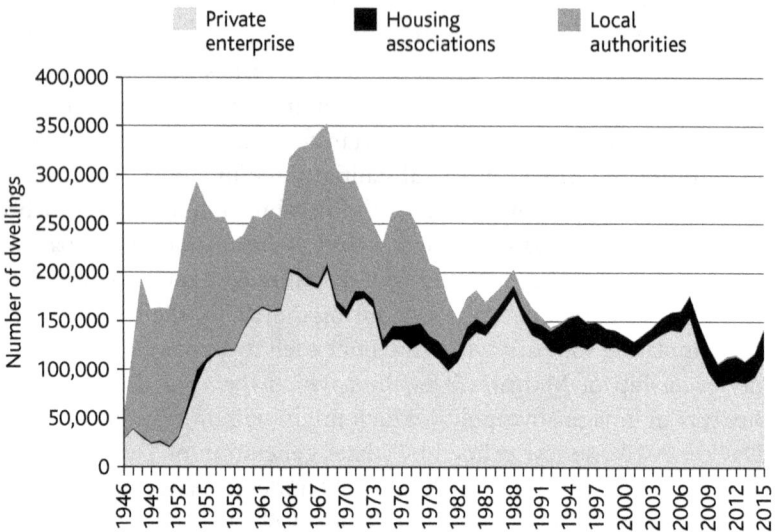

Source: DCLG, 'Live tables on house building, Table 244', https://www.gov.uk/government/
statistical-data-sets/live-tables-on-house-building

debt problems experienced in the NHS, alongside severe issues with contracts and repairs (Williams, 2017). ALMOs have also been associated with poor management and lack of accountability, with the consequence that local authorities have wound back almost half of the ALMOs outsourced since 2008 and taken back responsibility for their housing. In Kensington & Chelsea the council continued with its now infamous ALMO arrangements with the Kensington & Chelsea Tenants Management Organisation – the misleading name of the ALMO – widely regarded as contributing significantly to the lack of accountability Grenfell residents had to face (Power, 2017).

While social housing was sold off and privatised, the legislative and financial architecture laid down by the Conservatives in the 1980s enabled the private rented sector to take over where social housing had left off. This shift in policy is sometimes referred to as 'from bricks to benefits' (Minton, 2017a), as councils stopped building and began to rely on housing benefit to house tenants in the private rented sector, which took off as a result of Buy to Let. Introduced at the height of the Thatcher era in 1988, Buy to Let got going properly in 1996 when Buy to Let mortgages were introduced and a new Housing Act made the Assured Shorthold Tenancy the main type of tenancy. Today Buy to Let is booming, fuelled by demand in every part of the housing market from professionals to those in housing need, with a third of social housing tenants renting privately.

The unforeseen consequences of the interaction between Right to Buy and Buy to Let is that the sale of council homes, originally designed to shift wealth to the less well-off, now transfers it directly into the pockets of private landlords as the original beneficiaries of the 'property owning democracy' sell up, often to professional private landlords. In 2016, a House of Commons Select Committee Report found that 40% of council homes sold through Right to Buy are being rented out far more expensively by private landlords, some of whom own hundreds of properties (Communities & Local Government Select Committee Report, 2016). The rent increases are extreme, with figures for 2015 showing the average rent for a local authority two-bed flat in London at £417, compared with £1,500 in the private rented sector (Minton, 2017a). The result is a Housing Benefit bill which has doubled since 2005 to reach £9.3 billion in 2016, driven by councils which desperately need more housing – a crisis which is compounded by rising rents and the need for substantial deposits. The consequence is that nearly every local authority operates private sector leasing schemes, leasing back former council properties from private landlords – at huge expense.

Failed attempts to reduce the housing benefit bill by linking Housing Benefit to the market have resulted in a situation of extreme precarity for social housing tenants renting privately, who face frequent evictions. Known since 2008 as 'Local Housing Allowance', Housing Benefit no longer covers all the rent for a property. The rationale was that Local Housing Allowance would pay for the lowest thirtieth percentile of rents in an area, meaning that theoretically the cheapest 30% of properties in a local area would be available to tenants on benefit, which the government claimed would ensure that some rents would remain low. But it has not worked out like that, as rather than coming down, rents in every part of London and many other British cities have gone up. In London there are hardly any properties available at all which are affordable to people on Local Housing Allowance. In Westminster, for example, the rent in 2017 for a two-bedroom former council flat was £1,799 per month – £600 more per month than the Local Housing Allowance for a two-bedroom flat in London (Minton, 2017a). It is now official policy for Westminster to house people in cities outside of London (Butler and Booth, 2017). In Newham, 540 households were moved out of the borough between 2012 and 2015, with families going to Birmingham, Leeds and Middlesborough. But this creates a housing crisis in other cities such as Luton, where

London boroughs house families, which in turn means Luton has nowhere to put its own residents and exports them to Milton Keynes, Bedford, Northampton and Peterborough (Minton, 2017a). When I was researching *Big Capital* I was particularly struck by comments made by a Luton councillor who said:

> The Local Housing Allowance in Luton for a one-bedroom place will be around £650 and London Local Housing Allowance is £760, so the landlord can get an extra £110 by doing a deal with a London borough. But Luton also has a housing shortage so the stupid bit about it is we're having to do the same and move our people … so Luton people are further north and London people are moving north to Luton. (Minton, 2017a: 86)

This is the unintended consequence of treating social housing as a financial instrument, through the provision of benefits tied to markets.

'Placemaking'

All across London and in other British cities 'placemaking' strategies are reconfiguring areas and shaping new districts. It is not a new approach, pioneered by cities such as London, Liverpool and Manchester in different iterations in the 1980s, 1990s and 2000s. The 1980s were the era of the Conservative-led Urban Development Corporations, which began with Docklands and Merseyside and which were premised on 'property-led regeneration' and 'trickle-down economics' – the idea that the influx of private sector wealth and finance capital into an area would benefit the poorest communities which needed it the most. New Labour's concept of the 'urban renaissance' was accompanied by very different mood music, but was similarly underpinned by property-led regeneration which understood space primarily as a place for investment, with strategies aiming to lever in private sector investment to formerly run-down industrial areas with the potential for growth.

'Placemaking' is a vague term, which seems to have originated in the US in the 1990s at the behest of the American policy makers who have been so influential in shaping UK policy towards cities. It was popularised by Richard Florida's (in)famous book, *The Rise of the Creative Class* (Florida, 2002), which emphasised that knowledge workers – in design, technology, education, arts and entertainment – were the spur for growth through innovation, and that placemaking should aim to attract these types who power forward the new economy and cleave to hip locations. Creating 'innovation clusters', which ideally include a university, commercial space, shops, restaurants and perhaps an art gallery alongside housing in the form of luxury apartments, is the model generally favoured, most often in a Canary Wharf-style privately owned, high-security environment.

Bruce Katz and Jeremy Nowak (2018), the American authors of *The New Localism*, describe placemaking as a process where former industrial and inner city areas are regenerated by 'extracting value' through 'increasing commercial yield' – which means that the potential for relatively low-priced former industrial and inner city areas to produce far higher returns attracts developers. An alternative lens through which to look at similar processes is provided by the late geographer Neil Smith, who developed his theory of the 'rent gap' as far back as 1979 as an economic explanation for gentrification (Smith, 1979). This held that when the gap between the current 'rent' or income from a property and the potential income was large enough developers would become interested and private capital would flow in. And as property prices and rents increase, existing communities are priced out and displaced; rather than 'trickling down', wealth doesn't benefit existing communities, it moves them out.

The same model continues to drive contemporary regeneration at the Greenwich Peninsula, Kings Cross, Elephant & Castle and throughout London and in other British and North American cities. French sociologist Henri Lefebvre predicted that treating space purely as a product for investment would mean that everywhere would come to look the same, and this is what has happened and continues to happen. At Greenwich Peninsula, the presence of the art school Ravensbourne brings activity and a 'sense of place' to the area, which also boasts the O2 venue and Emirates Air Line, as part of the attractions for those seeking to invest in the forest of luxury apartment towers going up. At Kings Cross, another art school, Central Saint Martin's, provides the cultural capital for what is billed as the largest redevelopment in northern Europe, set in a private estate of 2,000 homes alongside an 'innovation cluster' which includes Google's headquarters, with Facebook apparently set to follow. The New Localism, which singles out the 'innovation cluster' at Kings Cross for particular praise, acknowledges that the outcome is to 'typically see tenant replacement' as 'yesterday's artists' lofts become tomorrow's investment banker's condos'. But while housing affordability is seen as an issue it is not addressed – almost as though it were collateral damage, the price that must be paid for this model (Minton, 2018).

In London, 'estate regeneration' programmes which have witnessed the demolition of up to 100 housing estates (Minton, 2017a) have also been part of the city's 'placemaking' strategies. The Heygate Estate in Elephant & Castle in south London is an instructive example. Formerly home to more than 3,000 people, the majority of whom were on low incomes, it was demolished in 2014 and replaced by luxury development Elephant Park. Of the 2,704 new homes at Elephant Park only 82 are social housing. While 25% are classified as 'affordable housing', since affordable housing was redefined by the Conservatives to mean up to 80% of market rent this places the properties out of reach not only to those on low but also on middle and relatively high incomes. According to a report by Transparency International, 100% of all properties in the first phase of the development were sold to foreign investors (Minton, 2017a) and it is commonplace for schemes of this nature to be marketed abroad before they hit the UK market.

It is a similar story in Poplar in East London where Grade II–listed Balfron Tower, Erno Goldfinger's modernist social housing masterpiece, has been repurposed as apartments for sale to finance professionals and investors. Around the corner, Robin Hood Gardens, another social housing estate hailed by architects and conservationists as a modernist masterpiece, failed to gain listed status and was at the time of writing in the process of demolition. It is being replaced by the new Blackwell Reach development which was marketed to Asian investors in Hong Kong in October 2017 before the bulldozers had barely got on-site, with the event boasting of 'East London's best value 2 bedroom apartments from £565,000' (Minton, 2018). The Victoria & Albert Museum's controversial decision to purchase a three-storey section of the estate, including the exterior facades and the interiors of a maisonette, sparked condemnation that a public institution is making cultural capital from a section of an iconic building which is deemed worthy of exhibit in a museum but not as housing for people to live in.

Student accommodation offers a microcosm of this picture of luxury placemaking on the one hand and displacement and exclusion on the other. Sitting alongside the commodification of university education and the business model UK universities now subscribe to, UK university student accommodation in luxury complexes with gyms, swimming pools and cinemas is amongst the most expensive in the world. A report by property consultants Savills described the 'flowering of student housing as it has grown from a niche investment opportunity to a global asset class', with the UK by far the most popular home for institutional and private capital, attracting almost $9 billion in three years. At $1,600 a month (Savills, 2016), which is significantly more than the value of a year's student loan, accommodation in halls of residence is limited largely to wealthy and overseas students. The consequence is that student accommodation is unaffordable to almost half of all students, who have to navigate the private rented sector where they often face appalling conditions, while rent strikes are becoming a regular feature of London campuses. One of my students admitted to spending three nights in the library after he came home one evening to find his landlord had changed the locks and put his possessions on the street.

'Housing insecurity'

The flip side of placemaking is precarity for the original residents of an area who are all too frequently forced to move out, either by rising rents or the demolition of their homes. Tenants forced to leave their homes on housing estates place further pressure on borough housing waiting lists, in the context of the already acute shortage of social housing.

But it is arguably not these private renters forced out of their homes and communities that have been worst affected. It is the leaseholders, Margaret Thatcher's Right to Buy owners, who have been the worst hit by demolition, with many having to move out of London as the compensation home owners receive as a result of compulsory purchase is very low. On the Heygate, Compulsory Purchase Orders averaged £107,230 for a two-bedroom flat; in December 2017, a two-bedroom property on Elephant Park, the development which replaced the Heygate, ranged in price between £890,000 to more than £1 million, according to the property website Rightmove. This meant that former Heygate residents who bought their own homes were through CPO-based gentrification priced out of the city and now live in Orpington, Sevenoaks, Thurrock and Rochester. A retired couple I interviewed for *Big Capital* who had lived on the Heygate for 34 years had been forced to move to Sidcup; both have suffered serious mental and physical health problems as a result of the move, including severe depression (Minton, 2017a).

Evictions are soaring across the world with mega events such as the World Cup or the Olympics witnessing placemaking strategies go into overdrive: 22,000 families were relocated as a result of the Rio Olympics for example (Madden and Marcuse, 2016). In the UK, multiple housing policies are causing increasing numbers of evictions, with the consequent emotional and mental health problems displacement from home and community brings. Loretta Lees is

Principal Investigator of the Economic and Social Research Council (ESRC)-funded project 'Gentrification, Displacement and the Impacts of Council Estate Renewal in 21st Century London', which has found that more than 135,000 London council tenants have been displaced since 1997. Interviews with tenants displaced from estates focus on the psychological impacts, with processes of attachment disrupted and ensuing problems of disorientation and alienation, with local GPs disturbed by the public health impacts in terms of anxiety, depression and suicide attempts (Lees, 2018).

The acute shortage of social housing, working in tandem with the capping of Housing Benefit linked to local market rents via Local Housing Allowance, is a key factor driving a cycle of continuous evictions as the private rented sector offers little security to tenants. While social housing has faced many assaults over the last 40 years, typically a council or housing association tenancy still offers considerably greater security of tenure than a six-month Assured Shorthold Tenancy; these are the shortest tenancies in the world, paralleled only by Australia.

In the private rented sector the situation is very different. One local authority cabinet member for regeneration I spoke to said: 'We think broadly a third of landlords are well meaning and do a good job, a third are well meaning and do a bad job and a third are rogue landlords, and at the fringes of that you have slum landlords and criminal human trafficking' (Minton, 2017a). Green Party London Assembly member Sian Berry conducted a 'Big Renters Survey' of more than 1,000 renters who described their experiences, highlighting rocketing rents compared to wages, poor conditions and the way lettings agents and landlords treat them. Rising rents were the most common problem and seven in ten renters suffered from repairs and maintenance not being done, with many reports of landlords who would rather evict tenants than carry out repairs (Berry, 2016).

For psychiatrist Dr Ciaran Abbey, stability of housing is the most important factor determining mental health. Abbey and Dr T.B.S. Balamuri are authors of *Housing the Mind*, which highlights the importance of security of tenure to general security and well-being. The report cites evidence that spending more than 30% of income on housing is associated with worse mental health: '[W]hen a disproportionate amount of income is spent on housing, this leaves people less able to purchase other necessities such as adequate food, increasing the family's vulnerability to disease but also the anxiety and sense of helplessness that results when unable to make ends meet' (Abbey and Balamuri, 2016: 109).

Helplessness, loss of control and shame are also at the heart of a report by social action centre Cambridge House and Leicester University, which investigated cases taken on by the Housing Law Centre at Cambridge House. A care worker on a zero-hour contract fell into arrears with her rent because her hours were not consistent and was asked by the judge if going to court meant she would be more likely to pay the rent. She responded:

> I was never in dispute of it; I just simply don't have enough money. I go to bed every night with a sandwich and a cup of tea [still crying], I can't even have a proper meal … I understand it's got to be done, but urgh … it just feels like a punishment for the poor. If I was in Dickensian times I would be in a debtors' prison. (Lees and White, 2016: 109)

The term 'ontological security', was initially proposed by the psychiatrist R.D. Laing and built on by sociologist Anthony Giddens to mean a sense of order and continuity in relation to experiences (Madden and Marcuse, 2016). Housing security is central to ontological security and the sense that the stability of an individual or family, their place in the world and their home, can be taken for granted. The privatisation and financialisation of every aspect of home is directly undermining ontological security, prioritising housing as a unit of profit for landlords, developers and investors rather than a social good and human right. Long before the fire, Grenfell residents' helplessness in the face of an unaccountable management company ensured that their safety concerns were not listened to and created fertile ground for the consequent catastrophe. In this context, the UN special rapporteur on the right to adequate housing, Leilani Farha, is investigating whether the UK government failed to comply with its international human rights obligations, voicing concerns that residents had told her they had been excluded from decisions about housing safety issues before the fire and not been engaged 'in a meaningful way' by the authorities in its aftermath, concerns which were confirmed by the expert report submitted to the Grenfell Inquiry by fire safety engineer Professor Barbara Lane.

Farha was struck by survivors' 'feelings of not being heard, of feeling invisible, and not being treated like equal human beings'. She was also concerned that they were stereotyped and discriminated against on the basis that they lived in social housing.

> Residents told me they feel the government's position is that they should feel lucky that they are going to be rehoused and that they should feel lucky that they had social housing. That doesn't suggest residents feel the government recognizes them as rights holders. The fact that so many residents have said to me they are not being treated as human beings is suggestive of a society that is structured in a way where those in social housing are viewed perhaps as counting less. And that is deeply troubling. (Butler, 2018)

The Grenfell fire shocked the UK to the core not just because of the scale and horror of the disaster but because it was a defining moment. It revealed a truth about the unaccountable and stigmatising nature of housing policy over the last generation which could not be denied even by a mainstream media keen to fall back on stereotypes. Or so it seemed at the time. A year later, on the anniversary of the tragedy, the *London Review of Books* dedicated an entire issue of the magazine to an unprecedented 60,000 word piece by Andrew O'Hagan which included a section called 'The Narrative' and a section entitled 'The Facts' (O'Hagan, 2018). According to O'Hagan 'The Narrative', that the local authority was responsible for the fire, was fuelled by activists who had long hated the Conservative-run council. His interviews with the dedicated public servants who ran the council told a very different story, in keeping with 'the way local authorities work every day in Britain, often demonstrating grace under pressure, without getting everything right, of course, but making a good effort'.

It is these same local authorities which have been at the forefront of stock transfer and the unaccountable private–public partnerships to promote spatial strategies such as 'placemaking' in 'opportunity areas' and it is notable that O'Hagan did not include the 'fact' that Grenfell Tower was managed by an Arms Length Management Organisation which repeatedly failed to listen to residents' concerns about safety. The piece, which shocked the left-leaning media of which the LRB is a part, included the description of activists 'throwing accusations into the air like confetti at a whore's wedding', revealing a contempt towards social housing residents paralleled by TV's 'poverty porn' programmes.

Grenfell has led to a shift in the political climate but has so far had little impact on policy, while the power of stigmatising narratives towards social housing and the people who live in it remains a dominant force. These narratives reflect exclusionary spatial strategies to promote 'placemaking' in 'opportunity areas' all around London and in other UK cities, strategies which create displacement and drive and promote the financialisation commodification of housing policy.

References

Abbey, C. and Balamuri, T.B.S. (2016) *Housing the Mind*. The Legatum Institute.

Berry, S. (2016) What are renters thinking? Briefing by Sian Berry, Green Party Member of the London Assembly.

Butler, P. (2018) UK may have breached human rights over Grenfell Tower, says UN. *The Guardian*, 9 March. www.theguardian.com/uk-news/2018/mar/09/grenfell-tower-uk-may-have-breached-human-rights-says-un

Butler, P. and Booth, R. (2017) Westminster council could send homeless families to Coventry. *The Guardian*, 15 January. www.theguardian.com/uk-news/2017/jan/15/homeless-families-coventry-westminster-council-london-cuts

Commons Communities and Local Government Committee (2016) Housing Associations and the Right to Buy: Second Report of Session 2015-16. London: House of Commons. https://publications.parliament.uk/pa/cm201516/cmselect/cmcomloc/370/370.pdf

Davies, A.R. (2013) Right to Buy: the development of a Conservative housing policy, 1945–1980. *Contemporary British History* 27(4): 421–444.

Department for Communities and Local Government (2017) Fixing our broken housing market. www.gov.uk/government/publications/fixing-our-broken-housing-market

Engels, F. (1936 [1872]) *The Housing Question*. Ed. C.P. Dutt. London: Lawrence and Wishart.

Florida, R. (2002) *The Rise of the Creative Class: And How It's Transforming Work, Leisure, Community and Everyday Life*. New York: Basic Books.

Grenfell Action Group (2016) KCTMO – Playing with fire! Posted 20 November. https://grenfellactiongroup.wordpress.com/2016/11/20/kctmo-playing-with-fire/

Harper, P. (2016) The housing crisis isn't a crisis, it's a design project. *Dezeen*, 30 September. www.dezeen.com/2016/09/30/phineas-harper-opinion-on-the-uk-housing-crisis-that-isnt-a-crisis/

Healey, J. (2018) Speech to the Labour Party Conference. https://labour.org.uk/press/john-healey-speaking-labour-party-conference-today/

Katz, B. and Nowak, J. (2018) *The New Localism: How Cities Can Thrive in the Age of Populism*. Washington DC: Brookings Institution Press.

Khan, S. (2017) We owe it to the Grenfell Tower victims to establish the full truth. *The Guardian*, 18 June.

Lane, B. (2018) Dr Barbara Lane's expert report. Grenfell Tower Inquiry. www.grenfelltowerinquiry.org.uk/evidence/dr-barbara-lanes-expert-report

Lees, L. (2018) *Challenging the Gentrification of Council Estates in London.* Oxford: Urban Transformations.

Lees, L. and White, H. (2016) *Why We Can't Afford to Lose It: Local Authority Housing in London Protects the Poor from Homelessness.* University of Leicester & Cambridge House report, in partnership with Lambeth County Court Duty Scheme.

Madden, D. and Marcuse, P. (2016) *In Defense of Housing.* London and Brooklyn: Verso.

Minton, A. (2017a) *Big Capital: Who Is London For?* London: Penguin.

Minton, A. (2017b) High-rise blocks like Grenfell Tower can be safe. The key issue is management. *The Guardian,* 14 June. www.theguardian.com/commentisfree/2017/jun/14/high-rise-grenfell-tower-safe-building-west-london-fire

Minton, A. (2018). Setting the scene: thirty years of regeneration in East London. In Duman, A., Hancox, D., James, M. and Minton, A. (eds) *Regeneration Songs: Sounds of Investment and Loss from East London.* London: Repeater.

O'Hagan, A. (2018) The tower. *The London Review of Books* 40(11).

Peck, J. and Tickell, A. (2002) Neoliberalizing space. *Antipode* 34(3): 380–404.

Power, A. (2017) How tenant management organisations have wrongly been associated with Grenfell. LSE Blogs. http://blogs.lse.ac.uk/politicsandpolicy/the-truth-about-tmos/

Savills (2016) *World Student Housing: Class of its Own.* https://pdf.euro.savills.co.uk/global-research/spotlight-world-student-housing-2016-2017.pdf

Smith, N. (1979) Toward a theory of gentrification: a back to the city movement by capital, not people. *Journal of the American Planning Association* 45(4): 538–548.

Stone, J. (2016) Tories refused to build social housing because it would 'create Labour voters', Nick Clegg says. *The Independent,* 3 September. www.independent.co.uk/news/uk/politics/tories-refused-to-build-social-housing-because-it-would-create-labour-voters-nick-clegg-says-a7223796.html

Watt, P. and Minton, A. (2016) London's housing crisis and its activisms. *City* 20(2): 204–221.

Williams, Z. (2017) The long read: The real costs of regeneration. *The Guardian,* 21 July. www.theguardian.com/society/2017/jul/21/the-real-cost-of-regeneration-social-housing-private-developers-pfi

5

Re-placing employment support: multi-spatial activation diorama

Adam Whitworth

Policy contexts across advanced economies have reconfigured welfare systems to consolidate paid work as the cornerstone of citizenship obligations. Yet unfulfilled or undesired employment situations – whether unemployment, underemployment, precarious employment, unhealthy (mentally or physically) employment or stalled employment – are pervasive features of capitalist economies.

In response, national governments cite a new need to reform welfare systems in order to create an 'activating' environment to drive maximum labour market participation. This is narrated in part as necessary in today's interconnected economy due to the disciplinary logic of global economic forces and in part as benevolent governance based on a paternalistic desire to enhance citizen well-being through supporting participation in paid work. There is some truth to both claims, but only in part. Whilst globalisation indeed brings new economic pressures on nation states it does not remove governments' capacity to act, though does offer them a conveniently self-constraining narrative to pursue already desired reforms. And whilst good work is on average known to be beneficial for health (Waddell and Burton, 2006), all work is not 'good' – indeed, a growing amount of the labour market is becoming 'bad' zero-hours and casualised employment – and nor are all individuals able to realise their employment aspirations.

Irrespective, 'activating' employment support and the underlying normalisation in policy that all adults should be in paid employment wherever possible have become central features of welfare states across advanced economies. However, the nature and balance of the elements that define the nature of the employment 'support' on offer vary across national regimes (Levy, 2004; Lindsay et al., 2007; Bonoli, 2010) – 'support' might in differing contexts read as voluntary help, mandatory coercion or financial incentivisation and reward. The devil, as ever, is in the detail. Particular attention has been paid by policy makers during this period to certain 'priority' groups – lone parents, individuals with health conditions and disabilities, the long-term unemployed and either end of the working age spectrum (young adults seeking to solidify their place in the labour market and older workers often struggling due to sectoral change or new skills demands). These groups have been depicted in policy strategies as a 'problem' due to their lower employment levels as well as the persistent failures of successive policy interventions to increase those levels.

An ongoing aspect to this activation debate has been the attention paid to ideas of geography in two related ways. Firstly, research and policy experience highlight the (often cyclical) waves of recentralisation and decentralisation as government's performance frustrations and policy priorities ebb and flow – standardisation, cost, value for money, provider flexibility, local discretion, and so on (van Berkel et al., 2011; Minas et al., 2012; Heidenreich and Rice, 2016). In some nations decentralisation of employment responsibilities approaches occur synchronically with multiple mutually reinforcing trends in the same decentralising direction. In contrast, in other contexts decentralising trends in some aspects of employment policy occur diachronically such that the centre retains or even increases control over local areas through central dominance of (possibly new) procedural steering mechanisms (Sweden), changes to funding (Netherlands) or definitions of the bounds of local remits (UK). In many contexts (de)centralising shifts are – in differing directions and for differing reasons – planned, though in other contexts (such as the Czech Republic) decentralisation occurs more organically as a result of a governance failure at the central level and the spontaneous unplanned emergence of more local actors in response. As this literature makes clear, whilst much experimentation of vertical scalar shifts is evident (back) down to localities and (back) up to central government few patterns are detectable other than continual motion.

Secondly, a separate but related set of debates has centred on the roles and possibilities of building better integrated employment approaches that bring together multiple services and partners that are presently fragmented into coherently connected well-functioning whole-person support (van Berkel et al., 2011; Minas, 2014; Heidenreich and Rice, 2016; Whitworth and Murphy, 2018). This type of integrated whole-person employment support model is of relevance to most service users given the prevalence of cross-cutting needs amongst these cohorts, and is of particular relevance to those 'priority' cohorts previously outlined, given that complexity and severity of barriers – health, childcare, experience, skills mismatch, travel, confidence, and so on – is the norm for such groups (Minas, 2016).

Significant learning has been gathered from these dual comparative policy trends and bodies of research. Less well discussed in these debates, however, are the multiple potential readings of 'space' at play within them and the relevance both for academic and policy learning of their fuller and more explicit examination. The remainder of this chapter explores one such reading and draws out its implications for a bottom-up focus on the perspectives and experiences of service users in modern activation programmes, in contrast to the more usual focus on the system level within these dual spatial activation debates.

Specifically, the chapter explores connections between the ideas of two leading critical geographical thinkers: David Harvey's work around absolute, relative and relative space and Torsten Hägerstrand's ideas and visualisations of space–time diorama. Although both are recognised key thinkers of twentieth century geography scholarship (Hubbard and Kitchin, 2011), this is not to suggest of course that these thinkers offer the only conceptual geographical richness that can be brought to bear on applied policy topics such as employment policy, quite the opposite. The range and depth of alternative conceptualisations of space combined with the openness yet often unexplored multiple spatial natures of social policies make this a rich and vast intersection to explore. Rather, the intention is to use these particular geographical ideas in relation to the specific policy case study of employment support to illustrate the interdisciplinary possibilities that exist between the disciplines of human geography and social policy and to encourage others to take up continued spatial exploration within their own policy scholarship.

Re-placing locally integrated employment support from a service user perspective

It seems apt to begin with a map. Hägerstrand's (1982) influential ideas around diorama are framed around the visual space–time depiction of his daily childhood rhythms growing up in a wooded valley in southern Sweden. The lower section of Hägerstrand's diorama shows the physical landscape of the valley and its key features – woods, roads, rivers, a farming settlement to one side, a denser factory settlement at the other, a school building in the middle of this diorama built centrally as a compromise between the two communities. The upper section of the diorama shows the three space-time pathways of Hägerstrand's sample sets of children as they move locations throughout this single Monday in view (although Hägerstrand's original article contains a full week of pathways). These time–space pathways are depicted by continuous lines running vertically down the page according to the running of time and moving across the page diagonally left and right according to the spatial movements of the individuals depicted in each time–space pathway. In the centre of Hägerstrand's original diorama is Hägerstrand's own pathway: his father was a teacher at the school, hence he lived above the school and so remains centrally located throughout this school day. Hägerstrand's pathway depicts him always nearby to the school, trapped there during the compulsory pace-setting hours during the daytime (denoted by the two central fixed rectangular blocks of time through with all children are required to pass) and remaining around home during the evening time, relatively isolated from the other children after they had returned to their farms or homes. To the left of the diorama the pathway of children from the farming community shows them waking on their farms in the morning, journeying into school for the day and then back to spend the evening and night back in their farming community. And to the right of the diorama a pathway showing children from the factory settlement similarly waking in their homes, travelling into school for the day and then travelling back home to have their evening.

Hägerstrand's diorama provides a powerful visual summary of the daily space–time rhythms of these three sets of children. More broadly, however, it also offers rich conceptual foundations for the enhanced spatial understanding of social and policy issues, including this chapter's focus on developing a multidimensional spatial perspective on locally integrated employment support from a service user perspective. To aid that analysis, Hägerstrand's ideas of space–time diorama are combined in the chapter with another key thinker of twentieth century human geography, David Harvey. Amongst Harvey's vast body of Marxist scholarship it is his ideas around distinct absolute, relative and relational conceptualisations of space that are of particular interest (Harvey, 2006).

For Harvey, absolute space is the familiar physical geography of discrete bounded territorial designations on maps – housing plots, administrative units, city boundaries, national borders, and so on. In this absolute view not only is space conceived as known territorial boundaries on maps but it is understood to be akin to a series of passive, empty containers to be filled up in order to give them content and identity. Social policy as both a professional practice and academic discipline clearly is spatial in many ways – policies happen in (sometimes targeted) geographies, local and regional policy partners work to spatially based targets and measures, funding flows to geographically bounded actors, national welfare states are categorised into nationally based welfare regimes, debates around citizenship and migration are rooted around the borders and units of nation states.

This is *a* spatial social policy, but it is an incomplete one dominated by a partial absolute view of space that neglects alternative spatial conceptualisations that offer new dimensions and richness for policy understanding and development.

In contrast, the relative view of space emphasises that understanding the value and meaning of space requires a focus not on the objects themselves but rather on the connectivity of those objects with respect to each other as well as on the circulations between those objects. To understand the elevated house prices of most global cities, for example, one has to see place not as a reflection of a house or area per se but rather their proximity – physically, temporally, culturally – to all of the high-value employment, resources, lifestyles and locational symbols of a pre-eminent urban location in the global network. It is through these proximities and circulations that places take their social, cultural and economic meaning and value. Relatedly, thinking about space relatively incorporates a dynamic emphasis on circulations, flows and processes – whether of people, money, knowledge, values, and so on – compared to the static absolute view of space. The circulatory potentials and frictions in turn relates to the nature of the objects in question, their relative positioning to other relevant objects, and the ease of movement between those objects.

Finally, the relational view of space has become something of a *cause célèbre* amongst human geographers since the turn of the century. Topology and not topography is the chief concern of the relational view (Jones, 2009), such that space comes to be seen as a series of nodes, networks and relations in which space is stretched, folded and in constant flux. As Amin (2007: 103) describes, the result 'is a subtle folding together of the distant and the proximate, the virtual and the material, presence and absence, flow and stasis, into a single ontological plane upon which location – a place on the map – has come to be relationally and topologically defined'. For relational thinkers spatial formations are not only open and discontinuous but also comprise histories, identities, meanings, emotions and characters. The interwoven journeys of people's lives in, through and with places have real effects on those individuals and their lives as distinct from if those places had been other (Massey, 1991). The delineation between people and place thus fractures: place is people, and people are place. This relational view opens space out not only to historical biographies but also to feelings, emotions and to the varying possibilities around the differing meaning of places – a 'ghetto' for one, a community for another. In doing so it incorporates into analysis what different individuals think, understand and feel within any spatially situated moment, event or interaction given their alternative past spatially rooted experiences and influences that combined shape them up to that moment in space–time (Harvey, 2006).

Each of these understandings offers distinct ways in which space can be considered and through which spatial policy analysis can be approached. And, as Harvey emphasises, there is also analytical and policy richness in the ongoing dialectical tensions between these three conceptualisations of space.

Consider the diorama presented in Figure 5.1. At its simplest this reflects the physical world in the realm of absolute space by defining the positioning of the key sites of relevance to an 'activated' service user's daily life – their home, key services, schools and childcare settings that together shape their daily rhythms, the location of the Jobcentre where they must attend regularly to maintain eligibility for their benefits and receive some employment support, and the location of key wraparound services such as health, housing and benefits advice to help resolve current barriers to work. This absolute view of space provides the physical anchors socially and economically that an unemployed individual must interact with as part both of their search for employment and their wider life activities. A range of relevant questions flow out from and around this absolute view of space.

A necessary starting point to understand the perspective of socially and spatially embedded service users in the activation diorama are the regular daily needs and daily rhythms of all our lives – home, school, nursery, shopping, parks, libraries, friends and family, and so on. These daily rhythms of life inevitably vary according to each individual's personal habits and family circumstances as well as the geographical locations and, to use Hägerstrand's lexicon, pace-setting timetables of the anchor institutions that they must interact with.

Figure 5.1: A service user's hypothetical activation diorama in absolute space

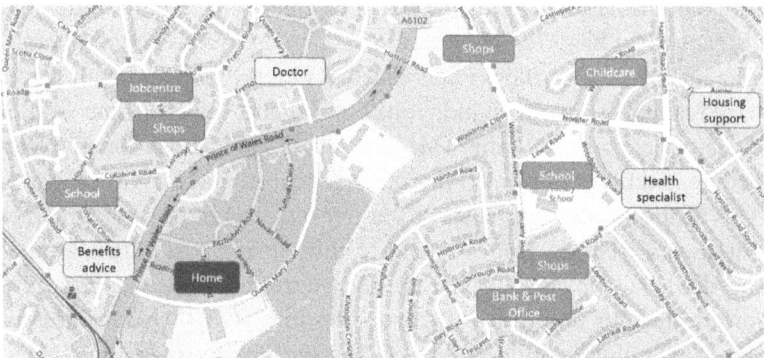

Taken together each service user's space–time rhythm can be traced onto the diorama in order to offer the socio-temporal building blocks of their engagement with activation policies.

Many features of these space–time rhythms are shared widely across the population – home, schools, shops, friends, and so on. Layered on top, however, is a specific set of absolute spatial considerations that can be traced for service users of activation programmes. These relate to the various support needs that different service users can face and the associated range of wraparound support services required, as well as attendance at employment providers to receive core employment support as well as to satisfy conditionality requirements for continued eligibility to social security benefits. Lives are complex and the list of wraparound support needs can be lengthy – mental and physical health, housing, debt advice, childcare provision, skills and learning, CV and interview skills, confidence and attitudes, family support, work experience, transport, and so on. Modern welfare systems have, understandably, evolved into complex specialist sub-systems delivering each of these support services separately across a whole panoply of public, private, third sector and informal provision. For many service users of activation programmes it is necessary therefore to interact with multiple different providers and each of these services is typically located in separate geographical locations. Exemplar separate service locations are displayed in Figure 5.1 to give a sense of the potential spatial distribution of a realistic activation diorama from a service user perspective. What becomes clear is how the fragmented and disparate reality of the system (or, more accurately, the non-system) for service users clashes with the simplified and homogenised top-down fiction typically held by activation policy makers and scholars alike.

As the diorama presented in Figure 5.1 illustrates, for many service users the absolute space–time requirements of engagement in activation programmes are extensive, disjointed, demanding, costly (in terms of time, money and energy) and typically utterly neglected by policy makers. Local integration can add value in this context. To seek to bring coherence and coordination for service users (and frontline practitioners) the idea of co-locating services has become a powerful discourse within employment policy debates. This may involve the physical co-location of particular key services, such as the co-location of employment staff within secondary mental health teams in the well-evidenced Individual Placement and Support (IPS) voluntary employment model for individuals with severe mental health conditions (Marshall et al., 2014; Modini et al., 2016). More ambitious co-location strategies might seek to bring together in a shared physical location a wider range of services, as in the popular idea of 'one stop shops' (Minas, 2014).

The perspectives of absolute space are also important to bringing in recognition of important structural economic demand-side issues about labour market opportunities within which any supply-side activation policy – irrespective of its quality – will inevitably be significantly affected. Unsurprisingly, evaluations of activation programmes repeatedly find that outcomes from activation programmes are lower in local labour markets with fewer opportunities and higher competition for job vacancies. Despite this, a notable element within virtually all activation policies internationally continues to be an elevation of individualistic supply-side narratives of worklessness alongside the simultaneous de-emphasis of structural demand-side issues around local labour market buoyancy and job availability. The changing nature of labour markets in advanced economies as a result of ongoing globalisation and rapid technological change continue to have significant impacts on those key demand-side issues, particularly for lower skilled individuals and in areas with a (previous) reliance on lower skilled heavy industries and manufacturing. The result has been highly uneven concentrations of economic buoyancy and weakness spatially. Yet activation strategies too often continue to respond reactively and individualistically to past realities rather than proactively to changing present and future structural realities. The lens of absolute space is able to bring into clear focus these key demand-side considerations and their spatial nature and implications for employment support systems, acting as they do to either significantly constrain or enable transitions into paid employment over and above the quality of any supply-side activation interventions.

Finally in terms of policy targeting and outcomes, if the ultimate aim of employment support interventions is to enable individuals to move into, retain and progress in paid employment that benefits their quality of life then the simplest (though by no means only) barometer of policy success is whether that is achieved. Alongside the focus on individuals a frequent way to assess this is within social groups of interest: age groups; gender; disability and health conditions; qualification levels, and so on. As with a wide range of other policy domains geography is of core interest within such aggregated analyses whether at the national, regional, municipal or neighbourhood level (which may or may not map onto the qualitative view of 'neighbourhood' that individuals themselves relate to and understand on the ground). Indeed, policy interventions might themselves be designed as area-based interventions aimed at deprived neighbourhoods. These might focus on employment alone or the interest in employment might coexist alongside an interest in other key policy domains within a broader multidimensional policy approach (for example employment, crime, health, skills). Moreover, the approach might focus only on individuals (whether within an area-based intervention or not) or might be combined with policies that seek to affect the areas in which people live (for example improving housing or the physical environment) in recognition of the interactions between individuals and their geographical environments. In both cases, and irrespective of how large or small those spatial boundaries of interest might be cast, it is the absolute conceptualisation of space that monopolises social policy thinking and approaches.

Interesting in this context is the mismatch between the dominance of absolute space within social policy decision making and analysis and conceptual scholarly debates within the discipline of human geography that often dismiss these absolute views as unduly partial and simplistic when considered alongside other alternative conceptualisations of space that exist within human geography scholarship. Indeed, this trend within conceptual human geography scholarship away from absolutist spatial thinking has led some conceptual thinkers such as Jones (2009) in his notion of 'phase space' to push back and re-emphasise the continuing importance of absolute concerns alongside alternative relative and relational conceptualisations of space.

The need for conceptual openness and balance having been noted, what value might these alternative relative and relational conceptualisations of space bring to our understanding of activation diorama for service users?

The relative perspective invites new questions and offers fresh insights to the analytical power of the diorama through its emphasis on the connectivity and circulations of service users around their spatially situated experiences of their activation diorama. What pathways are claimants following and who are they interacting with, supported by or constrained by as they do so? To what extent – and at what personal financial, temporal and emotional cost – are differently placed service users able to reconcile their employment support needs and activities with other needs and activities (such as school runs, caring duties) in any given context?

Diversity of experiences and likely outcomes are better able to be highlighted within the diorama when taking into account such relative views of space. The nature of each unemployed service user's personal support needs as well as their household circumstances play an important role in defining which locations each service user will need to engage with in the absolute space of the activation diorama. Whilst some service users may need only to attend an employment office to receive core employment support, others may require interactions with a whole range of support services and may, in addition, have caring and household responsibilities that require movement through space and time to nurseries, schools, residential homes or shops. Conversely, those ethical networks of friends and family might for some individuals (but not for others) provide important informal networks that aid – and in doing so shape the circulations of – service users. Travel and transport are key considerations too in this relative perspective, with road systems and public transport networks acting as important factors in shaping the viability as well as the financial, temporal and emotional costs of service user's differing space–time rhythms in their activation diorama.

The nature of the activation regime in each municipal or national context inevitably matters too. This regime context defines for service users what the expectations and requirements are in terms of the frequency and location of journeys required for employment support and to satisfy conditionality requirements. In the UK context, for example, the UK's tough approach to conditionality and sanctions within employment policy have been widely discussed (Eleveld, 2017; Fletcher and Wright, 2018). Yet this has not fed through to widespread awareness of the spatial dimensions to such critiques, which remain unduly neglected. These spatial dimensions – or, more fully and accurately, space–time dimensions – are however central to the lived realities of service users. How far, for example, are service users required to travel to search for jobs within the particular system's conditionality requirements? This varies across nations and is 90 minutes as default in the UK activation system. How does this compare to the average travel-to-work journeys of typical blue-collar workers in that same context (closer to 30 minutes in the UK)? And how far does this alter a service user's job search area and the range of job opportunities in scope for them, which itself depends on their mode of travel, scheduling needs and the nature of local labour markets?

Figure 5.2 layers these relative ideas onto the analytical framework to show the connectivity and circulations of a single service user dependent on public transport through their regular activation diorama (portions of two bus routes are shown by solid lines). Waking at home, getting the children ready, a morning bus ride together to drop one child at childcare with granny then a walk with the elder child to an early morning appointment at the health specialist to pick up some test results. Drop the other child at school and off to the Jobcentre for a late morning appointment (with a reasonable walk to get there as the bus routes don't connect them easily). A short visit to the benefits advice service to try and sort out a benefits problem then home for lunch. After lunch off to the doctor, collect the children from school and childcare, then back home for the evening before bed and starting all over again the next day with a new set of space–time circulations.

Indeed, one could expand the diorama in Figure 5.2 further than Hägerstrand's original work by using this relative diorama to show not only the circulations and connectivities but also their ease and effectiveness. This service user's pathway, for example, might be shown not as a single-sized line but, instead, as a pathway varying in thickness according to the functioning of the circulation and connectivity at the different points around its journey – thin for a poorly functioning/difficult connection, thick for a well-functioning/easy connection. The functioning and ease of this circulatory flow could itself be expressed in a variety of relevant ways, including knowledge and understanding, time, cost, access, energy, and so on.

Alternatively, alongside the flows of service users around the diorama the relative perspective enables a light to be shone on key issues around the circulation of a range of alternative items of crucial importance to service users in any modern activation system. These include in addition 'hard' items such as data, performance targets and money. Just as important from a service user perspective, they also include 'soft' items such as cultures, attitudes, aims, incentives, pressures and values.

Figure 5.2: Building up a service user's absolute and relative activation diorama

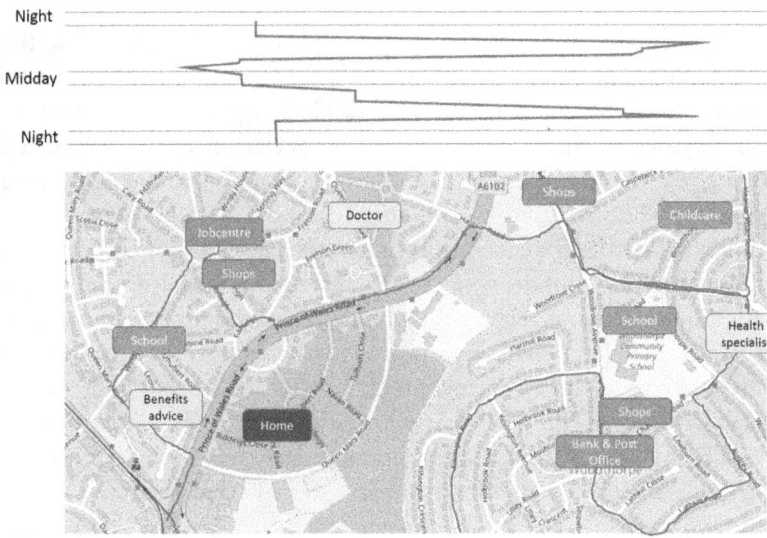

To focus on data, for example, to what extent are frontline practitioners in the employment support service and the range of wraparound services able to share information about each service user's needs, past support interventions, circumstances and action plans in a way that would enable them to work together more effectively and more seamlessly for service users? To take softer items, to what extent do complementary cultures, values and aims circulate between these ranges of services given that they relate to distinct types of frontline practitioners, teams and organisations? Where frontline staff work to performance targets or to payment-by-results models attached to specified outcomes, to what extent do those metrics and incentives align across the whole system of services of relevance to any service user's support experience? Such questions inevitably affect the extent to which frontline practitioners are enabled and incentivised to work collaboratively with other services in order to deliver the type of effective and seamless whole-person support that each service user needs and desires rather than to act in siloed, individualistic and potentially even competitive ways with other relevant services.

When considering the spatial natures and potential value-addeds of locally integrated employment support in terms of relative space, these multidimensional circulations around the activation diorama provide rich insights from service user and frontline practitioner perspectives. They help to identify the circulatory location of connective sources of effective, efficient, person-centred support or, conversely, of key blockages, mismatches, duplications and disconnects. The most visible and obvious element of locally integrated employment support may be that of co-located one stop shops in the frame of absolute space. Yet it is instead in the details of this complex multidimensional web of circulations and connectivities in the frame of relative space that the performance potential, but also policy challenge, of locally integrated employment support lies. For from a service user experience it is primarily through the seamless connections and alignment between the myriad set of absolute points of support within any activation diorama that the fragmentation of, and resulting 'distances' between, those differing support services are defined and experienced. These are the concerns of relative rather than absolute space – physical co-location may help real integration in a relative sense but they are not the same thing. It is by reconfiguring the nature of those various circulations and connectivities within the relative frame of space that locally integrated employment support systems might be transformed towards a single well-functioning system rather than the typical reality internationally of disconnected and often contradictory sets of services, cultures and practices within which service users and frontline practitioners alike feel (because they are!) neglected, depersonalised and poorly supported.

And it this final conceptual dimension of feelings and emotions – the relationalities of space in Harvey's conceptual triad – that enable a final shift in policy perspective to what are in many ways the key but frequently neglected drivers of 'performance' in any activation system. For as Harvey argues, if we are to fully understand the nature and performance of any policy system then for some questions it is surely central to understand the mental and emotional positions of individuals as they move through and engage with their own personal activation diorama.

What role might locally integrated approaches to employment support hold for service users in the frame of relational space? What impact do attempts to better align the nature and experiences of the myriad connections and circulations at play have on the emotions, attitudes and motivation of service users and frontline staff? What affect does the tendency for strong user-centred values and cultures within locally integrated approaches have? How does entry into an employment office, waiting to see an adviser, or the power dynamics at play within any employment meeting affect a service user? How does the lingering threat of conditionality and sanctions hanging over those conversations shape those engagements and outcomes? How do service users feel when their advisers move them mindlessly through bureaucratic processes or hurry them from their offices in order to move onto the next person or task? Or when their adviser truly recognises their needs and aspirations, connects with their dreams and takes meaningful personal steps to help them become real? Excitement? Hope? Fear? Opportunity? Despair? Exhaustion? Shame? Frustration? Demotivation? How do service users feel as they travel around the city from support service to support service interacting with receptionists and frontline professionals at each one? Or when a support service once again fails to operate in conjunction with other services or once again asks them for the same set of personal information or support needs for their database?

Layering on these relational ideas adds still further depth and analytical power for policy understanding and performance in the activation diorama. Visualising these ideas, one could imagine extending Figure 5.2 such that rather than pathways being of differing thicknesses but always solid black across the diorama they might instead take on different colours throughout to denote different emotions of service users at distinct points in space–time – green for hope, red for despair, blue for exhaustion, brown for excitement, yellow for fear, and so on. Indeed, Hägerstrand at one point mentions a desire to do just this by including the sounds and feelings of his own sample diorama (Hägerstrand, 1982: 331), although he does not in the end extend his work to include those relational considerations visually on his pathways.

Such an approach could again go further to also be used to visualise the connections and circulations of the various other items of relevance including data, cultures, objectives, incentives and so on that reflect the flow of different elements in the wider system from a service user perspective. For example, red lines might denote connections or flows that are aligned and functioning, brown for divergent but not conflicting, blue for conflicting but open to change, yellow for conflicting and currently blocked to change, green for in a process of joint change towards better integration, and so on.

Conclusion

Like many policy domains, employment support policy is an area of critical importance across all advanced economies to both makers and service users alike, supporting national governments to maintain economic prosperity and service users to improve their quality of life and realise their aspirations towards paid employment. As policy makers and academic researchers continue to experiment in their search for more effective activation approaches, this chapter has sought to illustrate the analytical and policy power that can be gained through a fuller conceptual exploration and empirical application of alternative views of space.

Taking as its focus a linked take on the works of two key spatial thinkers of the twentieth century – Torsten Hägerstrand and David Harvey – the chapter has sought to move through a discussion of the alternative spatial perspectives that can be brought to bear on policy questions such as this in order to enhance our conceptual and empirical understanding and policy practice. Whilst the activation literature focuses spatially on top-down system perspectives in an absolute view of space, this chapter's discussion has instead sought to leverage these richer spatial conceptualisations to inform understanding from the perspective of service users.

Though not without its challenges (van Berkel et al., 2011; Minas, 2014; Heidenreich and Rice, 2016; Whitworth and Murphy, 2018), local integration has been discussed widely in academic literature and policy debates as an important way in which activation policies should develop in order to enhance policy effectiveness and service user experiences. This is of particular importance for the now large group of unemployed service users with a range of more complex and/ or severe support needs whose employment aspirations have not always been well catered for in many previous employment interventions where effective connections to wider support needs are not present. The nature and evolution of locally integrated employment support is an important area of continued academic and policy attention. This chapter has sought in two key ways to contribute to that task by reflecting critically on the alternative perspectives and insights for employment support policy of these alternative absolute, relative and relational conceptualisations of space.

Firstly, it seeks to apply these alternative views to an evolving activation diorama in order to better understand the key questions and considerations that each spatial conceptualisation can bring to bear on effective employment support from a service user perspective. Secondly, through using these alternative spatial frames the discussion illustrates more precisely where and how local integration can add particular value to employment support systems. Interestingly, it becomes clear in doing so that whilst the academic literature and policy debate concentrates in its discussion of local integration on the absolute space of decentralisation, it is in fact in the relative and relational spatial frames that the true potential of locally integrated approaches to employment support rest. It is hoped that better understanding of the spatial natures and potentials of policy domains such as employment support can help policy makers think more fully about how those multiple – but frequently neglected and misunderstood – spatialities can be used creatively to enhance policy effectiveness and improve service user experiences.

References

Amin, A. (2007) Re-thinking the urban social. *City* 11: 100–114.

Bonoli, G. (2010). *The Political Economy of Active Labour Market Policy* (RECWOWE Working Paper No. REC-WP 01/10). Edinburgh: Dissemination and Dialogue Centre.

Eleveld, A. (2017) Activation policies: policies of social inclusion or social exclusion? *Journal of Poverty and Social Justice* 25(3): 277–285.

Fletcher, D. and Wright, S. (2018) A hand up or a slap down? Criminalising benefit claimants in Britain via strategies of surveillance, sanctions and deterrence. *Critical Social Policy* 38(2): 323–344.

Hägerstrand, T. (1982) Diorama, path and project. *Tijdschrift voor Economische en Sociale Goegrafie* 73(6): 323–339.

Harvey, D. (2006) Space as a keyword. In Castree, N. and Gregory, D. (eds) *Harvey: A Critical Reader*. Chichester: Wiley.

Heidenreich, M. and Rice, D. (eds) (2016) *Integrating Social and Employment Policies in Europe: Active Inclusion and Challenges for Local Welfare Governance*. Cheltenham: Edward Elgar.

Hubbard, P. and Kitchin, R. (eds) (2011) *Key Thinkers on Space and Place*. London: Sage.

Jones, M. (2009) Phase space: geography, relational thinking, and beyond. *Progress in Human Geography* 33(4): 487–506.

Levy, J. (2004) Activation through thick and thin: progressive approaches to labour market activation. In Ellison, N., Bauld, L. and Powell, M. (eds) *Social Policy Review 16*. Bristol: Policy Press.

Lindsay, C., McQuaid, R., and Dutton, M. (2007) New approaches to employability in the UK: combining 'human capital development' and 'work first' strategies? *Journal of Social Policy* 36(4): 539–560.

Marshall, T., Goldberg, R., Braude, L., Dougherty, R., Daniels, A., Shom Ghose, S., George, P. and Delphin-Rittmon, M. (2014) Supported employment: assessing the evidence. *Psychiatric Services* 65(1): 16–23.

Massey, D. (1991) A global sense of place. *Marxism Today* 38.

Minas, R. (2014) One-stop shops: increasing employability and overcoming welfare state fragmentation? *International Journal of Social Welfare* 23: S40–S53.

Minas, R. (2016) The concept of integrated services in different welfare states from a life course perspective. *International Social Security Review* 69(3/4): 85–107.

Minas, R., Wright, S. and van Berkel, R. (2012) Decentralization and centralization: governing the activation of social assistance recipients in Europe. *International Journal of Sociology and Social Policy* 32(5/6): 286–298.

Modini, M., Tan, L., Brinchmann, B., Wang, M.J., Killackey, E., Glozier, N., Mykletun, A. and Harvey, S. (2016) Supported employment for people with severe mental illness: systematic review and meta-analysis of the international evidence. *The British Journal of Psychiatry* 209(1): 1–9.

van Berkel, R., de Graaf, W. and Sirovatka, T. (eds) (2011) *The Governance of Active Welfare States in Europe*. Basingstoke: Palgrave Macmillan.

Waddell, G. and Burton, K. (2006) *Is Work Good for Your Health and Wellbeing?* London: The Stationery Office.

Whitworth, A. and Murphy, R. (2018) *An Employment System Fit for Today: Harnessing the Potential of Local Integration*. Sheffield: University of Sheffield. www.sheffield.ac.uk/polopoly_fs/1.820830!/file/Local_integration.pdf

6

Financialisation, Social Impact Bonds and the making of new market spaces in social policy

Jay Wiggan

Introduction: social impact investment and financialising social policy

Social impact investing (SII) is a mechanism by which governments seek to access and mobilise the resources of private for-profit and philanthropic capital to finance the pursuit and attainment of specific social and/or environmentally desirable outcomes, through various forms of investment activity (Social Impact Investment Taskforce, 2013: 1; HM Government 2014, 2016a, 2016b). This can include direct investment in charities and social enterprises; in funds geared to impact investing; in intermediary organisations that link potential financial investors with service providers in impact investment markets; or in the direct resourcing of SII interventions via new policy tools, such as Social Impact Bonds (SIBs) (Rosenman, 2019: 143–146). The focus of this chapter is on SIBs, which, as Whitfield (2015) has identified, are novel in that they do not require a wholesale transfer of a service between sectors – as under privatisation – or direction of public resources to a contracted service provider, as in public sector quasi-markets. Rather, an SIB is a variant of a payment by results (PbR) contracting agreement under which the state decides on the desired outcomes to be achieved to resolve a social problem, such as youth unemployment or homelessness and then contracts with providers to deliver these (OECD, 2015: 62–63; Wiggan, 2018).

Where an SIB differs from a standard PbR model is that neither the state nor the provider contracted to deliver a given service is responsible for providing the capital investment to get the service up and running. Instead this comes from a mix of for-profit and not-for-profit private investors who advance the resources to the provider on the basis they are repaid their investment and interest should programme outcomes be met (Whitfield, 2015: 7). The setting of outcome targets and the price the state is willing to pay for these are based upon a calculation of the future social and financial value these are expected to create. For example, in the case of a youth employability SIB this might be reductions in public spending estimated to arise from higher subsequent employment levels and fewer benefit claims over time. Like a PbR system an SIB concretises future value in the present (Esposito, 2011: 128) so as to enable value extraction prior to the material manifestation of value creation itself (that is participants entering and sustaining employment). The rationale advanced by advocates for SIBs is that they allow the state to draw upon much-needed additional resources for social programmes and provide an opportunity to harness investor expertise and rational self-interest which will, in turn, foster a rigorous pursuit of desired social outcomes and an efficient, effective use of resources (Joy and Shields, 2018; Wiggan, 2018; Sinclair et al., 2019). The separation of the role of investor and provider also means that it becomes more feasible for the state to contract with a wider variety of voluntary and community organisations to deliver services which might otherwise be excluded from outcome-funded programmes on the grounds of insufficient capital to cover start-up and running costs.

Government and other SII market actors have tended to provide somewhat boosterist accounts of the benefits of SIBs and there is now a burgeoning interest amongst academic communities concerning the role of the state in facilitating SIB expansion and questions regarding their effectiveness and value for money (Edmiston and Nicholls, 2018; Wiggan, 2018; Tan et al., 2019). Critical accounts have situated the SII turn as an attempt to manage tensions arising from austerity and fracturing societies while opening up new opportunities for capital accumulation (Bryan and Rafferty, 2014; Dowling and Harvie, 2014; Whitfield, 2015; Dowling, 2017; Harvie, 2019). Such accounts call to mind Harvey's notion of the 'temporal-spatial' fix (cited in Arrighi, 2006: 202; see also Sokol, 2013: 509) where contradictions within the process of capital accumulation are responded to by expansion of capital into new territory and through temporal shifts in investment – the logic being that, as new spaces are opened up and developed, opportunities for investment and production are renewed/expanded (Arrighi, 2006: 202–205).

The purpose of this chapter is to contribute to this debate through an analysis of the Innovation Fund (IF) SIB and the Youth Engagement Fund (YEF) SIB commissioned by the UK Department for Work and Pensions (DWP, 2017, no date) to improve youth employability. The aim is threefold. The first aim is to identify how we can understand the turn to SII as a distinct process of financialisation – *extensive financialisation* (Fine, 2013: 55; Fine and Saad-Filho, 2016: 153-157): that is, how the SIB marks the direct expansion of finance capital[1] into social welfare programmes in the form of finance as money capital and in doing so configures a new financialised market space (Fine, 2014; Fine 2010). The second is to unpack how the operation of the SIB as part of this process forges new financial chains of value (Sokol, 2015) that transform geographically rooted ('problem') populations and welfare delivery into investable products linked to mobile national and global financial market actors. Consequently, while sites and populations of investment potential remain bounded by the territoriality of the local and national state, the SIB permits investors to transcend these and avoid entanglement in the materiality of actual programme delivery in a specific locality. Finally, the chapter considers how the particular temporality of value creation and realisation associated with the SIB facilitates value reallocation to finance capital within the process of (re)producing labour and how rather than securing resources from finance capital *for* welfare provision appropriates additional public resources *for* finance capital.[2]

Conceptualising financialisation

Financialisation is a somewhat slippery concept which encompasses multiple meanings and variety of activity (French et al., 2011: 800; Christophers, 2015). Here financialisation is understood to refer to the growing importance of finance capital as a source of economic activity within contemporary economies and the diffusion of financial market rationales and practices throughout society, reshaping the state and the behaviour and expectations of individuals (Van der Zwan, 2014; Davies and Kim, 2015). In the UK, for example, the output of the finance sector prior to the financial crisis of 2008 is estimated to have grown at an average of 6% per annum compared to 3% growth in UK GDP (Burgess, 2011: 234). Data from HM Revenue and Customs indicates the banking sector paid £21.4 billion in taxation in 2013–14 and the financial services industry contributed 8% of the total Gross Value Added to the economy in 2014 (Tyler, 2015: 3–7). The UK is also home to one of the leading global centres of financial services, with London ranked number one in the 2016 Global Financial Centres Index, ahead of New York and Singapore (China Development Institute and Z/Yen, 2016: 4).

Meanwhile, scholars of 'everyday financialisation' (French et al., 2011: 804) have detailed how people have become reliant on financial products and services (credit cards, mortgages, unsecured bank loans, car finance, loans for higher education study) to meet immediate needs and access goods and services otherwise beyond their income level (Martin et al., 2008; Martin, 2013; Soederberg, 2015). The easy availability of credit and the willingness of people to take on debt to manage daily life is also integral to the form and condition of the UK economy. The level of total household debt as a proportion of household disposable income increased from 95–100% in the 1990s to reach a peak of 160% in 2007. Although the level of household debt subsequently declined, in 2016 total household debt as a proportion of household disposable income still stood at 143% (Harari, 2017: 8–9), with the Office for Budget Responsibility estimating this figure may rise above 150% by 2022 (Harari, 2017: 12). The salience of finance in the economy and society certainly captures the broad financialisation tendency (Christophers, 2015; Davies and Kim, 2015). To leave our understanding of the concept there, however, risks obfuscating the particularities of financialisation as a mix of distinct processes and practices which transverse social, political and economic space to connect disparate actors across global, national and local scales. Before proceeding to analysis of SIBs it is necessary to further unpack the concept of financialisation.

Fine (2013: 49–55), drawing on Marx, notes that finance can be distinguished between the advance of money as credit and the advance of money as capital (hereafter referred to as finance as credit and finance as capital; in practice they are understood to intermingle) (Fine, 2013: 49–55). The former can be understood as the taking out of a loan to resource the consumption of a particular good or service, with the originator of the loan receiving repayment of the principal advanced and agreed interest. Fine argues that in this form of 'finance as credit' the process involves the circulation of existing resources, but is not directly concerned with the enlargement of production in the pursuit of accumulation. Conversely, 'finance as capital' refers to the intention of the originator of a loan to invest in activities which increase productive capacity and contribute to expanding accumulation (see also Fine, 2012: 82–83). The expectation (and risk) is that investment leads to an increase in production and renewed accumulation of capital. It is through this process that finance inserts itself into production to occupy a position from which it appropriates a share of the additional value created and is indeed given first claim on this new value (Fine, 2013: 49–53). In the abstract at least, *finance as credit* is distinct from *finance as capital* and for Fine it is the spread of finance as capital (*extensively* – hereafter 'extensive financialisation') into new areas, including within social policy, that is a key feature of contemporary processes of financialisation (Fine and Saad-Filo, 2016: 161).

As extensive financialisation proceeds the markets colonised by finance become sites for a more thorough transformation of products and services, facilitating an expansion of *finance as capital* to occur 'intensively' (hereafter 'intensive financialisation') (Fine, 2013: 55). The latter, for example, could include the introduction of various financial practices such as 'securitisation', which packages together the income streams due a creditor (mortgages/student loans/credit cards) to create a suite of products marketable and tradeable in secondary markets to other investors. Such practices permit a thoroughgoing delocalisation process to occur, as immoveable sites of capital investment becomes transformed into liquid tradeable commodities, enabling a temporal and spatial reallocation of risk and profit as the originator of credit realises the (anticipated) future returns of the income stream in the present, while dispensing with the future risk of default by trading this on to other parties (Martin et al., 2008: 121; Martin, 2013: 90; Breger Bush, 2016). The more activities that can be commodified, unbundled into income streams, repackaged and traded then the greater the scope for de-territorialisation to expand accumulation and grow financial market opportunities, while also disciplining market actors to prioritise returns on investment (Bryan and Rafferty, 2015: 320; Davis and Kim, 2015: 207; Harvie, 2019).

While such developments are not guaranteed to flow from SIB, the argument here is that the insertion of finance *in the form of money capital* into the provision of social programmes at the work–economy–welfare nexus through SIBs is an example of extensive financialisation. That is, the making of a new market space in social welfare where territorial and sectoral boundaries are irrelevant and whose environment is necessarily conducive to a subsequent realisation of further financialising reforms (*intensive financialisation*) (Sinclair et al., 2014; Whitfield, 2015; Fine and Saad-Filo, 2016: 161). As a consequence, locales as fixed sites of specific programme intervention become opened up and linked to investors that are geographically dispersed and not involved in the sector as providers. In this way the geographically uneven development and underdevelopment of economies and communities and its manifestation in problems such as poverty, unemployment and low levels of educational qualifications can be reconstructed through SII as new spaces of capital accumulation *for* finance (Harvie and Ogman, 2019: 15).

The scale, scope and form of social impact investing and Social Impact Bonds

SII differs from mainstream financial investments by making the attainment of a demonstrable social benefit along with economic returns a requirement of investment (Social Impact Investment Taskforce, 2014: 1; City of London Corporation, 2015: 14). Assessment of the scale and scope of the domestic market for impact investing in the UK by the organisation Big Society Capital concluded that the total value of all forms of social investment in the UK up to the end of 2015 was worth over £1.5 billion (BSC, 2016a: 9). Of this, the largest proportion of investment activity was in the form of lending by banks to charities and social enterprises (36%). Direct investment in 'pay for performance' SIBs was comparatively minor, estimated to equate to less than 2% of this total of social investment (BSC, 2016a: 9).[3] Some caution should be exercised to ensure that interest stimulated by the novelty of SII does not lead to an exaggeration of the extent to which finance through SII has become pervasive in the UK social policy space. Yet being alert to this danger should not lead us to draw the opposite conclusion, as to do so would risk failing to grasp the salience of an emergent but accelerating process of financialisation taking place within a broader project of public service commodification (Whitfield, 2015; Dowling, 2017). SIB remains a minority form of investment, but this is not surprising given their recent introduction. The number of SIBs has experienced rapid expansion both domestically and globally (see below) (Social Finance, 2017b), and in the UK the DWP, focused on core social policy concerns around (un)employment, poverty, skills and health, has led experimentation with and investment in SIBs. Indeed, the UK is a global leader in developing and launching SIBs (Social Finance, 2017b) and is active in promoting these internationally as an innovative and effective policy tool and attractive financial product for investors (Wiggan, 2018). The decision to focus here upon Social Impact Bonds is not due to their existing share of all impact market activity. Rather, it is because they represent a policy technology and financial product that show the process of extensive financialisation taking place through the creation of new market spaces and accompanying financial chains of value (Sokol, 2015: 682) which point to the emerging scope for future intensive financialisation of social welfare (Harvie, 2019: 115-117).

The rationale for SIBs is similar to that advanced for other forms of payment by results: that rewarding organisations for delivering state-defined outcomes rather than simply delivering a state-stipulated set of services strengthens the incentives of the provider to achieve the desired outcomes. The reconfiguration and refinement of the payment by results contracting model in the British welfare state over the last ten years means that, though the outcome focus of SIBs is not new, it is able to draw on institutional familiarity and information built up through operation of 'welfare' quasi-markets of the various costs/ benefits of particular interventions (Rees et al., 2014; Bennett, 2017; Greer et al., 2017). This has allowed the UK government to construct and make available a 'unit cost database' incorporating information to assist potential SIB commissioners to decide whether an SIB is a financially viable option and then how to price it appropriately (Wiggan, 2018: 728). Through the SIB the state ostensibly seeks to lever philanthropic and/or for-profit capital investment for particular projects and thereby transfer the risk of a programme failing to achieve its targets to investors, who may lose some or all of their investment in the event of this occurring (Keohane et al., 2013). The attraction for investors is that if the programme outcomes identified by the commissioner[4] are achieved then the investor is paid a return on their investment that is more or less closely derived from state estimations of the long-term value this generates and which manifests as reduced public expenditure, more productive citizens and/or greater social cohesion (Social Investment Taskforce, 2010: 18; Secretary of State for Work and Pensions, 2015; Social Finance, 2017b). The money advanced can consequently be understood as a form of finance as money capital. It represents an investment made in expectation that expanded production of a given social good (more employable labour and hence more productive citizens) generates new value which enables repayment of capital advanced plus interest (Martin, 2013: 5).

The exact structure of a given SIB varies, but generally involves commissioners of a service, providers of a service, and the investors in the intervention. It may also include intermediary organisations which link these actors together, offer advice and information and arrange (independent) evaluation of programme performance (Keohane et al., 2013: 21; Dear et al., 2016; Berndt and Wirth, 2018: 28). As any of the roles in the SIB structure can in theory be fulfilled by actors from the public, private or third sector, the SIB fosters interchangeability and commensurability between sectors which creates a more dynamic and liquid market environment. By diminishing barriers to entry in any given SIB activity the future of discrete private-led social interventions – in addition to or in place of public provision – becomes feasible. It remains the case, however, that the state is the principal purchaser of contracted welfare services in the UK and acts as the 'payer' in the event of successful service provision under an SIB (Social Finance, 2016), although other non-state actors have also been involved as co-commissioners. The first UK SIB intervention, which sought to reduce reoffending rates amongst short-term prisoners following their release from HMP (Her Majesty's Prison) Peterborough, was commissioned jointly by the UK Ministry of Justice and the (non-state) Big Lottery Fund to achieve an overall reduction in reoffending rates of 7.5%, at which point outcome payments would be triggered (Dorsett, 2017: 4). The funding to resource this SIB was organised by the social economy organisation Social Finance, which, acting as a market intermediary, raised £5 million from 17 investors, all charitable trusts and foundations, and oversaw the intervention (Social Finance, 2017b: 1–4).

The growth of SIBs in the UK has typically revolved around the resourcing of welfare interventions, targeting a distinct subset of the population, often identified as at risk of socioeconomic exclusion due to personal, family and/or community behaviour, attitudes, characteristics, capabilities and/or environment (Dear et al., 2016: 12; Social Finance, 2016: 13). From one SIB in 2010 the number of SIBs in the UK has grown rapidly. The organisation Social Finance has created a public database of SIBs that have launched or are under development and this indicates that by October 2017 a total of 33 SIBs had been launched with funding of over £35 million in the UK (Social Finance, 2017a). Of the overall number of SIBs launched, the largest proportion (38%) related to employment, followed by housing (16%), families (13%), health (12%), criminal justice (8%) and education (8%), with central government dominant in the commissioner role in the majority of UK SIBs. The Department for Work and Pensions has been involved in the highest number of SIBs launched (14) in the UK to date (Social Finance, 2017a). This may reflect the links drawn by ministers between resolving unemployment and forging a stronger (Big) society and the positioning of the SIB as a mechanism to help realise this through using the resources of investors and their focus on securing returns to fund the operation of specialist voluntary and community service providers (Harvie, 2019; Wiggan, 2018).

Social Impact Bonds for 'employability': financialising the social (re)production of labour

The nature of the contracts and the pricing of outcomes

The SIB commissioned by DWP were initiated through two 'outcomes funds' – the Innovation Fund (IF) and the Youth

Engagement Fund (YEF). The IF was launched in 2012 as part of broader government measures to address youth unemployment, and had three objectives: to improve the employability of young people aged 14 and over, regarded as at risk of social and economic exclusion; to test the feasibility of impact investment to deliver social *and* financial benefits; and to support development of SIBs as a form of impact investment market interventions (DWP, 2016a: 22). Involving two rounds of commissioning and running for three years from 2012, up to £30 million was made available through the Innovation Fund, which acted as a pot of money dedicated to resourcing payments for outcomes achieved in the commissioned IF projects. The first round saw six projects commissioned across the UK (Greater Merseyside; West Midlands; Nottingham; two in East London; Perth in Scotland) with interventions encompassing the 14–24 age group. The second round involved the commissioning of a further four projects (Thames Valley/SE England; Greater Manchester; West London; South Wales), each targeted on the 14–15 age group.

The programme used a payment by results system of performance contracting. This meant outcome performance was assessed and differentially rewarded according to whether or not participants achieved one or more of the state determined (proxy) measures of improved employability. These included outcomes such as improved attendance/behaviour/attitudes at school; achievement of educational qualifications at either level 1, 2, 3 or 4; improved English language skills; and job/work-based learning sustainment for three or six months (DWP, 2016a: 95). Different projects were free to target whichever outcomes they preferred, in keeping with the non-prescriptive outcome-based black box approach taken by the DWP as a means to stimulate innovation. Each outcome measure had a value attached, relating to estimates of how the proxy measure of employability would translate into the accrual of savings in benefit payments made by the state over the course of two (round one) or three (round two) years (DWP, 2016a: 26). In round one, for example, those projects achieving improved school attendance for a participant could potentially unlock an outcome payment of £1,300, while achievement of a level 3 qualification for the first time could trigger an outcome payment of £3,300. The total price the DWP was willing to pay per participant in round one was set at £8,200, and in round 2 at £11,700 (DWP, 2016a: 95; DWP, no date: 9), though organisations bidding for IF contracts were encouraged to offer a discount on the DWP's stated rate for the different outcomes, meaning that in practice the amount actually received per outcome would be lower than the DWP's stated maximum (Carter, 2019: 11; and see DWP, 2016a: 95).

The UK Coalition Government followed up the 2012 launch of the IF with the commissioning in 2014 of additional SIB projects, this time resourced via a £16 million Youth Engagement Fund provided by the Ministry of Justice, Cabinet Office and the DWP. Beginning in 2014 for a period of three years, the YEF sought to further test an SIB approach to reducing the number of young people 'Not in Employment, Education or Training' (NEET) through resourcing four projects targeted at young people aged 14–17 years old (HM Government, 2014; DWP, 2017: 4). A total of 11 outcome measures were outlined for the YEF projects, again relating to improvements in school attendance and behaviour, the achievement of educational qualifications and job entry and sustainment (DWP, 2017: 37–49). Multiple outcomes could be claimed per participant, provided each was for a different outcome measure, with an overall maximum payment per participant of up to £11,800 (DWP, 2017: 15). In theory, the value accruing to public funds from the production of individuals (labour) deemed to be 'more employable', indicated by the achievement of various outcomes, permits the SIB to pull value that has yet to be realised into the present and transform a portion of this into income for the actors within the impact investment market.

The performance of the Innovation Fund

From the available public data it is known that desired outcomes were achieved across the ten IF projects. Up to September 2015 the DWP record 13,700 starts on the six round 1 IF projects and 4,600 starts on the four round 2 IF projects. The round 1 projects had recorded a total of 14,300 outcomes achieved as of September 2015 and the round 2 projects had delivered 9,300 outcomes achieved (DWP, 2016b: 5–6). The separate DWP-commissioned qualitative evaluation indicates that initial performance targets were met across all projects and either all investors had been repaid already, or were on track to be repaid. Interviews conducted with participating young people and staff in associated schools also reported changes in behaviour and attitudes relating to school, family and future employment prospects that imply the IF SIB, at least on the terms set, were contributing to the social reproduction of 'employable' individuals (DWP, 2016a: 14–15), though as indicated below this does not mean the SIB is a more effective mechanism than publicly funded alternatives or indeed no intervention at all. A more detailed overview of the performance of a specific round 1 IF project – 'New Horizons' in Greater Merseyside – has been provided by one of its investors, Bridges Ventures. Care must be taken here in the treatment of this data, given that this organisation has invested in multiple SIBs and is enthusiastic about their expansion. Having said that, it offers a useful insight into how IF SIBs have functioned in practice. For this IF project Bridges Ventures claimed a total of 4,200 participating young people and the achievement of just over 6,000 outcomes against a target of working with 3,928 young people and achieving 4,200 desired outcomes (Bridges Fund Management, 2016: 10).

As might be expected with the target group, over half (51%) recorded outcomes related to improved school attendance and behaviour, two-fifths (42%) for achievement of NVQ Level 1 or 2 qualifications, and with employment sustainment the remainder. If we take as an example the reported data on improved school attendance we can begin to see how a portion of estimated value created for the state from the production of (ostensibly) more employable individuals is channelled to providers/intermediaries/investors. The stated estimated value to government of an improved school attendance outcome in the Greater Merseyside IF SIB was £1,400, with the outcome payment per improved school attendance paid at £871 (Bridges Fund Management, 2016: 11). This implies that of the value accruing to government from each improved school attendance outcome in the Merseyside IF project, about 62% flowed to SIB providers, intermediaries and investors as an outcome payment. If we take the total value to government from the outcomes achieved in this IF SIB (£9.24 million) then the total paid out by government, calculated on the basis of stated outcome payments, was about 49% of this figure (£4.5 million) (Bridges Fund Management, 2016: 11). On their own these figures tell us nothing about value for money, the additionality of the intervention or how payment was distributed between different actors, or the rate of return on investment for investors, all of which remain unclear.

The quantitative analysis of the IF SIB projects in England commissioned by the DWP does though offer some indication of the overall 'value for money' of these SIB projects (Salis et al., 2018: 59). Note that the social return on investment analysis of the IF SIB programme suggests that the overall benefits-to-cost ratio of the programme was about 1:25–1.31 times what the DWP originally stated was the maximum it was 'willing to pay' providers to achieve the desired outcomes.[5] This indicates that the DWP was able to extract a higher amount of value from the IF SIB than it would have done had it actually paid the headline rate it was ostensibly willing to pay for different outcomes and which providers offered a discount against. We do need to be cautious here regarding what this means in terms of actual value generation, as becomes clear when exploring the question of overall programme 'additionality' below. The authors of the impact evaluation, for example, note that with the exception of level 1 (basic) educational outcomes it is likely that most of the positive outcomes achieved across the IF SIB projects would have been realised in the absence of the programme. Indeed, the quantitative evaluation suggests the IF SIB may actually have had a negative impact on the likelihood of participants securing more challenging outcomes, such as higher level qualifications, training and/or employment.[6] The earlier qualitative evaluation of the IF projects had also indicated that during round 1 of the IF pilots (set up to serve the 14–24 age group) a number of projects which initially proposed to focus attention on the 16 and above age group of those Not in Employment, Education or Training instead redirected their efforts towards recruiting school-age participants (Carter, 2019: 9). The quantitative evaluation confirmed this for the round 1 projects, suggesting that, as providers were not prevented by their contracts from prioritising lower level outcomes such as improved educational attendance and attitudes and attainment of level 1 qualifications, these seem to have been prioritised over achievement of more advanced qualifications or employment (Salis et al., 2018: 69).

In short, a spatially dispersed population of post-school-age participants, where the concomitant outcomes, in the form of employment or higher qualifications would likely prove challenging to achieve, were substituted for a spatially concentrated school-age population whose institutional embeddedness more readily facilitated mapping of, and access to, potential participants.[7] The nature of the IF SIB effectively permitted providers to (re)construct the space of intervention in response to whether the geographical fixity of different ostensible 'problem populations' made recruitment and attainment of outcomes more/less amenable. As Rosenman (2017: 147) observes, locales where SIBs are operationalised become (re)constructed as sites to mine for their profitable potential. In this case the decision to switch to the younger cohort in the face of difficulties with recruitment was essentially the search for a more accessible seam of material to mine. Of course, a consequence of the change in the composition of the target population was a change in the strategy of intervention and concomitant types of outcomes pursued. The scope to achieve higher individual payments associated with achieving employment and more advanced qualifications for participants diminished and for some providers was replaced by a focus on delivering a higher throughput of participants attaining lower value 'softer' outcomes as a means to maximise income (see Salis et al., 2018: 68). A spatial perspective then directs our attention to how space itself was used as a means of filtering programme recruitment and participation in this new social policy market to best configure a population likely to produce a payment to providers and a return on capital to investors.

Mapping the market space of the DWP IF and YEF Social Impact Bonds

This section considers the constellation of actors present in the IF and YEF SIB market to explore the patterning of roles and the flow of resources across this space and how extensive financialisation links actors together in a new market. As noted earlier, what is novel about an SIB is that investors advance money capital to providers of specific social programmes. In doing so they place a claim to the value seemingly generated with the production of the desired commodity (e.g. outcomes ostensibly indicating more qualified labour). From the perspective of UK government ministers, an SIB unlocks additional (private) capital and helps channel this into welfare provision (see Wiggan, 2018). Such a representation of the flow of money, however, obscures the fact that the advance of money as capital is intended to facilitate a flow of value *to* the investor (Sokol, 2013: 506) *from* the public realm. It is also worth reiterating that SIBs are not simply an expansion of the market space in social policy, but also a change in market form that entails a shift in which businesses can benefit from commodification of welfare provision and how. That is, the value extracted does not only flow to the providers contracted to produce the various state stipulated outcomes as a portion is now appropriated by investors. We can begin to see here how the development of the SIB involves the emergence of new financial chains of value that organise the creation, extraction and distribution of value by linking spatially contained sites of welfare intervention with diverse state, private and third sector actors who together traverse local, national and global scales (Sokol, 2017: 683). Table 6.1 details the actors involved in this new financialised market space for the DWP Greater Merseyside (GM) IF SIB. The (potential) breadth and diverse mix of investors in this emergent space is clear with this particular IF SIB involving charities, mutual organisations and private investors.

A disaggregation of the sectoral composition of investors in both the DWP IF and YEF SIB projects indicates, for example, that more than

Table 6.1: Structure of the Greater Merseyside Innovation Fund SIB

Role	Actors	Scale
Commissioner	Department for Work and Pensions	National
Investors	Bridges Ventures Big Society Capital Esmée Fairbairn Foundation Charities Aid Foundation Knowsely Housing Trust Helena Partnerships Liverpool Mutual Homes Wirral Partnership Homes	International-national-regional
Intermediary	Triodos Bank	International-national
Provider	Career Connect	Local
Programme population	Young people (Not in Employment Education or Training) in the Greater Merseyside area	Local

Source: Author's collation of information (see Bridges Fund Management, 2016; Government Outcomes Lab (n.d.))

half of IF and YEF project investors (55%) were registered charities and mutual organisations; about two fifths (39%) could be categorised as private sector organisations and the remainder (6%) were drawn from the public sector (see Table 6.2).

Given one rationale for SIBs is to facilitate smaller and specialist non-state organisations involvement in delivery, it is perhaps not surprising this is what we find in the DWP IF and YEF SIB projects. Of all named providers,[8] about three quarters were charitable or mutual organisations, with private sector organisations (often self-reporting as social enterprises) about a quarter. A caveat to the categorisation of actors in Table 6.2 is that the complex nature of the public, private and civil society nexus shifts over time meaning it is best to treat the information provided as indicative rather than definitive.[9-10] Across the YEF and IF, of the projects reporting use of an intermediary organisation to arrange and manage investment, liaison between service providers and commissioners and organisation and oversight

Table 6.2: Percentage of investors, intermediaries and providers in IF/YEF SIBs

	Sector	Public	Private	Charity and mutual
Role	Investors	6	39	55
	Intermediaries	8	83	8
	Providers	0	27	66

Source: Author calculation based on information on project stakeholders available in the Impact Bonds Global Database (Social Finance, 2017) and i-for-change (2016)[11]

of outcome assessment (See Bridges Ventures, 2016: 9) half employed the services of either *Social Finance* or *Triodos Bank* as intermediaries. In relation to investment, the social finance organisation Bridges Ventures, who were the co-lead investors in the Greater Merseyside IF SIB, have also developed a Social Impact Bond Investment Fund to offer other investors exposure to returns from impact investment. This fund has attracted UK pension funds and banks as well as charitable foundations and trusts, and in 2014 it was announced that this fund would finance investment in two of the four DWP YEF SIB projects that had been commissioned to build on pilots resourced through the previous DWP SIB Innovation Fund (Bridges Fund Management, 2015).

The process of extensive financialisation then is not simply constructed once by the state but is reproduced and expanded by the flow of resources within the market between state, private and social organisations. Moreover, it is arguably the involvement of a variety of state, market and social organisations and their interactions which co-constitute SII as a seemingly dynamic and innovative market space. The complex interplay of state, voluntary and not-for-profit and for-profit organisations and resources in this field is further indicated by the organisation – Big Society Capital – which contributed investment to four of the ten IF projects (Ronicle et al., 2014: 19). The role played by Big Society Capital in the impact investment market is, as Ronicle et al. (2014: 19) note, to operate as a financial 'wholesaler', provisioning various other (private and charitable) impact funds with the resources which allow them to develop their market capabilities and capacity to invest in specific social impact investment activities. While Big Society Capital is an independent organisation, it was brought into being by the decision and action of the UK Coalition Government to create a social investment bank, resourced through unclaimed funds drawn from dormant bank accounts in addition to injections of capital from four UK banks (Social Investment Taskforce, 2010: 17; Wiggan, 2018: 728). As Cahill (2019: 5) notes, markets are not ahistorical disembodied self-regulating institutions, but lived social relations embedded in temporally and spatially contingent rules, practices and expectations governing the exchange and movement of commodities that are frequently determined and guaranteed by the state.

Conclusions

Social policy has long been recognised as having a role in social reproduction that contributes to the maintenance and expansion of accumulation in capitalist societies. Public funding and/or provision of welfare can socialise the costs of services and supports that may otherwise fall upon individuals, families and business, with an attendant risk that underinvestment and under-provision would result (Smyth and Deeming, 2016). The general trend in the UK over the last 30 years has been to marketise and privatise various aspects of the state's role in social reproduction, and the turn to SII is commensurate with this (Harvie and Ogman, 2019; Sinclair et al., 2019). What is novel about the SII turn is that it marks a process of extensive financialisation (Fine and Saad-Filho, 2016) of social policy. Through new financial technologies such as the SIB, the state crafts a new market space conducive to insertion of finance as money capital into the process for the (re)production of labour, creating new opportunities for value reallocation, appropriation and extraction from the commodification of social welfare by finance. The development/ underdevelopment of different regions and populations that arise from a market economy mean that extensive financialisation of social policy is necessarily spatial. Geography is consequently integral to the making and management of the emergent financialised marketplace as the spatiality of 'social problems' provides a means to identify, compare and select/reject locales for SIB project development while detaching the resourcing of this from the place itself (Rosenman, 2017: 152). Populations that are geographically fixed within the territorial boundaries of a nation state meanwhile become, via the SIB, linked into a chain of financial value (Sokol, 2015) that traverses local and national boundaries.

Of course, this poses the question as to what we understand to be value creation in SIB and who such value flows to. As noted, the temporal reordering of value extraction within SIB transforms expected future value into profits in the present and opens up direct value appropriation by a new market actor – investors (finance as capital). Moreover, while money in the new social policy market is advanced by finance for increased production and expanded value creation, what counts in generating 'investor' returns are relatively narrow outcomes whose production are proxies for estimates of longer term value accruing to the state. As discussed, the UK government-commissioned quantitative evaluation of the IF SIB (Salis et al., 2018) does indicate that the DWP's stipulated outcomes were achieved and at a lower cost than DWP had been willing to pay. If the counterfactual was payment at the higher rate then, in this sense, value creation did occur and flowed to the DWP, while successful attainment of outcomes generated payments for providers and a return of – and on – capital advanced by investors. Yet the evaluation questions the actual improved outcomes realised by the IF SIB in relation to comparison groups, suggesting the value of participating in the programme for individuals was limited and hence the programme generated little new value over non-intervention. Given the performance of the IF and other UK SIB it is difficult to ignore the observations of Dowling (2017: 302) and Harvie and Ogman (2019: 13) that the principal innovation of this new market space is to transform future value imaginaries into legitimate claims in the present to the appropriation of additional public monies by finance capital, rather than unlocking additional monies for social welfare.

Notes

[1] Finance capital is used here as an abstraction of for-profit and not-for-profit investors in the SII process. How such organisations vary in terms of their structure, drive, practice and ethos would likely affect the nature of SII activity and further research into this would be a valuable addition to existing knowledge.

[2] Harvie and Ogman (2019: 13) similarly suggest that the Peterborough SIB largely enabled investors to capture a share of public funding rather than expand the total resources available for social welfare programmes.

[3] The majority of this SII is made up of lending by social banks and social and retail investment funds to social enterprise and charities with a minor amount relating to investment in Community Shares and Charity Bonds (see BSC, 2016b: Annex A1). The composition of 'on the ground' activities and organisations resourced by this SII is not recorded.

[4] Usually this is the nation state, but it could be philanthropic organisations, international governmental organisations or private for-profit organisations.

[5] The DWP provided an 'outcome rate card' listing the maximum price the DWP was willing to pay for each type of outcome achieved for each round of the Innovation Fund (DWP, 2016b: 95). Consequently the evaluators were able to calculate the outcomes achieved at the price DWP actually paid each project and compare this with DWP's 'willingness to pay' indicated by the maximum set out for various outcomes in the Outcome Rate Card.

[6] The authors caution that it is possible the profile of the matched (non-intervention) comparison group did not sufficiently reflect the 'disadvantage' of the participant group or that the former had access to other state programmes that IF participants did not (Salis et al., 2018: 68).

[7] The school essentially functions as a place-based mechanism for identification and referral of individuals with the characteristics relevant to participation.

[8] This does not include sub-contractors.

[9] The provider for the Birmingham IF project – the BEST Network – is constituted as a (not-for-profit) private company, but is an umbrella body of charities, community interest companies, co-operative and social enterprise organisations (it is included here as one body under the 'charity and mutual category).

[10] The Nottingham IF project was managed by the local authority and delivery was undertaken by a social enterprise spun out of, but owned by, local council making it more akin to a standard payment by results approach.

[11] The table and calculation exclude one IF project (Perth) and one YEF project (London) due to a lack of information (or clarity) as to investors in those projects. Assessment of organisational status was based on information available on organisation websites and consultation of information held by Companies House; the Charity Commission Register for England and Wales and the Financial Conduct Authority's Mutuals Public Register.

References

Arrighi, G. (2006) Spatial and other fixes of historical capitalism. In Chase-Dunn, C. and Babones, S.J. (eds) *Global Social Change: Historical and Comparative Perspectives*. Baltimore, MD: Johns Hopkins University Press, 201–212.

Bennett, H. (2017) Re-examining British welfare-to-work contracting using a transaction cost perspective. *Journal of Social Policy* 46(1): 129–148.

Berndt, C. and Wirth, M. (2018) Market, metrics, morals: the Social Impact Bond as an emerging social policy instrument. *Geoforum* 90: 27–35.

Big Society Capital (2012) *Annual Report and Financial Statements 2012*. www.bigsocietycapital.com/sites/default/files/pdf/BSC_AR_AW_forwebsite.pdf

Big Society Capital (2016a) *Annual Review – Social Investment Refocused*. https://www.bigsocietycapital.com/sites/default/files/files/Annual%20Review%20for%20web%20FINAL.pdf

Big Society Capital (2016b) *Social Investment Insight Series*. https://www.bigsocietycapital.com/sites/default/files/attachments/The%20size%20of%20and%20composition%20of%20social%20investment%20in%20the%20the%20UK.pdf

Breger Bush, S. (2016) Risk markets and the landscape of social change. *International Journal of Political Economy* 45(2): 124–146.

Bridges Fund Management (2015) Bridges backs world's first two 'follow-on' SIBs as concept proves its worth, 19 March , press release. www.bridgesfundmanagement.com/bridges-backs-worlds-first-two-follow-sibs-concept-proves-worth/

Bridges Fund Management (2016) *Better Outcomes, Better Values: The Evolution of Social Impact Bonds in the UK*. www.bridgesfundmanagement.com/wp-content/uploads/2017/08/Bridges-Better-Outcomes-Better-Value-2017-print.pdf

Bryan, D. and Rafferty, M. (2014) Financial derivatives as social policy beyond crisis. *Sociology* 48(5): 887–903.

Bryan, D. and Rafferty, M. (2015) 'Risk and value: finance, labour and production', *South Atlantic Quarterly* 114(2): 307–329.

Burgess, S. (2011) Measuring financial sector output and its contribution to UK GDP. *Bank of England Quarterly Bulletin*, Q3. https://www.bankofengland.co.uk/quarterly-bulletin/2011/q3/measuring-financial-sector-output-and-its-contribution-to-uk-gdp

Cahill, D. (2019) Market analysis beyond market fetishism. *EPA: Economy and Space*, 1–19, online first. https://doi.org/10.1177%2F0308518X18820917

Carter, E. (2019) More than marketised? Exploring the governance and accountability mechanisms at play in Social Impact Bonds. *Journal of Economic Policy Reform*. https://doi.org/10.1080/17487870.2019.1575736

China Development Institute and Z/Yen (2016) *Global Financial Centres Index 20*, Long Finance. https://en.cdi.org.cn/component/k2/item/309-the-global-financial-centres-index-20-gfci-20

Christophers, B. (2015) The limits to financialisation. *Dialogues in Human Geography* 5(2): 183–200.

City of London Corporation (2015) *Developing a Global Financial Centre for Social Impact Investment*. City of London/PWC. http://gsgii.org/wp-content/uploads/2017/07/Developing-a-global-financial-centre-for-SII.pdf

Davies, F.G. and Kim, S. (2015) Financialisation of the economy. *Annual Review of Sociology* 41: 203–221.

Dear, A., Helbitz, A., Khare, R., Lotan, R., Newman, J., Crosby Sims, G., and Zaroulis, A. (2016) *Social Impact Bonds – The Early Years*. Social Finance. https://www.socialfinance.org.uk/sites/default/files/publications/sibs-early-years_social_finance_2016_final.pdf

Department for Work and Pensions (2016a) *Qualitative Evaluation of the DWP Innovation Fund: Final Report*. Research Report No. 922. www.gov.uk/government/publications/qualitative-evaluation-of-the-dwp-innovation-fund-final-report

Department for Work and Pensions (2016b) *Youth Unemployment Innovation Fund Pilot: Starts and Outcomes*, January. www.gov.uk/government/statistics/youth-unemployment-innovation-fund-pilot-starts-and-outcomes-to-sept-2015

Department for Work and Pensions (2017) *Youth Engagement Fund Provider Guidance*, Version 12, May. https://www.gov.uk/government/publications/youth-engagement-fund-provider-guidance

Department for Work and Pension (no date) *The Innovation Fund Invitation to Tender – Specification and Supporting Information v1.0.* https://webcache.googleusercontent.com/search?q=cache:3sgU AjDUAPkJ:https://data.gov.uk/data/contracts-finder-archive/ download/344819/6767fc6c-ff3e-4f23-8a3a-bc065874a04e+&cd =1&hl=en&ct=clnk&gl=uk

Dorsett, R. (2017) *HMP Peterborough Social Impact Bond – Learning Exercise.* www.gov.uk/government/uploads/system/uploads/ attachment_data/file/633246/peterborough-social-impact-bond-learnings-report.pdf

Dowling, E. (2017) In the wake of austerity: social impact bonds and the financialisation of the welfare state in Britain. *New Political Economy* 22(3): 294–310.

Dowling, E. and Harvie, D. (2014) Harnessing the social: state, crisis and (big) society. *Sociology* 48(5): 869–886.

Edmiston, D. and Nicholls, A. (2018) Social Impact Bonds: the role of private capital in outcome based commissioning. *Journal of Social Policy* 47(1): 57–76.

Esposito, E. (2011) *The Future of Futures: The Time of Money in Financing and Society*, Cheltenham: Edward Elgar.

Fine, B. (2010) Locating financialisation. *Historical Materialism* 18: 17–116.

Fine, B. (2012) Financialisation on the rebound. *Actuel Marx* 51(1): 73–85. www.cairn.info/revue-actuel-marx-2012-1-page-73.htm

Fine, B. (2013) Financialisation from a Marxist perspective. *International Journal of Political Economy* 42(4): 47–66.

Fine, B. (2014) *The Continuing Enigmas of Social Policy*, Working Paper 2014–10, United Nations Research Institute for Social Development. http://www.unrisd.org/unrisd/website/document.nsf/(httpPublica tions)/30B153EE73F52ABFC1257D0200420A61?OpenDocument

Fine, B. and Saad-Filho, A. (2016) *Marx's Capital*, 6th edition. London: Pluto Press.

French, S., Leyshon, A. and Wainwright, T. (2011) Financialising space, spacing financialisation. *Progress in Human Geography*, 35(6): 798–819.

Government Outcomes Lab (no date) *DWP Innovation Fund Round I – Greater Merseyside (New Horizons)*, Project Database, University of Oxford. https://golab.bsg.ox.ac.uk/knowledge/project-database/

Greer, I., Breidahl, K.N., Knuth, M. and Larsen, F. (2017) *Marketisation of Employment Services in Europe: The Dilemma of Europe's Work-First Welfare States.* Oxford: Oxford University Press.

Harari, D. (2017) *Household Debt: Statistics and Impact on Economy.* Briefing paper No. 7584, House of Commons Research Library. http://researchbriefings.parliament.uk/ResearchBriefing/Summary/CBP-7584

Harvie, D. (2019) (Big) society and (market) discipline: social investment and the financialisation of social reproduction. *Historical Materialism* 27(1): 92–124.

Harvie, D. and Ogman, R. (2019) The broken promises of the social investment market. *Environment and Planning A: Economy and Space,* doi.org/10.1177/0308518X19827298

HM Government (2014) *Youth Engagement Fund Prospectus.* www.gov.uk/government/uploads/system/uploads/attachment_data/file/313589/youth_engagement_fund_prospectus.pdf

HM Government (2016a) *Social Investment: A Force for Social Change, 2016 Strategy.* www.gov.uk/government/uploads/system/uploads/attachment_data/file/507215/6.1804_sift_strategy_260216_final_web.pdf

HM Government (2016b) *Social Investment: The UK as a Global Hub – 2016 International Strategy.* www.gov.uk/government/uploads/system/uploads/attachment_data/file/507060/6.1806_CO_HMG_International_strategy_FINAL_web__3_.pdf

i-for-change (2016) *Social Impact Bond Market in the UK,* January. www.i-for-change.co.uk/resources/sib-market.html

Joy, M. and Shields, J. (2018) Austerity in the making: reconfiguring social policy through social impact bonds. *Policy & Politics,* 6(4): 681–695.

Keohane, N. Mulheirn, I. and Shorthouse, R. (2013) *Risky Business: Social Impact Bonds and Public Services.* London: Social Market Foundation.

Martin, R. (2013) After economy: social logics of the derivative. *Social Text* 31(1–114): 83–106.

Martin, R., Rafferty, M. and Bryan, D. (2008) Financialisation, risk and labour. *Competition and Change* 12(2): 120–132.

OECD (2015) *Social Impact Investment: Building the Evidence Base.* Paris: OECD Publishing. www.oecd-ilibrary.org/finance-and-investment/social-impact-investment_9789264233430-en

Rees, J., Whitfield, A. and Carter, E. (2014) Support for all in the UK WORK PROGRAMME? Differential payments, same old problem. *Social Policy & Administration* 48(2): 221–239.

Robinson, M. (2016) The size and composition of social investment in the UK. Social Investment Insight Series, March, *Big Society Capital*. www.bigsocietycapital.com/latest/type/research/size-and-composition-social-investment-uk

Ronicle, J. Stanworth, N., Hickman, E. and Fox, T. (2014) *Social Impact Bonds: The State of Play*. https://atqconsultantsblog.files.wordpress.com/2014/12/sibs_the-state-of-play_full-report.pdf

Rosenman, E. (2019) The geographies of social finance: poverty regulation through the 'invisible heart' of markets. *Progress in Human Geography* 43(1): 141–162.

Salis, S., Wishart, R. and McKay, S. (2018) *Evaluation of the Innovation Fund Pilot: Quantitative Assessment of Impact and Social Return on Investment*. Research Report No. 956, Department for Work and Pensions. www.gov.uk/government/publications/innovation-fund-pilot-assessment-of-return-on-investment

Secretary of State for Work and Pensions (2015) Speech at the Reform Conference: 'The welfare state – continuing the revolution', 4 February, London. https://www.politicshome.com/news/uk/economy/news/70392/full-iain-duncan-smith-speech-welfare-savings

Sinclair, S. McHugh, N., Huckfield, L., Roy, M. and Donaldson, C. (2014) Social Impact Bonds: shifting the boundaries of citizenship. In Farnsworth, K. Irving, Z. and Fenger, M. (eds) *Social Policy Review 26*. Bristol: Policy Press, 119–136.

Sinclair, S., McHugh, N. and Roy, M. J. (2019) Social innovation, financialisation and commodification: a critique of social impact bonds. *Journal of Economic Policy Reform*. https://doi.org/10.1080/17487870.2019.1571415

Smyth, P. and Deeming, C. (2016) The 'social investment perspective' in social policy: a *longue durée* perspective. *Social Policy & Administration* 50(6): 673–690.

Social Finance (2017a) *Database – Global Social Impact Bonds*. https://sibdatabase.socialfinance.org.uk/

Social Finance (2017b) World's 1st Social Impact Bond shown to cut reoffending and to make impact investors a return. Press release, Thursday 27 July. https://www.socialfinance.org.uk/sites/default/files/news/final-press-release-pb-july-2017.pdf

Social Impact Investment Taskforce (2013) *G8 Social Impact Investment Forum – Outputs and Agreed Actions*, Cabinet Office/G8. www.gov.uk/government/publications/social-impact-investment-forum-outputs-and-actions

Social Impact Investment Taskforce (2014) *Impact Investment: The Invisible Heart of Markets – Harnessing the Power of Entrepreneurship, Innovation and Capital for Public Good*, Report of the Social Investment Taskforce, 15 September. https://impactinvestingaustralia.com/wp-content/uploads/Social-Impact-Investment-Taskforce-Report-FINAL.pdf

Social Investment Taskforce (2010) *Social Investment Ten Years On: Final Report of the Social Investment Taskforce*, April. www.bigsocietycapital.com/sites/default/files/attachments/Social%20Investment%20Ten%20Years%20On.pdf

Soederberg, S. (2015) The US debtfare state and the credit card industry: forging spaces of dispossession. *Antipode* 45(2): 493–512.

Sokol, M. (2013) Towards a 'newer' economic geography? Injecting finance and financialisation into economic geographies. *Cambridge Journal of Regions, Economy and Society* 6(3): 501–515.

Sokol, M. (2015) Financialisation, financial chains and uneven geographical development: towards a research agenda. *Research in International Business and Finance* 39: 678–685.

Tan, S., Fraser, A., McHugh, N. and Warner, M. (2019) Widening perspectives on social impact bonds. *Journal of Economic Policy Reform*. https://doi.org/10.1080/17487870.2019.1568249

Tyler, G. (2015) *Financial Services: Contribution to the UK Economy*, 26 February. Standard Note SN/EP/06193, House of Commons.

Van der Zwan, N. (2014) Making sense of financialisation. *Socio-Economic Review* 12: 99–129.

Whitfield, D. (2015) *Alternative to Private Finance of the Welfare State: A Global Analysis of Social Impact Bonds, Pay for Success and Development Impact Bond Projects*. European Services Strategy Unit. www.european-services-strategy.org.uk/publications/essu-research-reports/alternative-to-private-finance-of-the-welfare/alternative-to-private-finance-of-the-welfare-state.pdf

Wiggan, J. (2018) Policy boostering the social impact investment market. *Journal of Social Policy* 47(4): 721–738.

7

A critical neuro-geography of behaviourally and neuroscientifically informed public policy

Jessica Pykett

Introduction: what scale for social policy?

The obvious starting point for social policy making is of course 'the social'. Social policies are aimed at improving the welfare and well-being of both societies and individual citizens (Alcock, 2016: 7). Throughout the history of social policy and around the globe, the appropriate balance to be achieved between the welfare of society and the individual are the subject of enduring debate. This chapter explores how behavioural and neuroscientifically informed public policies are reworking the parameters of this debate by carving out new spatialities of social policy. They do so by raising questions of scale and politics: at what scale is government intervention necessary, effective and efficient; who should be responsible for health, productivity and well-being in liberal societies – individuals, local communities, regional bodies, nation states, global institutions? The predominance of 'welfare retrenchment' – the gradual decline in state provision of welfare associated with contemporary neoliberal economies characterised by state austerity, contracting out of public services, managerial and marketised forms of workfare – has sharpened the focus on the latter question in particular. Yet the established economic and political orthodoxy of neoliberalism as a deregulating, marketising and privatising impetus since the 1980s is being somewhat eroded. Today neoliberalism faces new challenges on several fronts: the rhetoric of economic protectionism in Trump's America; disaffection with free movement and free trade associated with Brexit; recognition of the perpetual economic crises caused by unfettered capitalism, most recently in the global financial crisis of 2008. Acknowledgement of the failure of both markets and governments to correctly understand the behaviours, preferences, motivations and decision-making capacities of citizens is at the centre of these challenges.

Specific developments in the behavioural sciences and neurosciences concerning the nature of decision making have been pivotal in acknowledging the new challenges faced by social policy. The primary contention of these scientific insights is that human behaviour can no longer be understood, as within neoliberal thinking, as being economically rational – rather, people's behaviour is subject to psychological heuristics and biases which are intuitive and automatic rather than deliberative and considered. Whilst such decision-making shortcuts often work well, they are subject to systematic errors. A dual system conception of human decision making is now broadly accepted in the behavioural economics literature (though less so in the neurosciences) and is often described using the shorthand of 'thinking fast and slow' (Kahneman, 2012). This body of knowledge is said to justify the use of psychologically sophisticated policy tools including 'nudges' and cleverly designed 'choice architectures' which can either overcome these biases or make use of them in order to help citizens to make decisions which will be in their own best and long-term interests, as judged by themselves (Thaler and Sunstein, 2008). Amidst this growing enthusiasm for the application of behavioural, psychological and neuroscientific insights in social policy, there has been a shift in emphasis from structural, through individuated and towards neuromolecular scales of explanation for social problems. This chapter develops a 'critical neuro-geography' (Pykett, 2018) to highlight the strategic but typically overlooked importance of spatialities – including sites and milieux, scalar claims and distributed assemblages of policies and power – to these new and growing forms of governance targeted at the brain, behaviour and soul.

The brain and behaviour in policy around the world

Post-war social policy in the UK was largely shaped by Keynesian economics and the academic discipline of social policy or 'public administration' itself (Alcock, 2016). But since the turn of the century, the explicit reference to behavioural economics and psychology in policy-making discourse, documentation and practice has become prevalent (notwithstanding a much longer history of the psy-sciences in social policy and governance; Rose, 1996). The UK is often regarded as something of an experimental laboratory for the application of behavioural insights in policy (see Jones et al., 2013; Halpern, 2015 for overviews). In 2004, the UK government's strategy unit at the Cabinet Office published *Personal Responsibility and Changing Behaviour*, a document which highlighted the mistaken assumptions about 'rational man' which had plagued neoliberal public policy up to this point. It described the moral, political and cost-based arguments for increased personal responsibility and co-production of public services, said to reflect changes in public attitudes away from reliance on the state as well as more sophisticated understandings of behaviour itself:

> it has become increasingly clear that government cannot simply 'deliver' key policy outcomes to a disengaged and passive public. ... We should have in mind that most of our behaviours are so deeply rooted that they are more akin to 'habits' and unspoken assumptions than carefully considered, fully-conscious choices. (Halpern et al., 2004: 14)

Between 2004 and 2010 various UK government departments had policy initiatives which drew on behavioural insights. The Department of Health's *Change for Life* campaign was a social marketing initiative based on mobilising social norms and people's stated commitments to increase physical activity and eat more healthily. The Department for Environment, Food and Rural Affairs' (DEFRA, 2007) *Framework for Pro-Environmental Behaviours* also discussed behavioural models at length, including the non-rational motivations (for example social norms, 'feel good factors', ease, feeling part of something) and barriers (for example habit, scepticism, disempowerment, lifestyle fit, self-identity, cost, infrastructure) to change. But despite some piecemeal efforts to embed behavioural insights across government departments through networks, training and secondments, there lacked a central driving force and organisation to push the 'Behaviour Change Agenda' forward.

This driving force was to come in 2010, when several things came together to promote the rolling out of behaviourally informed public policy making in the UK. First, the publication of *MINDSPACE* (Dolan et al., 2010), co-published by the Cabinet Office and Institute for Government, provided a cutting-edge overview of the potential value of behavioural insights in policy making, and a guiding framework for policy makers. Second, the head of the Civil Service, Cabinet Secretary Sir Gus O'Donnell, publicly promoted a behavioural approach to policy, and finally he set up the world's first national behavioural insights unit within the Cabinet Office, to be headed by David Halpern – a former Cabinet Office adviser himself, chief executive of the Institute for Government and co-author of *MINDSPACE*. The Behavioural Insights Team (BIT) – or so-called 'nudge unit' – was later 'spun out' as a social purpose company, owned by the Cabinet Office, Nesta (a third sector innovation foundation) and the staff (Halpern, 2015: 350). BIT's work has addressed policy areas such as tax compliance, reducing missed hospital appointments, public health campaigns, adult literacy/numeracy programmes, increasing charitable giving and improving completion rates for army reservist applications, more recently expanding their work into workplace diversity, widening participation in higher education and early childhood development amongst Syrian refugees.

The BIT quickly established a reputation for advising governments around the world (for example Australia, New Zealand, USA, Singapore), and now has offices in Sydney, New York, Wellington and Singapore. Moreover, behavioural insights to public policy making quickly became an object of rapid policy transfer, circulating through interconnected global policy networks. A number of countries have developed their own similar government units or non-state organisations and networks. The USA's Social and Behavioral Sciences Team was set up in the White House in 2014, achieving success with the passing of an Executive Order on 'Using Behavioral Science Insights to Better Serve the American People' in September 2015, only to be disbanded by the Trump administration in 2017. The Netherlands government set up a cross-departmental network for behavioural insights 'BIN-NL' in 2014. NudgeFrance was established in 2015 as a not-for-profit organisation to promote nudge approaches in France, and its team includes former and current staff from the French government, the European Commission and the BVA market research company. The Australian government has a central 'Behavioural Economics Team of the Australian Government' (BETA), including 17 government agencies (OECD, 2017: 26). Singapore has behavioural insights teams within several government departments, and a 'human centred design approach' to policy promoted through its 'Human Experience Lab' within the Prime Minister's Public Service Division. The first Middle Eastern Behavioural Insights Unit was launched by Qatar's Supreme Committee for Delivery & Legacy in 2016. These developments take behavioural public policies beyond liberal democratic contexts, the social policy rationales, implementation and impacts of which are not well researched (but for a comparative analysis of BITs in Singapore and the Netherlands, see Whitehead et al., 2018: chapter 5).

There has been an impressive cross-scalar movement (Peck and Theodore, 2012: 22) of behaviourally and neuroscientifically informed public policies. Supranational institutions have achieved this by promoting specific forms of policy learning, knowledge production, epistemic communities and communication which have seen nudge-type policy travel and transform from the relatively libertarian context of the USA to the social democracies of the European Union (Jones et al., 2014, discuss the specific spatialities of this kind of policy *translation*). In 2015 the European Commission launched the EU Policy Lab within the Joint Research Centre which uses foresight, behavioural insights and design thinking in combination to find new ways to solve policy problems. The EU Policy Lab has collated approaches and examples of 'behaviourally tested', 'behaviourally informed' and 'behaviourally aligned' public policies (referring to the degree to which the policies draw on evidence, research literature and in situ evaluation/experimentation) as well as information on national BITs across Europe (Lourenço et al., 2016). Development organisations and supranational bodies such as the OECD and the World Bank have also developed programmes of work which promote behaviourally informed public policy (international compendia of case studies examples include Whitehead et al., 2014; World Bank, 2015; Lourenço et al., 2016; OECD, 2017; the European Nudge Network, http://tenudge.eu). The use of 'behavioural change' techniques within the international development sector has been well established over several decades. Behavioural public policy has also become a profitable business venture – a behaviour change industry has responded to a global market for innovative social purpose products, services and consultancy, and one of the most important annual events now on the behavioural public policy calendar, the Behavioural Exchange, charges over £1,000 for admission. As such, the globalisation of behavioural and neuroscientifically informed public policy has been as much about exploiting and developing existing networks of not-for-profit NGOs and global corporations as it has been about the simple transfer of policy ideas from one nation state context to another. In this sense, the global upscaling and travel of such policies brings with it new legitimising ideas, objects, practices and allegiances which 'stick' to these policy agendas as they move across and beyond national borders (Freeman, 2009).

It is worth giving some brief examples of policies identified as broadly behaviourally aligned or oriented in the aforementioned compendia, specifically the European Commission Joint Research Centre *Behavioural Insights Applied to Policy* (Lourenço et al., 2016), the OECD *Behavioural Insights and Public Policy: Lessons from Around the World* (OECD, 2017) and the *Nudging All Over the World* report (Whitehead et al., 2014). There are more than 100 policy examples outlined in each of the EC and OECD reports, and 136 countries identified by Whitehead and colleagues where the behavioural sciences have influenced government policy to any extent. Here I pick out some of the initial policy areas and those related to heath and unemployment as areas most pertinent to social policy. The European Commission began its work in 2009 with a Directive on Consumer Rights limiting the use of defaults, or 'pre-checked boxes', in consumer contracts (Lourenço et al., 2016: 8). Defaults are administrative mechanisms which tend to 'lock in' habitual behaviours because it is easier to 'go along' with a particular bureaucratic process rather than make an active decision to 'opt out'. In the employment sector, initiatives in the UK, Hungary, Germany and the Netherlands have used public pre-commitments, framing, targeted information and group personal skills training respectively to increase employment amongst recipients of unemployment benefits. In Hungary, as in the UK, unemployment benefit has been renamed 'Job Seekers' Benefit' to highlight active job searching behaviour. In the health sector, common behaviourally aligned policies include display bans for tobacco products (in Iceland, France, the UK, Ireland), and presumed consent (opt-out) schemes for organ donation. The EC's taxonomy reports on policies which use mechanisms including defaults, framing, affects, social norms, anchoring, simplification, pre-commitments and choice architectures – all noted as policy levers which address behavioural errors such as salience (where obvious/prominent phenomena seem more likely), status quo bias (habitual tendencies), loss aversion (as opposed to seeking gains), overweighting of small probabilities (such as overconfidence in winning lotteries) and present bias (lack of long-term thinking). Specific 'welfare' policies referred to in the OECD report include the BITs Randomised Controlled Trial in JobCentrePlus offices in Essex, which in 2013–14 set out to reduce the number of people receiving unemployment benefits by increasing the number of people able to find jobs. It did this by 'simplifying' the job search process, and developing a 'commitment pack' to help job seekers plan their job search. It led to a 1.7% increase in those no longer receiving unemployment benefits at 13 weeks after the trial (OECD, 2017: 289), though this is of course not an indication of whether the *need* for such benefits declined. Notably, there are no policies described under a welfare category in either the EC or OECD documents, and the words 'welfare' and 'well-being' do not appear in *Behavioural Insights Applied to Policy* (Lourenço et al., 2016).

Whilst the sectors in which behavioural public policies have been applied indicate something of the kind of ideals and notions of public good being pursued, it is arguably in their separation of ends and means that such policies have enjoyed such global success across diverse policy sectors. The specific policy-making methodologies associated with behavioural public polies are arguably the most important factor in their capacity to jump policy scales and jurisdictions. The use of Randomised Controlled Trials – as in the JobCentrePlus case – has been one significant development in the application of behavioural insights to public policies. The BIT's *Test, Learn, Adapt* paper argued that RCTs should be used in public policy in order to improve policy effectiveness, to understand what works and what does not (Haynes et al., 2012: 6). This emphasis on policy experimentalism has been central to the global influence of the UK's particular approach to behavioural public policies, and is described by the chief executive of the BIT, David Halpern (2015: 298), as a 'quirky empiricism' – a challenge to 'brash' and overconfident traditional politics. It is an approach which is now widely used in assessing the value and impact of policies in education (through Education Endowment Fund projects), 'What Works' centres and international development organisations such as J-PAL (Abdul Latif Jameel Poverty Action Lab; see Halpern, 2015: chapter 10). Halpern (2015: 291) terms this approach 'radical incrementalism', meaning 'systematically testing small variations in everything we do'. This idea of small tweaks to policy and procedure, experimentation and learning from failures, spreading and sharing the results and building an evidence base has been an important part of countering criticisms that behavioural public policy initiatives have been too trivial to achieve large population-based and long-term effects. On the other hand, it has also been argued that the experimental approach to policy making needs its own normative considerations, given its potential to change the relationship between state and citizen (Whitehead et al., 2018: 126).

Although there has been much commentary on the rise of these behavioural forms and methods of governance, not least their affinity with individuated and behaviourist psychological theories rather than more socio-spatial conceptions of habit or social practice (Pedwell, 2017; Reid and Ellsworth-Krebs, 2018; Whitehead et al., 2018), less well known is to what extent specifically *neuroscientific* knowledge has influenced public and social policies in different national contexts. Whilst the international reports on behavioural public policies often refer to neuroscience and cognitive science as academic fields within the behavioural sciences (Lourenço et al., 2016: 9; OECD, 2017: 3), evidence on the application of neuroscientific claims on actual policies is scant. Clear lines of distinction are often drawn between the behavioural sciences, which study observable behaviour, and the neurosciences, which are more focused on the (internal) biochemical and physical mechanisms of the brain (only indirectly 'observable' through representations provided by neuroimaging technologies and experimental research techniques). But in reality the boundaries between these approaches are increasingly blurred, and focal points such as the 'decision-making sciences' and neuroeconomics muddy the waters further (Pykett, 2013). At heart, the behavioural and neuroscience disciplines both emphasise the irrationality of human decision making, our tendencies to make poor, ignorant or overly optimistic, ill-founded choices, and the ways in which policy could ameliorate our choices to combat such global crises as climate change and the obesity epidemic. In this sense, both the behavioural and the neuroscientifically informed policy agendas make quite explicit scalar leaps from individualised behaviours to global change, with little regard for all the geographical and political complexity of decision-making contexts that must necessarily bridge these scales.

Only a small number of studies to date have explored the impact or potential impact of neuroscience on social policy, with commentary tending to focus on societal, political or cultural impacts (Royal Society, 2011; Rose and Abi-Rached, 2013; Pitts-Taylor, 2015; Rose and Rose, 2016). More specifically, research has begun to consider the impact of neuroscientific discourse in public policy across the life course, including early years, adolescents and older adults (Broer and Pickersgill, 2015), and in different spaces, such as schools, cities and workplaces (Pykett, 2015). Education, child development and family policy have been common sites for critical ethnographic, interpretive and historical work. This work has considered whether we have been 'blinded by science' (Wastell and White, 2017), or have become hostage to new expert forms of self-knowledge used to govern our conduct towards neoliberal ends (Edwards et al., 2015; Gagen, 2015).

More recently, behavioural scientists themselves have begun to identify the potential for combining behavioural and neuroscientific insights for public policy (Seymour and Vlaev, 2012; Felsen and Reiner, 2015). Although Seymour and Vlaev surmise that there is thus far very little evidence of neuroscience directly informing behaviour change policy, Felsen and Reiner (2015: 470) conclude that: 'Neuroscience can contribute to both empirical and normative questions about nudging: Specifically, how to make nudges more effective, and how to understand whether they are consistent with our ethical principles'. For them, it is by understanding the biochemical mechanisms of decision making that we can really know how to design rational nudges and avoid any unwanted side effects. Animal models, psychological experiments and identification of causal relationships between neuronal activity and decision variables through neuronal stimulation, they argue, lend considerable weight to the liberal claims of nudging; that they do not restrict free choices (Felsen and Reiner, 2015: 472). Somewhat controversially and perhaps in contradistinction to this, they conclude that neuroscientific agreement on our diminished capacity for free will should in fact lead us to rethink the value we place on autonomy. The far-reaching implications of seeking a neuroscientific rationale for taking a particular ethical position will not be lost on those who are familiar with debates on medical ethics, bioethics, the science–policy nexus and the politics of knowledge production. Ethical issues are paramount, but it is far from clear why a neuroscientific account of decision making should form the basis for our normative frameworks – as a key proponent of behavioural and neuroscientifically informed public policy, Harvard Law School professor Cass Sunstein (2013: 3) himself has argued, what is needed is 'not a psychology of moral argument, but a moral argument'.

Spatialities of behavioural and neuro-governance

All too often the shift towards behaviourally and neuroscientifically informed public policies has been discussed without reference to their spatial dimensions, yet, as this section outlines, such neglected spatialities are key to fully understanding both the insights and potential risks of behavioural policy making. By taking a spatial approach to social policy, we can begin to see the active role that space plays in shaping not only social policy outcomes, but also the approaches and agendas which are pursued, and the strategies and techniques of governance posited as the most effective means for achieving policy goals at particular points in time and in specific national contexts. By challenging the idea that space is a mere container for social processes, policies and patterns, geography has the capacity to look across sites, sectors, scales, territories and networks, shedding new light on cultures and techniques of governance and opening out existing and future oriented social policies for political, ethical and pragmatic dissection.

Sites and spaces of neurogovernance

Geographers have begun to consider what contributions they can make to analysing and engaging with contemporary developments in the cognitive and neurosciences (for example Callard and Fitzgerald, 2015; Pykett, 2018), and in particular assessing the impact of their applications on public policy. Gagen has for instance demonstrated how Social and Emotional Aspects of Learning (SEAL) programmes in English secondary schools have been shaped by unacknowledged spatial assumptions in neuroscientific knowledge. Her approach is spatial in terms of considering the school as a site of governmentality – a site in which techniques of self-governance are promoted through the alignment of emotional techniques, neuroscientific knowledge and neoliberal forms of subjectivity, which she explores by looking at schools as sites in which we can discern 'the shifting locus of governmentality from targeting minds and bodies to insinuating itself at the molecular scale of subjectivity as it is newly rendered by neuroscience' (Gagen, 2015: 141). I have also focused on schools as spaces in which neuroscientific narratives, imaginaries and cultures have shaped policies and practices such as brain-based teaching and learning, on workplaces where organisational neuroscience and positive psychology have influenced training and management practices, and on neuroarchitectural approaches to urban design in cities (for example Pykett, 2015; Pykett and Enright, 2016; Williamson et al., 2017). I have drawn on Foucauldian geography and sociologist Nikolas Rose's analyses of the role of the neurosciences in subject formation, in order to consider how the orchestration of spatial relationships has been integral to the securing of power over individual bodies (anatamo-politics) and the management of populations (biopolitics) (Pykett, 2015: 63). In terms of the anatomy of the state, this analysis understands the mobilisation of certain academic knowledge sources (in this case, behavioural economics) as fundamental to the shaping of conduct, as set out by Foucault in his essay on governmentality:

> To govern a state will mean, therefore, to apply economy, to set up an economy at the level of the entire state, which means exercising towards its inhabitants, and the wealth and behaviour of *each and all*, a form of surveillance and control as attentive as that of the head of a family over his household and his goods. (Foucault, 1994: 207, emphasis added)

This type of indirect governance – the arrangement of people and things in specific institutions and sites – makes the idea of a spatial *milieu* central to understanding the politics of neurogovernance. Given that individuals' subjectivities and behaviours are always spatially rooted and networked, a geographical approach is important to help us to understand how behavioural drivers are both embodied and discursive, shaped by long-running and large-scale social, political, economic and cultural factors *in situ* as well as by psychological heuristics and neurobiological mechanisms of decision making (Pykett, 2015: ix). This offers something of a challenge, or at least a refinement, to dominant aspatial accounts of behaviour and decision making offered in the contemporary neurosciences, which explicitly tend towards acontextual internal, proximate, immediate and of course brain-based explanations for behaviour, often regarded as universal in nature and lacking a comprehensive theory of the role of the social in behaviour and change.

Politics of the neuromolecular scale

A second spatiality relevant to understanding the significance of the behavioural and neuroscientific influence on social policy is that of scale. In approaching human behaviour and decision making from a behavioural or neurobiological perspective, the scope for incorporating longer term and broader scale drivers of human and social action is diminished. There is no adequate behavioural or neuroscientific theory of social structures such as capitalism, colonialism, sexism, heteronormativity, racism – notwithstanding some strong claims to have identified, through psychological experimentation, the sources of economic self-interest, and unconscious gender and racial bias. Put simply, to explain these social phenomena and their power dynamics at a neuromolecular or behavioural scale is to risk universalising human experience, ignoring or indeed pathologising complex biographies of cultural difference, and leaving structural inequalities irrelevant and thus intact (Pitts-Taylor, 2015: 5; Pykett, 2015: 27). This is not to oppose the individual to the social scale of explanation, nor to impose a fixed division between the biological and social, but to reclaim some of the complexity with which we might understand the behavioural as shaped by economic, cultural, political, environmental organising frameworks, institutions, discourses, practices and embodied encounters – that is, the complex ecological milieu in which behaviours are *enacted* and decisions *take place*. So, too, it is to reclaim a level of analysis which incorporates multiple scales, to provide less partial insight into the politics of social policies which are derived from behavioural models and neuromolecular explanations. There are very real consequences of taking a naïve view of the politics of scale within social policy, as can be seen for instance in the popular idea within behavioural public policy of shaping the 'choice architectures' in which people make decisions. Famous examples include placing healthy food choices in prominent positions (at eye level), banning visible tobacco products at the point of sale, and changing the layout, order, colour or subtle linguistic cues of tax return forms. These operate at the scale of the immediate perceptual environment, in the latter case at the scale of a piece of paper, making no inroads into obesogenic environments and the profit-seeking imperatives of the food and drinks industry, or the social inequalities in tobacco use, or issues of tax fairness and reform – all of which operate at a larger scale.

There has been extensive discussion of the 'politics of scale' within human geography. Essentially, geographers have been concerned with the opposite problem to the reductive scalar thinking that I have just identified. Rather, some have argued that the global (read as structural) scale of explanation has been privileged over considerations of everyday life, micro-political practices and accounts of resistance and agency at the local level (see Marston et al., 2005, and Leitner and Miller, 2007, for two opposing sides of this argument). At a narrower scale yet, McCormack (2007: 364) has maintained that scientific discoveries at the neurochemical level since the 1950s have made the possibility of describing, intervening in and governing molecular affects a possibility, pointing towards a need in the discipline of geography for new analytical tools to understand governing, management and modification at a neuromolecular scale. As Leitner and Miller (2007: 120) show, an appreciation of the ways in which neoliberal globalisation 'hollows out' nation state responsibilities (and social policies) is not incompatible with a sense of human agency and the potential for political transformation. Rather, an attention to multiple scales – connoting a sense of 'level', 'size' and/or 'reach' – is crucial to be able to 'identify constraints to individual practices and behaviour in their spatial and temporal scales' (as Leitner and Miller, 2007: 121, suggest, paraphrasing John Protevi). Whilst their arguments are related specifically to the social and material construction of scales of political struggle, they are equally applicable to the contemporary struggles over the *scales of (scientific) explanation* which are characteristic of the behavioural and neuroscientific influence on social policy identified in this chapter. Indeed, an essential part of questioning this influence rests in carefully describing the way in which the behavioural and neuroscientific turn reframes the drivers of some intractable and 'global' social problems (crucially actually neither experienced nor caused uniformly) – such as the obesity epidemic, environmental and financial crisis – as at once the responsibility of individuals (in terms of their behaviour, psychological character and neural processes) and simultaneously as the target of a globalised industry of behaviour change and neuroscientific experts and consultants who can best advise states and devise tactics which are suited to governing global (universalised) emotions, decisions and behaviours. Instead, by looking at, *through* and *across* scales of explanation, data sources, evidential claims, agenda setting and social policy targets, we can begin to identify the significance of broader policy trajectories which may hitherto have been overlooked.

'Neuroliberal' governmentality: policy mobility, networks and assemblage

Within this social policy trajectory – the focus of this chapter – is the establishment of a global governmental infrastructure which aims to shape citizenly conduct through affective mechanisms and is inspired by the behavioural and neuro-sciences. This has been labelled 'neuroliberal' (Jones et al., 2011: 489; Whitehead et al., 2018). This term is at once a comment on the political-economic thinking behind public policies aimed at shaping the brain and behaviour whilst preserving freedom of choice, a description of an internationally evident set of techniques of self-governance targeted at the interface of conscious and unconscious neural activity, and hints at a critique of the sense of neurosis which may be created by constant invocations to manage one's own inbuilt biases, habitual or mistaken behaviours, brain processes and 'choice environments'. Let us consider these three aspects of neuroliberalism in detail.

First, neuroliberalism has – since around 2010 if not well before – been based on policy experimentation within a 'libertarian paternalist' political economic framework which in many respects leaves intact the neoliberal emphasis on market-based solutions, the preservation of free choice and the limited role of the state in welfare provision which has dominated the 'advanced liberal democracies' since the 1980s. At the same time, however, it has posed a challenge to neoliberal thought by contesting the rational economic man on which such theories have been based. As such, it cannot be seen as an adaptation or mutation of neoliberalism, not least because it recognises that it was a neoliberal economic rationality which caused many of the global social problems (market failures) which behavioural and neuroscientific public policy has set out to address, and because these forms of public policy preserve an important (if altered) role for the state in governing decisions and behavioural change. Second, neuroliberal governmentality describes initiatives, policy tools and techniques which govern individual citizens and populations through cultivating and systematising particular forms of self-conduct which use imagery and knowledge about the brain and ingrained behaviours as their rationale (Jones et al., 2011: 490).

This works either by bringing to conscious awareness the brain's troublesome biases, habits and inertia, or by using affective means to override conscious awareness entirely, preferring to directly target the emotions, the preconscious and automatic neural mechanisms driving behaviour. Finally, the term neuroliberalism suggests the ways in which these kinds of self-governing techniques can produce new anxieties, inequalities of psychological capital and self-knowledge, and patterns of exclusion. This can lead to a sense of neurosis among citizens, who are required to change their behaviour 'not via *calculating* habits but by soothing, appeasing, tranquillizing, and, above all, *managing* anxieties and insecurities' (Isin, 2004: 226, emphasis added).

These three elements of neuroliberalism have significant, if often neglected, geographical implications. The spatialities implied here relate to the *diffuse* and *networked* power through which neuroliberal governmentality is exercised; it is distinctly not a programme of government for which state regulation is at the *centre*, but what Foucault called a *dispositif* or an apparatus of power involving 'discourses, institutions, architectural forms, regulatory decisions, laws, administrative measures, scientific statements, philosophical, moral and philanthropic propositions', which are intended to shape the field of possibility for other actions (Foucault, 1977: 214, cited in Greco and Stenner, 2013: 2). By identifying behavioural and neuroscience-informed public policy as *dispositif* or apparatus of power, we can begin to think of these phenomena not as state-directed political agendas, but as *distributed assemblages* of ideas, expertise, people, institutions, techniques, objects and subject positions which, whilst they might tend to endure, and resonate with neoliberal economic imperatives, can also be riven with tensions, contradictions and paradoxes, gaps and sites of potential dissonance. This leads to a geographical perspective on social policy which highlights the spatial *embeddedness* and spatial *mobility* of particular policy ideas: how they are incubated, move, 'stick' to key personnel and events, gain currency, adapt or change in different policy sectors and sites, are mediated through policy networks and institutions. In doing anthropological work of this nature, we can identify the political rationalities, mechanisms and potential unintended consequences of social policies, pick out *geographical variation* in policy assemblages, and consider how they might have been and be assembled differently.

Conclusions: notes for critical neuro-geography

The appropriate balance between collective and individual responsibility and welfare has long been the concern of social policy scholars and a recurrent theme in political debate worldwide, not least in current policy preoccupations with 'well-being' and its multiple actors, agencies, partnerships and sponsors, in a place previously occupied by the 'welfare state'. So, too, geographers have contributed a great deal to these debates. They have mapped and measured spatial inequalities in welfare and well-being, resource allocation and distribution of social benefits and disadvantage. They have identified objective indicators of quality of life, and shown how place can drive and shape experiences of poverty (Pacione, 1982; Powell et al., 2001). The behavioural and neuroscientific developments in public policy outlined in this chapter provide new impetus to interrogate 'who gets what where, and how?' (Smith, 1974). Investigating *how* social problems are framed, *how* policy solutions are scaled, *how* sites are shaped as new spaces of neurogovernance is essential if we are to understand the global imperative to govern through neuromolecular affects as opposed to resource distribution.

As the chapter has argued, there are significant political implications of an approach to social policy which is based on a reductive scale of scientific explanation, which tends to see the governing of self-conduct and the design of immediate choice architectures as the principal focal points of libertarian paternalist governments. By personalising the roots of social problems in behavioural mistakes, defects in character and lack of psychological capital, what could be radical and progressive about behavioural economics (its appreciation of the potential diversity of human experience, attention to the non-rational/non-utility-maximising components of decision making, a [limited scale] commitment to shaping the contexts in which these decisions are made) is lost in its continued adherence to an a priori individualistic notion of the economic agent and the ideal attainment of an economic rationality above other (political, cultural, environmental, social) senses of reason. The abandonment of 'the social' and the failure of neoliberal social policies to increase welfare or decrease inequalities in well-being have been evident in political discourse for several decades. Take this quote from Margaret Thatcher, reflecting on her own moral and political-economic thought after her first two years of office:

> What's irritated me about the whole direction of politics in the last 30 years is that it's always been towards the collectivist society. People have forgotten about the personal society. And they say: do I count, do I matter? To which the short answer is, yes. And therefore, it isn't that I set out on economic policies; it's that I set out really to change

the approach, and changing the economics is the means of changing that approach. If you change the approach you really are after the heart and soul of the nation. *Economics are the method; the object is to change the heart and soul.* (*Sunday Times*, 1981, emphasis added)

If behavioural public policy, whether supported or supplanted by neuroscientific insights, is to avoid further abandonment of the social in the name of an embodied, emotional and psychological politics, then greater attention needs to be paid to the geographical sites, scales and diffuse forms of power indicated by these 'heart and soul'-based solutions to political-economic problems.

References

Alcock, P. (2016) What is social policy? In Alcock, P., Haux, T., May, M. and Wright, S. (eds) *The Student's Companion to Social Policy*, 5th edition. Chichester: Wiley-Blackwell, 7–13.

Broer, T. and Pickersgill, M. (2015) Targeting brains, producing responsibilities: the use of neuroscience within British social policy. *Social Science & Medicine* 132: 54–61.

Callard, F. and Fitzgerald, D. (2015) *Rethinking Interdisciplinarity across the Social Sciences and Neurosciences.* Palgrave Macmillan. www.palgrave.com/us/book/9781137407955

DEFRA (2007) *A Framework for Pro-environmental Behaviours.* London: Department for Environment, Food and Rural Affairs.

Dolan, P., Hallsworth, M., Halpern, D., King, D. and Vlaev, I. (2010) *MINDSPACE: Influencing Behaviour Through Public Policy.* London: Institute for Government and Cabinet Office.

Edwards, R., Gillies, V. and Horsley, N. (2015) Brain science and early years policy: hopeful ethos or 'cruel optimism'? *Critical Social Policy* 35(2): 167–187.

Felsen, G. and Reiner, P.B. (2015) What can neuroscience contribute to the debate over nudging? *Review of Philosophy and Psychology* 6(3): 469–479.

Foucault, M. (1994) Governmentality. In Faubion, J.D. (ed) *Power: Essential Works of Foucault 1954–1984.* London: Penguin, 201–222.

Freeman, R. (2009) What is translation? *Evidence and Policy* 5: 429–447.

Gagen, E (2015) Governing emotions: citizenship, neuroscience and the education of youth. *Transactions of the Institute of British Geographers* 40(1): 140–152.

Greco, M. and Stenner, P. (2013) Happiness and the art of life: diagnosing the psychopolitics of wellbeing. *Health, Culture and Society* 5(1): 1–19.

Halpern, D. (2015) *Inside the Nudge Unit*. London: Penguin.

Halpern, D., Bates, C., Mulgan, G., Aldridge, S., Beales, G. and Heathfield, A.(2004) *Personal Responsibility and Changing Behaviour: The State of Knowledge and its Implications for Public Policy*. London: Cabinet Office.

Haynes, L., Service, O., Goldacre, B. and Torgerson, D. (2012) *Test, Learn, Adapt: Developing Public Policy with Randomised Controlled Trials*. London: Cabinet Office Behavioural Insights Team.

Isin, E. (2004) The neurotic citizen. *Citizenship Studies* 8(3): 217–235.

Jones, R., Pykett, J. and Whitehead, M. (2011) Governing temptation: changing behaviour in an age of libertarian paternalism. *Progress in Human Geography* 35(4): 483–501.

Jones, R., Pykett, J. and Whitehead, M. (2013) *Changing Behaviours: On the Rise of the Psychological State*. Cheltenham: Edward Elgar.

Jones, R., Pykett, J. and Whitehead, M. (2014) The geographies of policy translation: how nudge became the default policy option. *Environment and Planning C. Government and Policy* 32(1): 54–69.

Kaheman, D. (2012) *Thinking Fast and Slow*. London: Penguin Books.

Leitner, H. and Miller, B. (2007) Scale and the limitations of ontological debate: a commentary on Marston, Jones and Woodward. *Transactions of the Institute of British Geographers* 32: 116–125.

Lourenço, J.S., Ciriolo, E., Almeida, S.R. and Troussard, X. (2016) *Behavioural Insights Applied to Policy: European Report*. Brussels: Joint Research Centre, EU.

Marston, S.A., Jones, J.P. and Woodward, K. (2005) Human geography without scale. *Transactions of the Institute of British Geographers* 30: 416–432.

McCormack, D. (2007) Molecular affects in human geographies. *Environment and Planning A* 39: 359–377.

OECD (2017) *Behavioural Insights and Public Policy: Lessons from Around the World*. Paris: Organisation for Economic Co-operation and Development.

Pacione, M. (1982) The use of objective and subjective measures of life quality in human geography. *Progress in Human Geography* 6(4): 495–514.

Peck, J. and Theodore, N. (2012) Follow the policy: a distended case approach. *Environment and Planning* 44: 21–30.

Pedwell, C. (2017) Habit and the politics of social change: a comparison of nudge theory and pragmatist philosophy. *Body and Society* 23(4): 59–94.

Pitts-Taylor, V. (2015) *The Brain's Body: Neuroscience and Corporeal Politics*. Durham, NC: Duke University Press.

Powell, M., Boyne, G. and Ashworth, R. (2001) Towards a geography of people poverty and place poverty. *Policy & Politics* 29(3): 243–258.

Pykett, J. (2013) Neurocapitalism and the new neuros: using neuroeconomics, behavioural economics and picoeconomics for public policy. *Journal of Economic Geography* 13(5): 845–869.

Pykett, J. (2015) *Brain Culture: Shaping Policy through Neuroscience*. Bristol: Policy Press.

Pykett, J. (2018) Geography and neuroscience: critical engagements with geography's 'neural turn'. *Transactions of the Institute of British Geographers* 43(2): 154–169.

Pykett, J. and Enright, B. (2016) Geographies of brain culture: optimism and optimisation in workplace training programmes. *Cultural Geographies* 23(1): 51–68.

Reid, L. and Ellsworth-Krebs, K. (2018) Nudge(ography) and practice theories: contemporary sites of behavioural science and post-structuralist approaches in geography? *Progress in Human Geography* 43(2). https://doi.org/10.1177/0309132517750773

Rose, H. and Rose, S. (2016) *Can Neuroscience Change Our Minds?* Cambridge: Polity Press.

Rose, N. (1996) *Inventing Ourselves: Psychology, Power, and Personhood*. Cambridge: Cambridge University Press.

Rose, N. and Abi-Rached, J.M. (2013) *Neuro: The New Brain Sciences and the Management of the Mind*. Woodstock: Princeton University Press.

Royal Society (2011) *Neuroscience, Society and Policy*. London: The Royal Society.

Seymour, B. and Vlaev, I. (2012) Can, and should, behavioural neuroscience influence public policy? *Trends in Cognitive Sciences* 16(9): 449–451.

Smith, D. (1974) Who gets what where, and how: a welfare focus for human geography. *Geography* 59(4): 289–297.

Sunday Times (1981) Mrs Thatcher: the first two years. *Sunday Times*, 3 May.

Sunstein, C.R. (2013) Is deontology a heuristic? On psychology, neuroscience, ethics, and law. 1 August. http://dx.doi.org/10.2139/ssrn.2304760

Thaler, R.H. and Sunstein, C.R. (2008) *Nudge: Improving Decisions about Health, Wealth and Happiness*. London: Yale University Press.

Wastell, D. and White, S. (2017) *Blinded By Science: The Social Implications of Epigenetics and Neuroscience*. Bristol: Policy Press.

Whitehead, M., Howell, R., Jones, R., Lilley, R. and Pykett, J. (2014) *Nudging All Over the World: Assessing the Impacts of the Behavioural Sciences on Public Policy*. https://changingbehaviours.wordpress.com/2014/09/05/nudging-all-over-the-world-the-final-report/

Whitehead, M., Jones, R., Lilley, R., Pykett, J. and Howell, R. (2018) *Neuroliberalism: Behavioural Government in the Twenty-First Century*. London: Routledge.

Williamson, B., Pykett, J. and Nemorin, S. (2017) Biosocial systems and neurocomputational governance: brain-based and brain-targeted technologies in education. *Discourse* 39(2): 258–275.

World Bank (2015) *Mind, Body and Society – World Development Report*. Washington, DC: World Bank.

PART III:

Methods

8

Not just nuisance: spatialising social statistics

Richard Harris

Introduction

This chapter is about treating space seriously within quantitative methods and thinking. It argues that geography is a fundamental characteristic of society, and of the social processes studied in the social sciences. However, the sorts of statistical techniques typically taught to social scientists, and used to inform social policy, either ignore the spatial dimension entirely or regard it as a nuisance. Neither of these acts of geographical short-sightedness is adequate, and both can result in misunderstanding about what is happening, where and why.

A few years ago, concern about these inadequacies might have been dismissed as part of a wider disinterest in (and distrust of) quantitative methods within the social sciences. However, this chapter is written at a time when statistical teaching has returned to prominence, reinvigorated by a resurgent interest in quantitative social science (broadly defined as the application of quantitative data, computation and statistics to probe areas of disciplinary and interdisciplinary interest). To a large degree (and to mutual relief), past antagonisms between quantitative and qualitative approaches have been set aside in favour of a shared interest in evidence-based knowledge, critical enquiry and empirically informed understanding of socio-spatial processes.[1]

There is much to gain from this rapprochement. Reasoning with numbers is a vital skill for any student of the social sciences. Lynch makes the case, after Kant, that although we cannot defend scientific methods (including quantification) as more rational than other methods, we '*can* show that that they are more democratic, more respectful of basic human autonomy' because 'observation and logic are strategies that everyone can, at least to some extent, use themselves and employ in their social networks, and that can be made at least a little more effective with training' (Lynch, 2016: 59–60, original emphasis).

Unfortunately, insofar as that includes statistical training, the tools and methods can act to disregard the very thing that motivates their usage – the study of a geographically varied and spatially embedded social world. If a key role of quantitative social science is to measure, to explain and to offer insight into the socio-spatial differentiations, inequalities and variations that characterise society then to do so is at odds with the sorts of spatially myopic methods that are characteristic of textbook introductions to statistics and applied policy analysis. The disjuncture arises because many methods involve a naïve or dismissive view of geographic space, of geographical relationships and of geographical interdependencies whereby the geography is averaged away, ignored or treated as a statistical inconvenience. Numeric reasoning is important but it needs to be coupled with spatial reasoning too.

With that in mind, this chapter reviews some alternative approaches, discussing the conceptions of geography they entail. The focus is upon regression which, as the most widely used method of statistical modelling in the social sciences, routinely and widely is applied to the study of geographical data and relationships. Yet it is an essentially non-spatial method of analysis which tends to assume that what is measured at any one location is independent of (neither connected to nor interacting with) what is measured at other locations around it. This is a view of geographic space in which 'things' exist in a spatial vacuum, shielded and in isolation from one another. But in the real world, people and places are not hermetically sealed, and so location, geographical context, interactions and the distances between things matter. Recognising that they do takes us in this chapter from ignoring geographic space, through treating it as a statistical problem for which technical solutions are sought, to better appreciating the substantive richness and importance of geography, and to a spatialisation of quantitative approaches. Textbook introductions to these methods include Brunsdon and Comber, 2018, Lovelace et al., 2019, and Chi and Zhu, 2019.

Understanding the problem

Consider the relationship shown in Figure 8.1. The data are from a set of tables published by the Social Mobility and Child Poverty Commission and used to create a social mobility index for local authorities (LAs) in England.[2] Figure 8.1 plots the percentage of pupils in each LA that achieved a benchmark for what was then regarded as a target level of success in examination at age 16: five or more

(GCSE) exam passes at levels A⋆ to C in subjects that include English and mathematics. Aside from a few missing cases, the percentage is provided separately for each of two groups of pupils per LA: those who are known to be eligible for free school meals (FSM eligible, here the *Y* variable) and those who are not (the *X* variable). FSM eligibility is a proxy indicator of household poverty.

Figure 8.1 includes the line of best fit that arises from regressing the first variable against the second. There is no claim that the *X* variable is causative upon the *Y*. The attainment of FSM eligible pupils is unlikely to be affected directly by the attainment of non-eligible ones. Instead, any relationship is likely to be mediated through 'hidden' variables such as unmeasured attributes of the LAs and the populations they contain. The logic of the regression is that in places where non-FSM pupils benefit from an increased propensity to meet the target, whatever caused it ought to benefit FSM eligible pupils too. Where the percentage of FSM eligible pupils meeting the target

Figure 8.1: The relationship between the percentage of free school meal eligible pupils per local authority meeting the target examination grades and the percentage of non-eligible pupils achieving the same

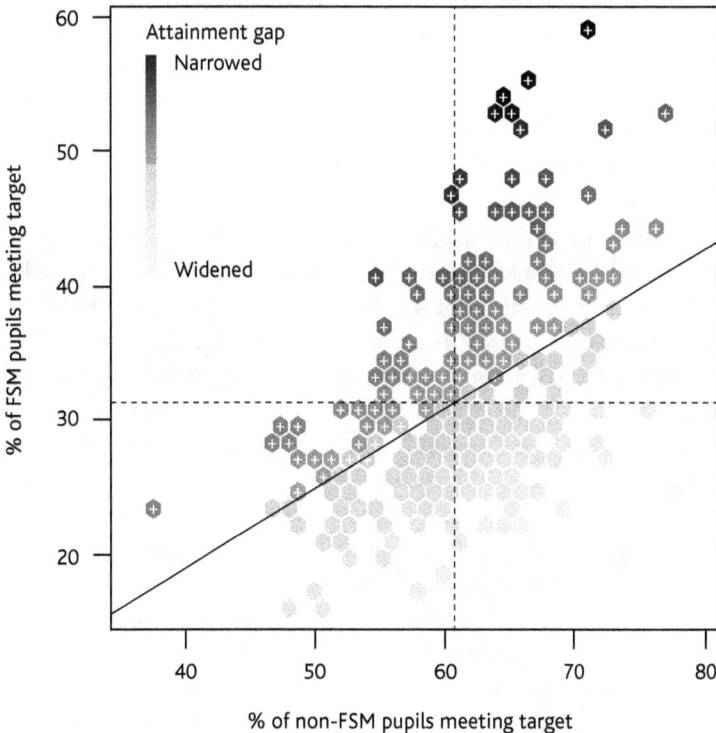

is above the regression line in Figure 8.1, it may be interpreted as a narrowing of the attainment gap between FSM eligible and ineligible pupils compared with what is expected given the percentage for the non-eligible group. In short, for places above the line, the percentage for the FSM group is higher than expected.

Looking at Figure 8.1, it can be determined that a FSM eligible pupil has, on average, half the chance of a non–FSM pupil to meet the exam target: the average LA has 31% of FSM pupils meeting the target and 61% of other pupils. The upwards sloping line suggests 'a rising tide lifts all boats' because where the percentage is higher for ineligible pupils it tends to be higher for eligible pupils too. Consequently, the two variables are correlated, $r = 0.503$ [95% CI, 0.415 to 0.581].[3] It is possible to predict the percentage for FSM eligible pupils from the percentage for ineligible pupils using the equation of the line, the gradient (which is the effect size, $\hat{\beta}_1$) and the y-intercept ($\hat{\beta}_0$) of which are estimated by the regression.

Even so, it is evident from the points both above and below the line that whilst it may be best fitting it is not a perfect fit. The deviations from the line – the variation – are the numeric differences between what is predicted by the regression line and what is observed in the actual data. These are the residual differences. Usually the residuals are of interest only insofar as they are checked to see whether they meet the assumptions of regression, which, stated simply, require the residuals to be random 'noise' around what is of most interest, the (average) relationship between the two variables.

This practice risks a dismissive view of geography. It acts to discount what the residuals represent, which are geographic differences in the attainment gap from one local authority to the next. Those local authorities have a geography (they also assign location to the schools and pupils they contain) but standard usage of regression is either blind to or simplistic in its treatment of this geography. The same is true of many other statistical techniques prevalent within the social sciences. The reason is that the statistics operate solely on the attributes of the places; on *what* is measured, not on *where* it was measured. Their locations are treated either as irrelevant by analysts or as a potential problem undermining the validity of the analysis. The problem is that traditional statistics assert an assumption of independence. For regression analysis, it lies with the residuals. If that assumption is valid then the residuals cannot have a spatial structure because the structure means the residuals are not just random noise. That is a bold assumption to make if what is studied is underpinned by any of the various socioeconomic and other geographies that characterise society.

If any of the variables measures something that is a geographically patterned outcome of one or more socio-spatial processes, then it is likely (although not inevitable) that some of that pattern will filter through into the residuals.

For the present (and admittedly simple) case study, it is an unwarranted assumption. Figure 8.1 has been shaded in a way that emphasises the places (to the top right of the graph) where the attainment gap between the two groups is less than expected. Is there a spatial pattern to those places? Figure 8.1 cannot say, but mapping the residuals – a process that employs both the attribute and locational information – can. Figure 8.2[4] reveals two things: spatial variation and spatial clustering. It shows that not every value is the same (there is spatial heterogeneity) but there is a tendency for similar values to be

Figure 8.2: Mapping the residuals from the regression model to reveal their spatial patterning

located together. Spatial autocorrelation is when there are geographical patterns in the data, most typically when similar measurements cluster together on the map, which is known as positive spatial autocorrelation and best summed up by Tobler's well-known 'first law' of geography – everything is related to everything else but near things are more related than distant things (Tobler, 1970). It is, of course, not really a law (that was just a turn of phrase) and it is not always true. Nevertheless, it has merit as a rule of thumb observed in the real world, and it informs the spatial methods of analysis that are discussed below.

More broadly, what the map suggests is that the residuals are spatially patterned and not, as regression analysis assumes, independent of one another. As a technical issue these spatial dependencies may lead to overestimation of the statistical significance of the X variable as a predictor of Y, and greater instability in the measurement of the effect size (the slope of the regression line, $\hat{\beta}_1$). However, to regard it only as a technical issue is to miss the point. Geography is not merely a statistical inconvenience; for better or worse, geography is a distinguishing feature of society. It is frequently key to the processes and patterns that policy makers and analysts wish to understand and to affect.

Object-based views of geographic space

The corollary of what has been discussed is that many statistical methods are not merely agnostic towards geography, they are non-spatial in the sense that the presence of geographical patterns undermine the statistical foundations upon which they are based. For the present case study and for the regression analysis, one straightforward but simplistic way to proceed is to incorporate into the model knowledge of the geographic hierarchy of administrative areas within England, whereby LAs group into regions at a more aggregate scale. The regional effects can then be estimated using additional predictor variables which are dummy variables coded 1 if an LA belongs to a given region, otherwise 0. This calls upon an object-based view of geographic space where the regions are treated as discrete (polygonal) objects with boundaries between them. It entails a change to Tobler's law because everything is not related to everything else, only LAs within the same region are, and near things are no longer related if they fall either side of a regional boundary. It conceives of the connections between places in the way they appear in Figure 8.3 for the northern parts of the map. The space is highly regionalised and discontinuous.

An object view of geographic space informs geographical applications of multilevel models (also known as hierarchical models) which are a

Figure 8.3: An object-based, regionalised and hierarchical view of geographic space

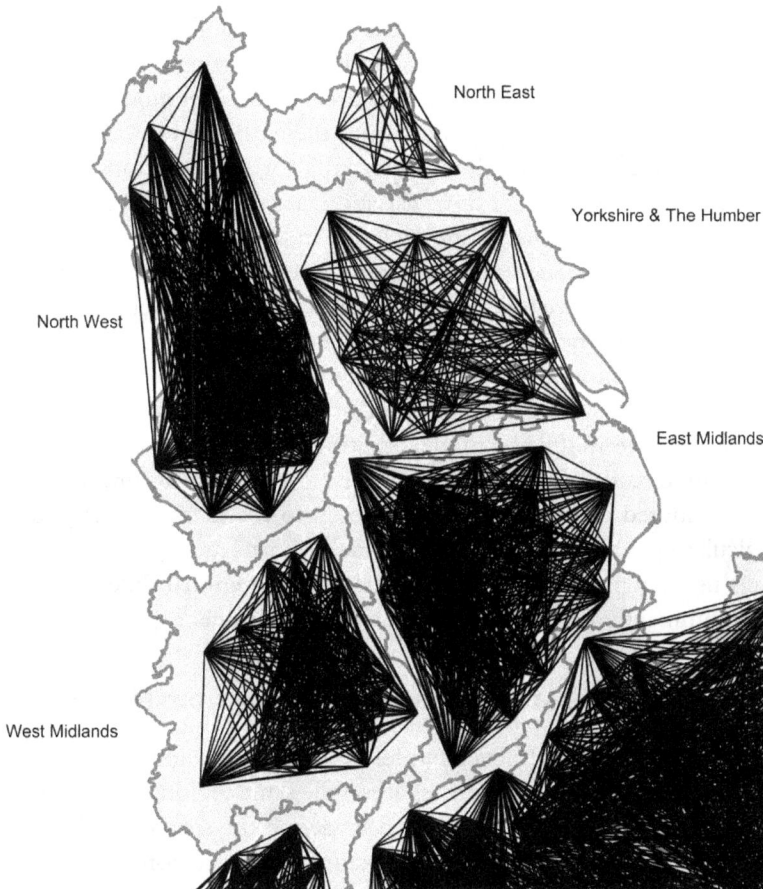

more advanced form of regression analysis that has become popular in the social sciences in looking for neighbourhood, contextual or other geographical differences between places (in regard to health or educational outcomes, for example) and/or exploring the importance of scale (for measuring and understanding segregation, for instance: Harris and Owen, 2017).

The structure of space shown in Figure 8.3 is hierarchically ordered: LAs within regions; or even pupils within schools, within LAs, within regions. From a geographical perspective the attraction is obvious: the levels of the model can represent various levels of a geographic hierarchy, the importance of which can be examined. For example, in the English and Welsh census, small areas (Output Areas) group into larger Lower Level Super Output Areas, then into Middle Level Output

Super Areas, and further into Local Authorities and Regions. Using the multilevel model, data can be 'mixed and matched' at the various levels with the aim to improve the predictive ability of the model. Time periods can be included as levels also, allowing for longitudinal analysis to understand changes over time. Multilevel models work by slicing time and geography (and, from these, the regression residuals) into discrete analytical 'chunks', looking for the variations between them and asking whether those variations are explained or remain after various predictor variables are included in the model.

For the present case study, a regression model with dummy variables produces substantively similar results to a two-level model (LAs within regions). Both reveal the substantial narrowing of the attainment gap in London and its widening (although not to the same extent) in the South East of England, and in Yorkshire and The Humber. However, the multilevel model additionally allows determination of the percentage of the variance around the regression line that can be attributed to the regional as opposed to the local authority scale, calculating what is known as the intraclass correlation. It is about 37% in this example, which is substantial. Those regional differences are predominantly due to London where the attainment gap is smallest.

What makes a statistic spatial? Learning from Moran's *I*

Intrinsic to the multilevel model is a spatial weights matrix that indicates which local authorities are in the same regions as each other. The spatial weights matrix is used to define the spatial relationships between people and places – for example, their regional groupings, the connections, the flows or the interactions between them.

The presence of a spatial weights matrix is found in the formula for Moran's correlation coefficient *I*, which is often used to measure patterns of spatial autocorrelation in data.[5] The idea is that if there is no pattern of spatial dependency in what has been measured then there will not, on average, be any similarity between locations and their neighbours. Alternatively, if like values cluster together then locations will exhibit a positive correlation with their average neighbour (positive spatial autocorrelation); or if there is a pattern of opposites coming together then the correlation will be negative (negative spatial autocorrelation). A definition of neighbours is required to calculate the correlation – for example, locations that are contiguous (share a border). Defined in this way, the *Y* values from the initial regression model have a Moran's value of 0.356 [95% CI, 0.286 to 0.425], the *X* values have 0.250 [95% CI, 0.180 to 0.320] and the difference in attainment between the two groups, $(Y - X)$, has 0.286 [95% CI, 0.216 to 0.356]. There is a considerable spatial dimension to these data patterns. It is not surprising to discover that these geographical patterns enter the regression residuals, with a Moran's value of 0.332 [95% CI, 0.262 to 0.402].

Although the interpretation of Moran's I is not as straightforward as for a standard (non-spatial) correlation coefficient, it can be used to compare models for the same study region and with the same definition of neighbours. In comparison to the initial regression model, the spatial patterning of the residuals is much reduced by the multilevel model (see overleaf), to a Moran's I value of 0.071 [95% CI, 0.001 to 0.141] once the regional variations are accounted for.[6] What remains is still statistically significant though. Looking again at Figure 8.2, this is most likely because the geographic patterns it displays do not map exactly to regional boundaries. Therein lies the problem with an object-based view of the world: it imposes what are often unrealistically hard boundaries, forcing geographical divisions upon the data that may not correspond well with the actual spatial connections, processes and relationships of what is being studied.

For the current discussion, Moran's I is of interest not only as a measure of spatial autocorrelation but more especially because of how it incorporates the spatial relationships between locations within its calculation. It does so through the spatial weights matrix, which may be understood as an n by n matrix (where n is the number of locations), assigning to row i, column j a value greater than zero if the locations represented by i and j are deemed to be connected in some way, else zero (if they are not). The matrix is symmetric when based on contiguity because if i and j have a common border then so, equivalently, must j and i. This will not be the case for every expression of neighbours. For example, trade between any two places can be unidirectional or unequal, as can migration or other flows of people, goods, services, natural resources and information.

The key points are that the spatial weights matrix encodes what are defined to be neighbours and that it provides the flexibility for analysts to change how they conceptualise and define the relationships between the people and places included in the spatial weights matrix. For example, Figure 8.4 shows the links between places that share a border for the same part of the map that is in Figure 8.3. Unlike the previous example, this moves beyond a simple, regionalised space, although still there are geographical cut-offs. Some of those are natural boundaries (note the effects of the coastline) and some are imposed by the weights specification. There is now partial adherence to Tobler's

Figure 8.4: A view of spatial relationships based on contiguity

North East

Yorkshire & The Humber

North West

East Midlands

West Midlands

'law': near things are related but only to the limit of any shared border. The matrix underpinning Figure 8.4 is binary because locations either share a boundary or they do not. In practice, that means the places with the most neighbours will have most influence on the Moran's coefficient because the sum of the weights is greater where there are more neighbours. To address this problem, weights are often row-standardised. If a location has six neighbours then each will be given a weight of $1/6$; if it has four then $1/4$. The consequence of row-standardisation is that the weights are no longer binary and the matrix is unlikely to be symmetric because adjoining locations need not have the same set or number of neighbours.

A further interest in Moran's I is that whilst it provides an example of what is called a global statistic – meaning it provides one summary value (of spatial autocorrelation) for the whole study area (in this case the country) – it need not be restricted to the global statistic because it can also be used to calculate localised estimates of spatial autocorrelation for sub-areas of the map. These local estimates show how the similarity of each place and its neighbours varies across the study regions. Localised Moran values belong to a wider class of statistics showing how the spatial patterns in data vary across a map. Collectively these statistics are known as local indicators of spatial association (LISAs) (Anselin, 1995).

Figure 8.5 shows the local Moran's values for the current data. Not all the localised values are statistically significant but amongst those that may be judged to be so, the clustering of positively correlated values in London is particularly evident.[7] Local statistics unpack their global 'whole map' equivalent to look for geographic variations in local spatial connectedness that are concealed by the global view.

Spatial regression

Having defined a spatial weights matrix it can be brought into the regression analysis, with two of the more basic methods (used in spatial econometrics) to do so being the spatially autoregressive error model and the spatially lagged Y model (Ward and Gleditsch, 2008; Kelejian and Piras, 2017). In the first of these, the regression residuals are divided into two: a spatially correlated part and a spatially uncorrelated one. This allows the strength of the (unexplained) spatial correlation to be investigated, as well as offering potentially more reliable estimation of the regression coefficients and their statistical significance. In the second, a process is conceived whereby the outcome at each location 'overspills' into surrounding neighbourhoods – for example, if processes of gentrification increase neighbourhood prices in one location then that rise is likely to ripple outwards into surrounding areas.

By design, spatial statistics such as Moran's I, LISAs and spatial regression models are affected by how the spatial matrix is defined: change the matrix and it changes the conceptualisation and definition of spatial connectedness between the geographical areas studied, which in turn affects the findings. In the examples, neighbouring LAs are those that share a border. This is perhaps the simplest specification of spatial connectedness but it is not the only possibility and it may well not be the most appropriate for a given policy issue. We might instead consider the neighbours of neighbours, all locations within a certain distance or journey time away from a boundary or centre point, or identify each of the k nearest neighbours for each location.

Figure 8.5: Local Moran values showing the clustering of places with similar percentages of FSM eligible pupils meeting the exam target

There are other possibilities – financial, cultural, commuter, trade, relational or digital flows for example (Bivand, 2017) – and there is not always a good reason for choosing one specification of the weights matrix over any other. Ideally it is tied to an underlying knowledge of the nature of the spatial landscape and of the spatial relationships that play out upon it. In practice, there is an element of circularity if the spatial weights matrix is used both to define and to explore the spatial patterns in the data – if what is measured geographically is linked to what was assumed of the geography in the first place. However, by thinking conceptually about the nature of the processes, patterns and flows at play in the particular policy case and by testing different conceptually informed specifications of the spatial weights matrix, richer understandings of those process, patterns and flows can emerge: where are they strongest? What are their spatial limits? How do they vary? And so forth. In this regard, spatial statistics operate at least as much on a conceptual and exploratory basis as a confirmatory and technical one. Working through these linked conceptual and technical spatial considerations for the study at hand helps to explore and better understand the nature, strength and variability of the spatial relationships, processes and outcomes seen across different fields of social policy making and analysis.

Regarding the spatial regression models, what differentiates them from the standard regression model and its naïve or dismissive view of spatial relationships is that through the inclusion of the spatial weights matrix they explicitly allow for the possibility that the data are spatially interdependent. The cause of the interdependence is not specified by the error model but for the spatially lagged Y model it is modelled as a feedback loop between locations, with the amount of feedback typically attenuated by their distance apart. That could be a simple straight-line distance but other metrics can be employed, including measures of social distance (which could be used to model friendship networks and whether those 'bridge' over social classes, for example).

From a geographical perspective, spatial regression offers a step towards a more nuanced appreciation of spatial relationships. Nevertheless, the models are, like standard regression, global models, estimating a single regression relationship for the entirety of the study region. What they will not consider is the possibility that the nature of the relationship is dependent upon the locational context and, as such, varies across the study region. To explore that possibility, geographically weighted regression and a field-based view of geographic space can be adopted.

Field-based views of geographic space

An alternative to an object-based view is a field-based view of geographic space. In the context of regression, rather than assuming the relationship between a Y and an X variable is constant across a study region (or within higher-level units such as regions), it can be allowed to change continuously from one part of the map to another. This means that instead of calculating a single set of estimates of the regression coefficients, $\hat{\beta}$, for the whole area study region (the whole country), localised estimates are obtained for specific locations within it, $\hat{\beta}_{(u,\, v)}$ where $(u,\, v)$ is a geographical coordinate. Those estimates can then be compared to see where and by how much they vary across the map, which is unlike the forced spatial uniformity of a single regression coefficient in a standard regression analysis.

This is the thinking behind geographically weighted regression (GWR; Fotheringham et al., 2002), which works by taking a location on the map, finding all the observations within a certain distance of it (either within a fixed geographic distance or one of the k nearest neighbours), fitting the regression to those data and then assigning the results to the location at the centre. The process is repeated for other locations across the map. In each case, the regression is weighted, giving most weight to observations closest to the target location and decreasing with distance apart. The weights become zero at a threshold that usually is determined by an automated process of calibration. This amounts to saying that near things are more related than far things but there is a geographic limit beyond which things are not related at all.

Figure 8.6 arises from applying GWR to the simple relationship of Figure 8.1 but this time including an additional X variable, which is the percentage of FSM eligible pupils per LA that achieved the target grades in reading, writing and mathematics in the final year of primary school in 2014. A useful feature of GWR is that the regression coefficients can be estimated separately at any location upon the map, not just those for which the data were collected. Figure 8.6 takes advantage of this additionality.[8] A standard regression shows, as before, that the percentage of FSM eligible pupils meeting the educational target at secondary school (GCSE level) is approximately half that of ineligible pupils but now also reveals that it rises with the percentage of FSM eligible pupils meeting the target at primary school. The global estimate of this new relationship is $\hat{\beta}_2 = 0.457$. Crucially, however, where GWR excels is in highlighting that the relationship is not immune to location but varies from place to place: most typically from 0.154 to 0.550 (where the weights meet zero at the 58th nearest neighbour from a total of 314 locations). This is the interquartile range of the geographically varying estimates of $\hat{\beta}_2$; the full range is from −0.397 to 1.113. This provides evidence that the otherwise positive correlation reverses in some parts of the North West of England between the percentages of FSM eligible pupils meeting the targets at primary and secondary school. There, unusually, an increased percentage for primary schools is associated with a decreased percentage for secondary schools. The implication is that educational trajectories from primary to secondary school vary with the geographical context within which they are situated – a variation in relationships across space that geographically sensitive

Figure 8.6: Geographically weighted regression adopts a continuous view of geographic space that allows the modelled relationship to change from one place to another

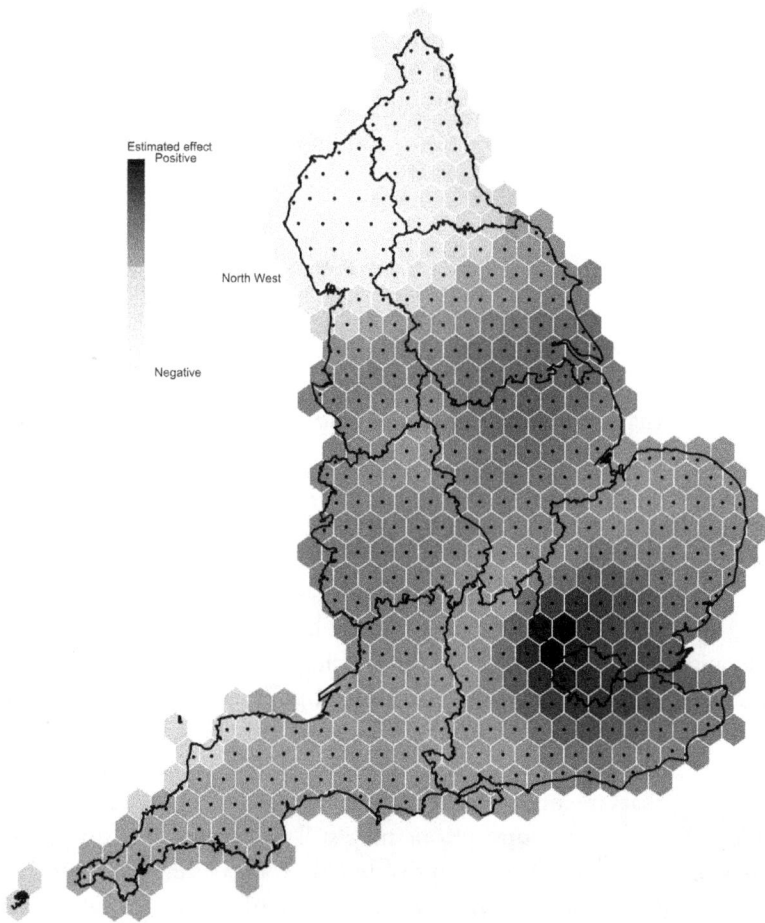

methods such as GWR are able to identify but that standard statistical thinking typically neglects.

GWR is one of a set of geographically weighted statistics that includes geographically weighted averages, measures of spread and geographically weighted principal components analysis (Gollini et al., 2015). Each adopts a view of geographic space that leans more closely to Tobler's 'law' than any of the other approaches discussed here, recognising that the nature of social and statistical relationships can vary according to the geographical context but without being strictly bounded in the way an object-based view presumes. The methods do not discount geographical variation or treat it as a nuisance. To the contrary, they seek to reveal and to study it as something of substantive purport. Nevertheless, this relational view of space is not always appropriate because the assumption that near things are more related is not always true – think, for example, of stark social, cultural or economic divisions that can exist in cities between neighbourhoods and across physical divides such as rivers, major roads or railways. Under such circumstances the spatial weights matrix can be modified to allow for spatial breaks and discontinuities (Mitchell and Lee, 2014; Harris, 2016).

Conclusion: not nuisance but explanation?

The argument raised in this chapter is one that highlights the disconnect between quantitative social science with its study of socio-spatial phenomena and the sorts of aspatial or spatially naïve statistical methods that typically have been taught to generations of social science students. The worry is that the severe spatial limits of those conventional approaches – both intellectual and methodological – lead to ignorance of, disinterest in or lack of proper appreciation of the role of geography within the social world and in the social policies that seek to affect that social world. If the spatialisation of social policy that is discussed in the book is to be informed by quantitative evidence – as I would argue it must be (not to the exclusion of other approaches but as a complement to them) – then it is important to work with more spatially informed foundations to our statistical enquiries.

The spatial approaches discussed in this chapter adopt conceptions of space that are brought into the heart of how the statistics are undertaken. Those conceptions may still be regarded as simplistic, constraining or overly prescriptive but they are better than ignoring geography altogether, with the dismissal of spatial context that it implies. Localised approaches also challenge the lingering but anachronistic belief that the uses of quantitative methods in the social sciences are for purposes that are positivistic and nomothetic. To the contrary, they adopt a mindset that is cautious of 'one size fits all' explanations and is instead interested in the wide range of circumstances that give rise to geographic variation and difference.

Three views of geographic space have been outlined in this chapter. The first sees it as an inconvenient truth, wherein geography is nuisance violating statistical assumptions and for which technical solutions are sought. The second and third are the object- and field-based views, which were linked especially to multilevel models in the former case and to geographically weighted approaches in the latter. In practice, the distinctions are blurred: for example, multilevel models can employ geographically overlapping and distance weighted groupings at a higher level, thereby mimicking the more continuous view of space adopted by geographically weighted regression (Owen et al., 2015); models exist that consider the similarities of neighbours that are geographically close but belong to different groups at a higher level in the hierarchy (the approach combines spatial econometric and multilevel thinking: Dong and Harris, 2015); and both the object- and field-based views can be brought together under a view of geographic space that sees it as a network of nodes and connections, and where the difference lies in how the connections are made (compare Figures 8.3 and 8.4, for example).

However, in arguing for more spatially savvy statistics, and in stating that geography is not nuisance, might it equally be said that it is not an explanation either? After all, finding evidence of geographic variation does not, of itself, reveal the causal factors or processes creating those geographic variations. Although it might be argued that identifying spatial patterns is a first step towards understanding the processes that generated those patterns, in practice the link between the two is far from straightforward, not least because the same pattern can have multiple and competing explanations for its cause.

One response to the question is to treat spatial variation as a surrogate for missing information. Then the spatial approaches can be used as diagnostic tools to check for a mis-specified model, notably one that lacks a critical explanatory variable or where the relationship between the X and Y variables is non-linear. The limitation of this thinking is that is still treats geography as an error to be resolved and/or it rests on the belief that with sufficient information the geographical differences will be explained. That may be true but what geographically weighted regression, for example, reminds us is that the nature of the relationship may be complex because it is changing in form across the study region as the socio-spatial causes also vary from place to place. Such spatial complexity may be challenging to accommodate within the parameters of conventional aspatial or spatially naïve statistical thinking but ignoring the geographical variation is not a solution if what results is a 'stylised fact' that is too simplistic and general to inform social policy (Bell et al., 2014). What spatial thinking brings to the table is the recognition of geographical context and the knowledge that geographically rooted social outcomes are not independent of where the processes giving rise to those outcomes are taking place. Combined with computational tools and spatial methods, including quantitative and qualitative GIS (see Chapter 9), new approaches for spatialising policy analysis continue to be created (Harris et al., 2017b).

Notes

[1] Within the UK, undergraduate teaching initiatives such as Q-Step (www. nuffieldfoundation.org/q-step) and postgraduate funding targeted at advanced quantitative methods seek to address an ongoing statistical skills shortage arising from a lack of numeracy amongst British social scientists. Commenting on the situation in 2015, the British Academy said that 'there is a need to transform the UK's quantitative skills: our ability to reason using numbers' (British Academy, 2015: 2).

[2] www.gov.uk/government/publications/social-mobility-index

[3] 95% CI is the 95% confidence interval.

[4] The map has been slightly distorted using the method outlined by Harris et al. (2017a). This is to aid the visualisation of the results – it enlarges small areas that would otherwise be concealed – and does not affect the analysis, which is based on the unaltered map.

[5] The formula for Moran's I is:

$$I = \frac{n}{\sum_i \sum_j w_{ij}} \frac{\sum_i \sum_j w_{ij}\left(x_i - \overline{x}\right)\left(x_j - \overline{x}\right)}{\sum_i \left(x_i - \overline{x}\right)^2}$$

where x is the variable being tested for spatial autocorrelation, i and j are two locations on the map, and – critically – is the part of the spatial weights matrix that defines the spatial connection between those locations.

[6] The complication with Moran's I is it is not expected to be zero under a null hypothesis of no spatial autocorrelation. Instead, it will be a value less than but tending towards zero as the sample size increases, $E(I) = -1/(n-1)$. In addition, although interpreted as a correlation coefficient, values of I need not lie within the range -1 to $+1$ (de Jong et al., 1984; Brunsdon and Comber, 2018) and a slight correction to the measures of statistical significance ought to be made when applied to regression residuals (Hepple, 1998).

[7] A problem when considering the statistical significance of localised statistics is the issue of repeat testing: with n locations, there are n separate tests so the probability that any one or more of them would appear significant by chance is higher than the $p = 0.05$ implied by a 95% confidence interval. Brunsdon and Comber (2018) suggest ways to address this issue.

[8] A disadvantage of this spatial interpolation is that there is no observed value at each interpolation point to compare with the predicted value, measures of statistical significance are not calculated. That problem does not arise if GWR is fitted only at the places measured in the data.

References

Anselin, L. (1995) Local indicators of spatial association – LISA. *Geographical Analysis* 27(2): 93–115.

Bell, A., Johnston, R. and Jones K. (2014) Stylised fact or situated messiness? The diverse effects of increasing debt on national economic growth. *Journal of Economic Geography* 15(2): 449–472.

Bivand, R. (2017) Creating neighbours. https://cran.r-project.org/web/packages/spdep/vignettes/nb.pdf

British Academy (2015) *Count Us In: Quantitative Skills for a New Generation*. London: The British Academy.

Brunsdon, C. and Comber, L. (2018) *An Introduction to R for Spatial Analysis & Mapping* (second edition). London: Sage.

Chi, G. and Zhu, J. (2019) *Spatial Regression Models for the Social Sciences*. Thousand Oaks, CA: Sage.

De Jong, P., Sprenger, C. and van Veen F. (1984) On extreme values of Moran's *I* and Geary's *C. Geographical Analysis* 16(1): 17–24.

Dong, G. and Harris, R. (2015) Spatial autoregressive models for geographically hierarchical data structures. *Geographical Analysis* 47(2): 173–191.

Fotheringham, A.S., Brunsdon, C. and Charlton, M. (2002) *Geographically Weighted Regression: The Analysis of Spatially Varying Relationships*. Chichester: Wiley.

Fry, R., Orford, S., Rodgers, S., Morgan, J., and Fone, D. (2018) A best practice framework to measure spatial variation in alcohol availability, *Environment and Planning B: Urban Analytics and City Science*, online first. https://doi.org/10.1177/2399808318773761

Gollini, I., Lu, B., Charlton, M., Brunsdon, C. and Harris, P. (2015) GWmodel: an R package for exploring spatial heterogeneity using geographically weighted models. *Journal of Statistical Software* 63(17). www.jstatsoft.org/article/view/v063i17

Harris, R. (2016) *Quantitative Geography: The Basics*. London: Sage.

Harris, R. and Owen, D. (2017) Implementing a multilevel index of dissimilarity in R with a case study of the changing scales of residential ethnic segregation in England and Wales. *Environment and Planning B* 45(6). https://doi.org/10.1177/2399808317748328

Harris, R., Brunsdon, C. and Charlton, M. (2017a) Balancing visibility and distortion: remapping the results of the 2015 UK General Election. *Environment and Planning A* 49(9): 1945–1947.

Harris, R., O'Sullivan, D., Gahegan, M., Charlton, M., Comber, L., Longley, P., Brunsdon, C., Malleson, N., Heppenstall, A., Singleton, A., Arribas-Bel, D. and Evans, A. (2017b) More bark than bytes? Reflections on 21+ years of geocomputation. *Environment and Planning B* 44(4): 598–617.

Hepple, L. (1998) Exact testing for spatial autocorrelation among regression residuals. *Environment and Planning A* 30(1): 85–108.

Jones, M., Orford S. and MacFarlane V. (eds) (2015) *People, Places and Policy: Knowing Contemporary Wales Through New Localities*, Regions and Cities Series. London: Routledge.

Kelejian, H. and Piras, G. (2017) *Spatial Econometrics*. London: Academic Press.

Lovelace, R., Nowosad, J. and Muenchow, J. (2019) *Geocomputation with R*. Boca Raton, FL: CRC Press.

Lynch, M.P. (2016) *The Internet of Us: Knowing More and Understanding Less in the Age of Big Data*. New York: Liveright Publishing Corporation.

Mitchell, R. and Lee, D. (2014) Is there really a 'wrong side of the tracks' and does it matter for spatial analysis? *Annals of the Association of American Geographers* 104(3): 432–443.

Orford, S. (2018) The capitalisation of school choice into property prices: A case study of grammar and all ability state schools in Buckinghamshire, UK, *Geoforum* 97: 231–241.

Orford, S. and Webb, B. (2018) Mapping the interview transcript: identifying spatial policy areas from daily working practices, *Area* 50(4): 529-541.

Owen, G., Harris, R. and Jones, K. (2015) Under examination: multilevel models, geography and health research. *Progress in Human Geography* 40(30): 394–412.

Tobler, W.R. (1970) A computer movie simulating urban growth in the Detroit region. *Economic Geography* 46(supplement): 234–224.

Ward, M.D. and Gleditsch, K.S. (2008) *Spatial Regression Models*. Thousand Oaks, CA: Sage.

Xiao, Y., Orford, S. and Webster, C. (2016) Urban configuration, accessibility and property prices: a case study of Cardiff, Wales, *Environment and Planning B* 43: 108–129, doi:10.1177/0265813515600120

9

Situating social policy analysis: possibilities from quantitative and qualitative GIS

Scott Orford and Brian Webb

Introduction

Geographic information systems (GIS) use maps and spatial analysis as a way of investigating real-world problems. Although traditionally associated with the geographical disciplines, it has since been adopted and used throughout the social sciences, including urban and environmental planning, public and community health, political and social studies, crime prevention and transport to name a few (Longley et al., 2015). GIS originally developed out of computerised cartography and it still uses maps and mapping as a way of structuring, managing, visualising and analysing data. A GIS stores a map as a series of separate map layers, with each layer containing data on a particular theme. A theme could relate to the population of an area, such as population density or percentage of children of school age; physical infrastructure, for instance the road network or public transport routes; or the environmental quality of an area, such as the location of parks and green space or the concentration of air pollution. By layering these themes one on top of the other within the GIS digital mapping, it is possible to see how they relate to each other across an area and to produce composite maps that can reveal spatial patterns and relationships. GIS contains tools that allow the data to be manipulated and analysed spatially and statistically so it is possible to determine, for example, how many people live within five minutes' walk of a bus stop or how many children in low-income households live in a particular school catchment area. This combination of mapping and spatial analysis makes GIS a powerful tool when researchers are investigating how social and economic problems vary across space, how spatial areas relate to one another, or how policy interventions may have different outcomes geographically. And as GIS can map and analyse data at a variety of spatial scales it is possible to investigate problems at the very local level through to the national and international level.

Traditionally, GIS has been a predominately static tool – it emphasises variation across space rather than change over time. This has partly been a reflection of data availability – socioeconomic data collection tends to be cross-sectional rather than longitudinal and in terms of mapping, data are usually only available aggregated into predefined geographical areas whose boundaries often change, hampering comparisons between time periods. These areas are usually designed for a particular function (for example wards for electing local councillors) and so often their boundaries do not reflect the underlying structure of the local population or the social process being investigated. This can result in the geographic areas distorting or unduly influencing the display and analysis of the populations and social processes of interest. This is called the modifiable areal unit problem (MAUP) and it continues to be an innate issue in social applications of GIS. The ecological fallacy (EF) is related to MAUP and occurs when data aggregated to areas are used to make inferences about individuals who live in those areas. So although we may observe that areas which have high unemployment rates may also have high crime rates we cannot say that it is the unemployed that is the cause of crime, merely that the two have an association at that geographical scale. Again, EF, like MAUP, is a reflection that socioeconomic and demographic data geographically referenced to individual persons and households has traditionally not been available in GIS and rather is supplied at some level of geographic aggregation.

But GIS, socioeconomic data and geographical data are all evolving and there is now increasing capabilities for dynamic mapping, interactive mapping and animated visualisations (for example Andrienko et al., 2016) allowing researchers to investigate how spatial patterns and relationships change over time, and in a finer detail, improving the analysis of the outcomes of policy interventions. These and other issues are addressed and reflected upon throughout the chapter. It will argue why GIS is a useful tool for spatial social policy analysis, looking at how maps and mapping can change the way we see and understand spatial relations between people and places. It will discuss how recent innovations in qualitative GIS are opening up the field to new academic and policy areas that benefit from a mixed method approach to understanding social policy. It will provide many examples from across broad policy themes that illustrate the advantages of exploring the impact of social policy from a geographic perspective within the context of maps, mapping and spatial analysis. It concludes with a reflection and discussion of the issues raised in the chapter and looks towards the future in terms of how recent innovations and trends could further the use of GIS in the field of social policy.

Why is GIS a useful tool for spatial social policy analysis?

The way in which we 'see' and 'understand' the spatial relationships that exist within the world has changed over the last 50 years (Davoudi and Strange, 2009) and influenced the evolution and use of GIS. GIS is utilised to overlay different datasets in order to not only represent information, as the discipline of cartography typically does, but also to query and analyse the relationship between those different layers of information. Some of the earliest uses of this more dynamic analysis of spatial data date back to the interpretation of health information collected as part of cholera outbreaks in Paris and London. Most famously, in 1854 the London physician John Snow mapped the locations of cholera victims and nearby water sources in Soho to identify a contaminated water pump where concentrations of victims lived. In doing so, he demonstrated the potential analytical capabilities of overlaying different data sources to identify spatial patterns that may not have traditionally been represented and analysed together on the same map (Snow, 1855; Orford, 2005) and he also provided a timely public health intervention by disabling the pump, preventing its further use.

Through the layering of data in computer-assisted environments, modern GIS provides the ability to represent the spatial distribution of people, resources and information in a single, easy to understand map (Wong et al., 2015). These visualisations are useful means to distil large amounts of information into a single image that can be easily understood by a wide range of non-technical audiences, from policy experts, to politicians, to local citizens. Despite improvements in the analytical capabilities of GIS software, it continues to be used more for spatial *information visualisation* rather than as an *analytical tool* to support decision making (Gilfoyle and Wong, 1998; Vonk et al., 2005). This is often the result of a lack of technical expertise of individuals within the public and private sector working in the fields of social science, a point which is discussed later. From a social policy point of view, the layering, analysis and visualisation of data can provide an important means of identifying areas for policy intervention (van der Horst, 2007), allocating resources (Ashby and Longley, 2005), understanding long-term trends (Rebel, 2007) or programme evaluation (Fischer and Nijkamp, 1993). Further innovative uses of GIS beyond these mainstays provide a glimpse of how it might add particular value to social policy analysis. However, GIS remains a strikingly niche method across the social sciences and largely overlooked within social policy research and practice. Yet, as discussed below, both quantitative and qualitative GIS offer considerable potential for such policy making and analysis, examples of which are highlighted in the next section.

As with any methodological field, GIS techniques, thinking and capabilities continue to evolve, opening up new opportunities for rich spatial insights into social policy issues. Increasingly, for example, more traditional quantitative GIS representations of containerised Cartesian spaces are being challenged through attempts to characterise the relationship between places by mapping flows of data – trade, people, finance, information and so on – rather than displaying static representations of place (Orford and Webb, 2018). Most commonly, flow maps are utilised to map commuting patterns of workers, showing how many people travel from home to work (Rae, 2017) in order to understand the functional geographies of cities and regions – Figure 9.1. Flow mapping has been used to understand the spatial extent of areas that cross local boundaries in order to demonstrate the need for different governments to coordinate public policy, particularly in relation to infrastructure provision. Yet, conversely, it also holds potential for understanding the isolation of communities, nodes of intense activity, and the interaction, or lack thereof, between prosperous and more deprived areas.

In a similar vein, GIS is being used beyond its positivist origins to support the creation of more qualitative diagrammatic or conceptual maps that draw together a range of secondary data to construct a single, more artistic image of an overall idea. Such a process is useful for defining potential policy problems that need to be addressed or as a baseline for a visioning process to engage different actors about initiatives (Wong, 2006). The process brings together multiple layers of spatial data about a place and then works to analyse and simplify that information into more basic representations of space, such as by identifying core problem areas, key strategic corridors, or relationships between places. In 1989 French geographer Roger Brunet developed a conceptual metaphor of Europe drawn from a range of spatial socioeconomic data and historical information, identifying a 'Blue Banana' (due to its shape and the colour used to map it) stretching from North West England around France's north-eastern border to northern Italy as a means of highlighting the lack of European socioeconomic integration and inequality between European countries (RECLUS, 1989). This simplification of spatial data was not processed through

Figure 9.1: Tract-to-tract commutes of 80km/50 miles or less in the Bay Area, California, USA

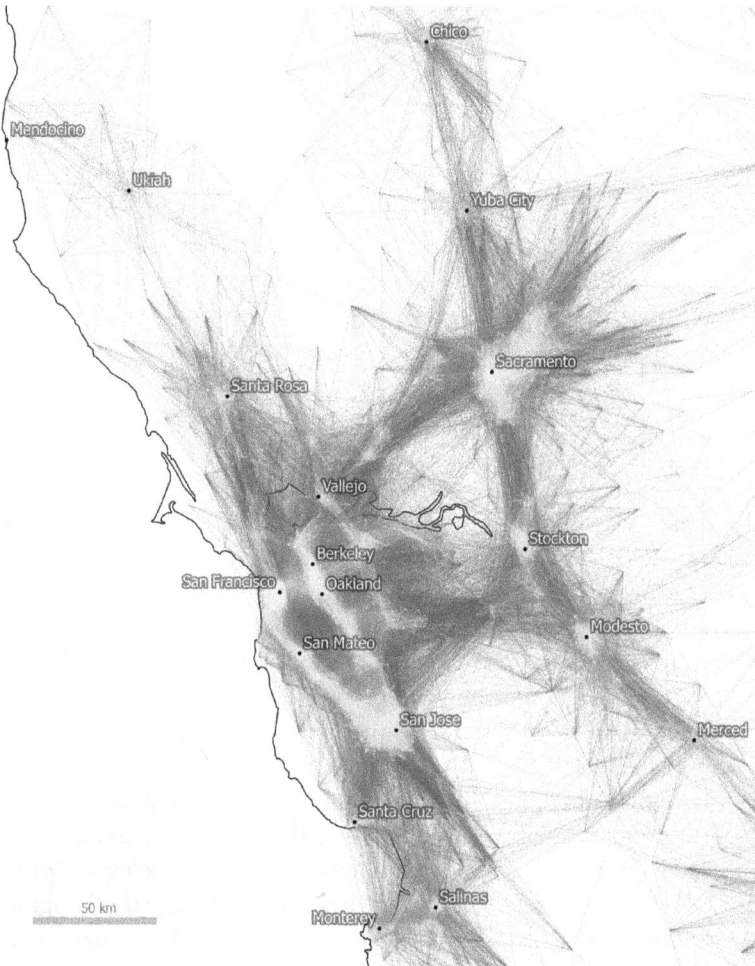

mathematical equations but rather was informed qualitatively by individual experiences, value systems and professional norms which interacted to generate a new way of thinking built through social practices rather than positivist representations of space.

Furthermore, the last decade has seen various innovative attempts to use GIS for qualitative data management and analysis (for example Kwan and Knigge, 2006; Pavlovskaya, 2006; Elwood and Cope, 2009). By adding geo–references to place names within a document, transcript or social media content, for instance, it is possible to use the GIS to map the textual data and add value and additional insights into the understanding and interpretation of the text. Other types of data promoted by qualitative GIS include photographs, video footage and audio clips that can add depth and context to the statistical data traditionally associated with GIS. Moreover, Global Positioning System (GPS) trace data of the movements of people or people's perceptions of the place in which they live collected through cognitive mapping exercises may provide methodologies and approaches that go beyond the static and Cartesian framework of most GIS. Hence qualitative GIS lends itself to those aspects of social policy research that, for example, emphasise the importance of lived experiences when addressing social problems and the effectiveness of policy interventions, or that seeks to identify differences between objective knowledge provided by quantitative GIS data and people's partial, subjective knowledge and experience of place.

Case studies of indicative examples

The previous section has provided an overview of some of the major ways in which quantitative and qualitative GIS are used and their potential to enrich applied social and policy analysis. This section moves on to provide a broad overview of different examples of social policy research with reference to both quantitative and qualitative GIS. The aim in doing so is to illustrate some of the specific insights and opportunities that such GIS methods can bring to social policy making and analysis.

A common use of GIS in social policy is to research people's ability to access public amenities such as post offices, GP surgeries, libraries, sports facilities, polling stations and good schools (for example Orford et al., 2011; Singleton et al., 2011; Higgs et al., 2015, 2017; Langford et al., 2016). This has important implications for the spatial equity of access with people from poor backgrounds or living in poorer neighbourhoods often finding it more difficult to access essential or good-quality services. It is possible to use GIS to generate a wide variety of accessibility measures from simple straight-line distances, to road network and footpath distances, as well as travel time measures. Increasingly, these metrics include the use of public transport, such as buses and trains, to capture those households which do not have access to private transport. More sophisticated accessibility measures will model the supply as well as the demand for public amenities to reflect competition, congestion and the allocation of scarce resources (for example Langford et al., 2016). These measures have been used as variables in statistical models that have quantified the effects of accessibility by different groups of people to different types of amenities. For instance, Figure 9.2 illustrates how voter turnout to local elections in London could be improved by siting polling stations closer to where most voters live in terms of voter density.

Another example is to understand the spatial implications of school choice on the educational performance of children in the state school sector. In many Western countries including the UK, parents have a choice as to which state school their children may attend and this can lead to competition for the more popular schools and thus the application of admissions criteria to select students. These criteria usually include catchment areas and distance to school

Figure 9.2: Percentage differences in the predicted probability of turnout at polling district level when re-siting polling stations at the maximum voter density locations for the 1998 local elections, London Borough of Brent, UK

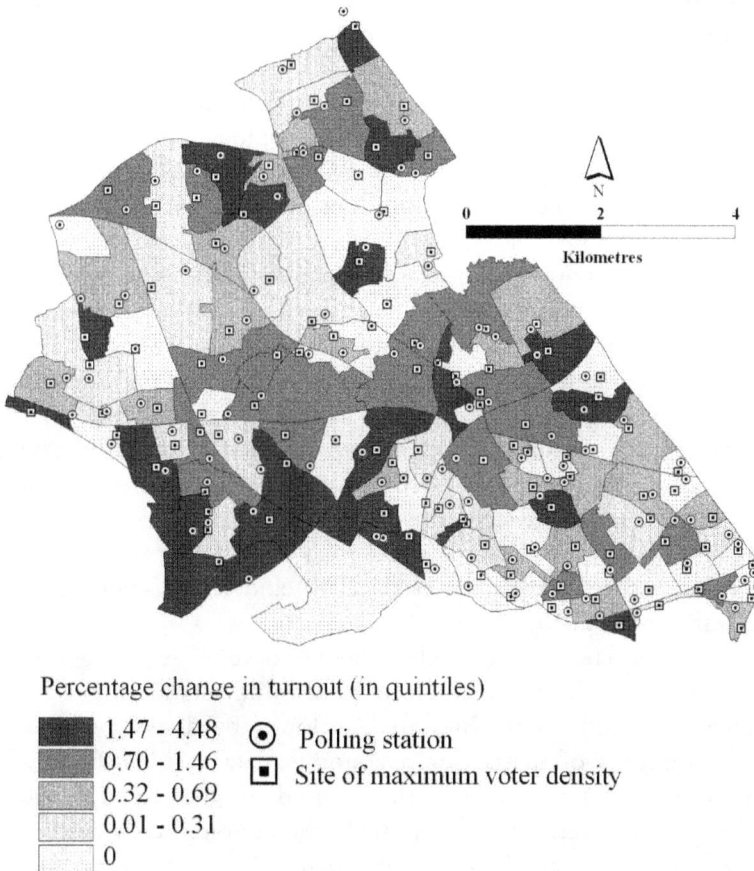

Percentage change in turnout (in quintiles)

1.47 - 4.48   ⊙ Polling station
0.70 - 1.46   ▣ Site of maximum voter density
0.32 - 0.69
0.01 - 0.31
0

Source: Orford et al., 2011

(Singleton et al., 2011) and this can lead to some parents moving close to good schools, pushing up house prices and rents in those local areas (Cheshire and Sheppard, 2004; Glen and Nellis, 2010; Orford, 2018). This 'selection by mortgage' (Harris et al., 2016) can lead to residential sorting of neighbourhoods, reinforcing social class differences and, as a consequence, exacerbating existing inequalities in the state education system. GIS can also be used to model both catchment areas and distance and relate this to educational performance (for example Burgess and Briggs, 2010), income identifiers (such as children in the receipt of free school meals – see Chapter 8 and also Hamnett and Butler, 2011) and house prices (for example Glen and Nellis, 2010; Orford, 2018).

Accessibility measures have also been used in the construction of the Indices of Multiple Deprivation (IMD) for England, Scotland and Wales. More broadly, an IMD has been utilised in a number of countries to map and target a range of policy initiatives. This approach divides deprivation into a range of domains that comprise different socioeconomic indicators at different spatial scales. One set of indicators relates to service deprivation measured by GIS analysis of reasonable access to key services using some of the measures previously outlined. The domains are then merged and weighted depending on perceived importance to develop a single deprivation ranking of all small areas in a given location (Noble et al., 2006). When mapped, geographical variation in social and economic circumstance between areas becomes apparent and it is often used as a means of understanding the spatial inequality present between places (Figure 9.3). In order to reduce spatial inequality, the measure has been used as a means of targeting funding to places in need as well as for area-based policy initiatives, such as urban regeneration and improvements in service provision (Deas et al., 2003). IMDs have seen particular use to map health inequalities (Mackenzie et al., 1998; Saunders, 1998) and understand factors related to issues such as mortality (Smith et al., 2014), breastfeeding (Brown et al., 2010) and cardiovascular disease (Ramsay et al., 2015).

GIS has also been increasingly utilised to develop geodemographic typologies of places in order to better understand their spatial make-up. Geodemographics are developed by drawing together large amounts of spatial socioeconomic data to identify 'types' of similar areas and classify them based on like characteristics (Vickers and Rees, 2011). Identified areas are often then described based on their overriding features, such as 'Aspiring and Affluent Cosmopolitans', 'Urban and Professional Families' or 'Constrained

Figure 9.3: Index of Multiple Deprivation Ranking for Manchester, UK at local level super output area level (2015)

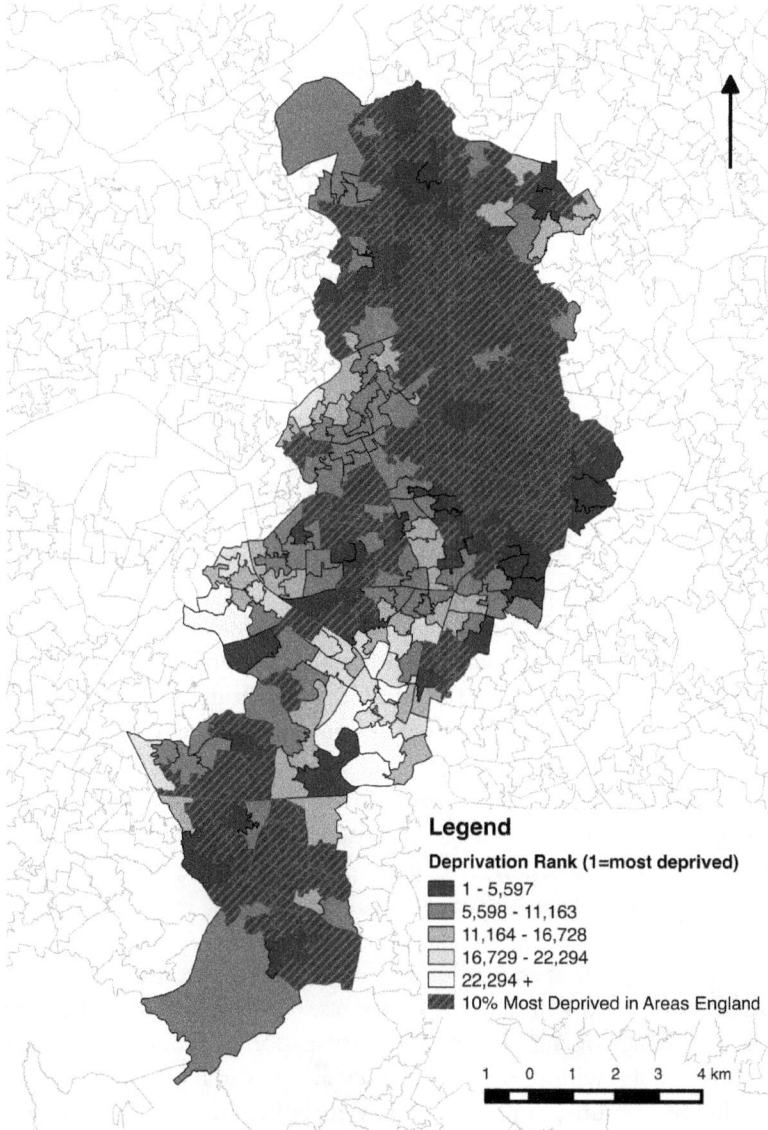

Legend

Deprivation Rank (1=most deprived)
- 1 - 5,597
- 5,598 - 11,163
- 11,164 - 16,728
- 16,729 - 22,294
- 22,294 +
- 10% Most Deprived in Areas England

Ageing City Dwellers'. Such an approach stems from the idea that 'where you are says something about who you are' (Harris et al., 2005: 2). Whilst this is to some extent inevitably a simplification of complex neighbourhood dynamics, such classifications have been widely used in policy and practice, including crime and retail analysis, urban policy and regeneration, through to marketing and environmental management (see Singleton and Spielman, 2014). Recently, geodemographics have been extended to explore not just the places that people live but also the ways they travel to work. This approach links demographic data to commuting flows, allowing researchers and policy makers to understand not only the number of people commuting between places but also who those people broadly are (ethnicity, occupation, gender, and so on) and what mode of transportation they use (Hincks et al., 2018). This data has then been linked into an online interactive GIS system, providing users the ability to visualise the flows between places dynamically.

At a more technical level, GIS systems have also been developed to help professional planners and other policy makers to make decisions. These 'planning support systems' (PSS) incorporate a wide range of spatial data about places that they can overlay and manipulate to help them make better informed decisions (Geertman and Stillwell, 2004). Unlike traditional GIS, such systems are customised to the task of decision making, incorporating a range of different components with specifically developed tools, models and analytical capabilities unique to the solving of problems. These systems help decision makers in two main ways, first to identify the problem, its causes and what can be done about it, and second to learn about other stakeholders' views by facilitating the exchange of information between professional as well as lay groups (Pelzer et al., 2014). Examples range from systems that allow the impact of transportation interventions on land use to be modelled (Arampatzis et al., 2004), to measuring and targeting sustainability measures and the potential impact of policy changes (Graymore et al., 2009). A key challenge with these systems stems from the wide range of disciplinary clients, which, as they become more developed and complex, must balance software capabilities with the levels of expertise present among potential users.

In this respect, there are examples of innovative qualitative and participatory GIS within social policy research and practice, reflecting the importance of engagement and participation of community groups and the public within planning, policy and research processes. There has been a tradition of participatory mapping in local government planning as a means of engaging local communities, particularly in the consultation process of local plan and decision making. These tend to use various 'mental mapping' exercises (such as sketch maps) as a means of getting local people to elucidate their thoughts, perceptions, opinions and local knowledge of an area being affected by a planning decision (Cinderby and Forrester, 2005; Dennis, 2006). The spatial representations created through these mapping exercises are digitised and incorporated into the GIS for further analysis. An example of participatory mapping is in the analysis of crime and neighbourhood safety. Orford and Leigh (2014) analysed over 700 maps based on residents' perceptions of the neighbourhoods in which they lived and worked in Cardiff, created as part of a wider research project on the role of neighbourhood intelligence in combating crime. The maps were generated by the residents during in-depth interviews using a mobile GIS interface which allowed them to draw neighbourhood boundaries onto a digital base map and annotate the map with insights and knowledge about their neighbourhood (Figure 9.4). This allowed maps of different crimes to be analysed with respect to resident-defined neighbourhoods and revealed the importance of local knowledge in explaining patterns and occurrences of crime at different times of the day and night. Other examples include the work by Pain and colleagues (2006), who found that crime hotspots identified by GIS crime data mapping did not match up with residents' experience of crime or their satisfaction with crime prevention measures, such as good street lighting, which has important implications for future policy interventions.

The adoption of GIS in local planning authorities saw a movement away from information gathering solely using participatory mapping approaches to public participation GIS (PPGIS), where local

Figure 9.4: Self-reported neighbourhoods with residential/work locations in Cardiff, UK

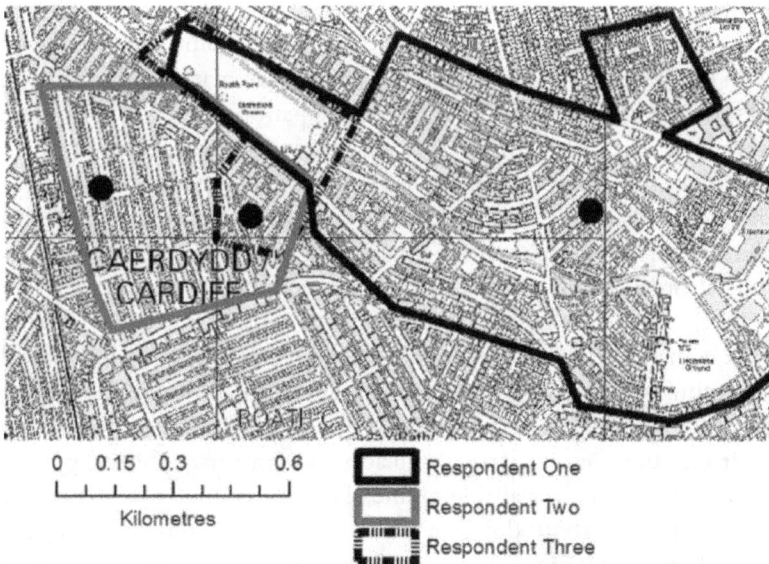

communities and citizens are involved in an iterative process before the final maps are produced (Kwan and Ding, 2008). Some of the first usages of more community-based PPGIS in the UK were to engage communities in local problem identification. For example, in the 'Shaping Slaithwaite' project residents of the West Yorkshire village were asked at a local fair to contribute to ideas about ways to improve their village. As part of this, computers were provided and an online interactive GIS system of the local area was created. Residents were asked to interact with the online map and leave comments about the different places, such as what areas should be developed or protected or what a particular building means to them, which were then fed into the local planning process (Kingston et al., 2000). At a larger scale, a woodland regeneration in the Yorkshire Dales National Park Authority also highlighted the early potential of PPGIS by allowing users to interact with an online map to select relevant factors to consider for an expansion in woodland tree planting and weighting their importance to generate different possible scenarios and preferred options (Carver et al., 2001).

Despite their democratic, policy and analytical appeal, there is however a potential danger with such approaches as projects may be based on explanatory information and maps that support the arguments of the planning authority rather than those of the communities involved and does nothing to address the inherent power relations in the decision-making process (Perkins, 2007). It is therefore necessary to carefully consider how such systems are designed and for whom. With the advent of Web 2.0 and neogeography (Haklay et al., 2008) citizens increasingly have the opportunity to become more involved with the collection, analysis and presentation of mapping data than in PPGIS in a field referred to as GeoParticipation (Panek, 2016). Here new (and often free) geospatial technologies such as GPS receivers on smart phones allow members of the public to generate and analyse their own maps and upload them onto online community sites to allow others to engage with them without the constraints imposed by official organisations. Probably the best example is OpenStreet Map (OSM) but others include FixMyStreet, by the charity mySociety, which makes it easier for people to report problems in their local community via a map-based platform. Less formal is EmoMap (Ortag and Huang, 2011; Gartner, 2012) that allows local people to map their emotions about particular places using a smart phone app and make them publicly available online. This can be used to visualise the way people feel about different parts of their local community which could form an additional layer of information for planners and decision makers. GeoParticipation is a call for a more humanised approach to mapping information and technology in an attempt to democratise the spatial decision-making process of planners and policy makers (Panek, 2016). The results of these different types of participatory mapping are often the reflections of the social and cultural backgrounds of the communities and their understanding of spaces and spatial relations (Corbett and Rambaldi, 2009).

In a related field, geo-narrative is a GIS-based approach to narrative analysis based on oral histories, life histories and biographies (Kwan and Ding, 2008). Here GIS is used to handle, visualise and analyse the chronology of people's experiences and the sequence of events. An example of this is research into the lives of 37 Muslim women in Columbus, Ohio, US in 2002 and the effects of the 9/11 attacks in terms of hostility and hate crimes (Kwan, 2008). The life paths of the 37 women were generated in the GIS based on a variety of multimedia data, including: survey diaries about activities and trips undertaken on designated days; oral histories through in-depth interviews based on how their lives had changed post-9/11 and their perception of safety and risk of where they lived; sketch maps of neighbourhoods including areas which they considered unsafe before and after 9/11; and photos and voice clips to contextualise their experiences. The life paths and associated geo-narratives of the women's lives revealed that space and time played a significant role in shaping the participants' post-9/11 experiences and that specific spatial and temporal experiences and events could be identified that were common to several of the women.

Finally, a slightly different example of qualitative GIS in social policy research comes from Orford and Webb (2018) and their mapping of social policy areas identified from the daily working practices of public policy practitioners in Wales. Here practitioners were interviewed in depth about their daily working lives and were encouraged to talk about the places that were significant in their activities. These places were geo-referenced and then mapped using spatial ellipses (Alexander et al., 2011) as a way of aggregating the individual places into regions. Different maps were produced for different policy areas and these were overlaid to compare and contrast how practitioners working in different fields had different activity spaces even though they may work for the same local authority and be based in the same location (Figure 9.5). The maps identified core and peripheral areas of working in the local authority which did not necessarily match up with the practitioners' official job demarcations and instead reflected historic ties with former administrative areas long since abolished and

Figure 9.5: Spatial ellipses of stakeholder interviews by policy area for North Wales, UK

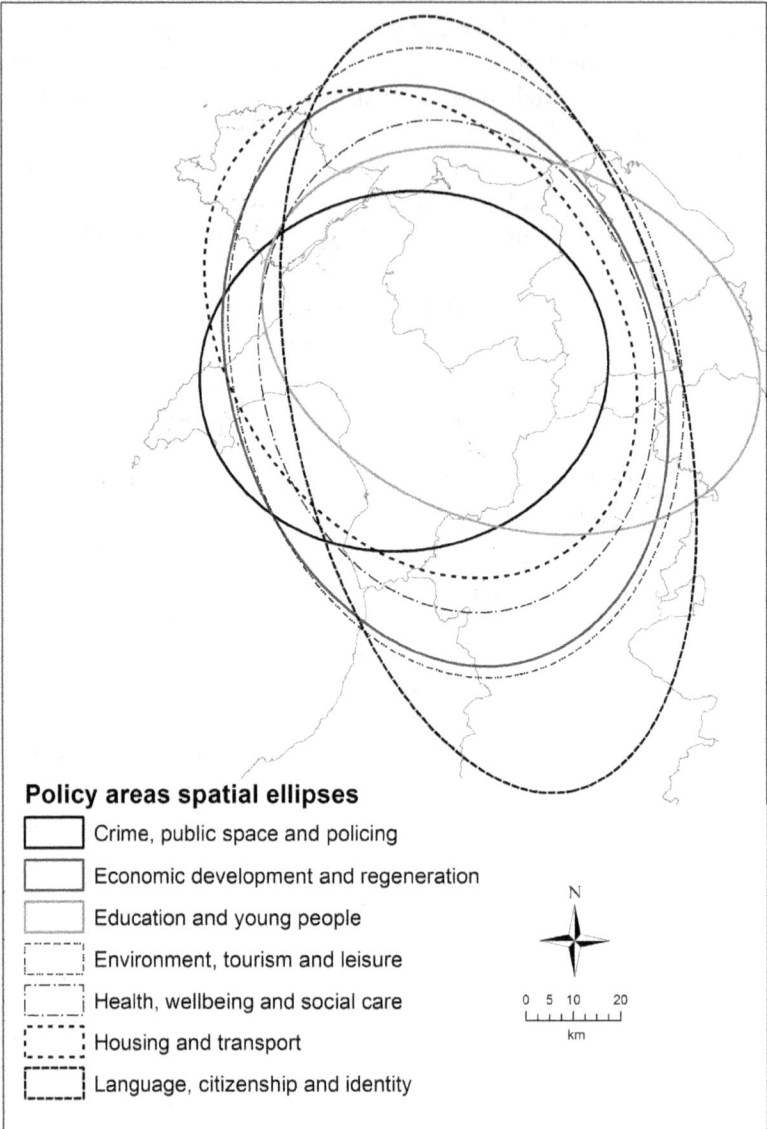

Policy areas spatial ellipses

Crime, public space and policing

Economic development and regeneration

Education and young people

Environment, tourism and leisure

Health, wellbeing and social care

Housing and transport

Language, citizenship and identity

N

0 5 10   20
km

collaborations with new organisations. They emphasise the fuzziness in the spatial working practices of policy practitioners and how these are difficult to change even with the implementation of new geographic regimes.

The future of GIS in social policy and analysis

This final section looks towards the future of GIS in social policy and analysis and briefly discusses continuing challenges and some developments that may help address these issues. Traditionally there have been many barriers to the adoption of GIS in social research and policy fields (for example Göçmen and Ventura, 2010). These include the costs of hardware and software, the costs and availability of data, knowledge and awareness of what GIS can do within an application domain, and the training and skills to use the GIS. Over the years some of these barriers have been reduced or removed entirely, whilst others remain in place. GIS software now runs on a standard PC or laptop and the emergence of free and open-source software such as QGIS means that significant financial costs have been removed. Spatial data, such as digital boundary data, are increasingly available under Open Data licence agreements (including UK Ordnance Survey data), whilst many government statistical data sources have standardised geographical references associated with their data records and are available on open platforms (such as data.gov and data.gov.uk).

However, there are many types of data that social policy researchers may find useful, such as survey or administrative data records, where the geographical references may not be of good quality or are non-existent and mapping of the data remains problematic (see Fry et al., 2017, and Bright et al., 2018, for recent commentaries on the issues of mapping alcohol licence records collected by local authorities and alcohol outlets available from OSM respectively). Added to this is the general rule of thumb that the more fine-grained the spatial data the less likely it is to be current and the fewer types of data that are available. The quantity, variety and currency of social policy data are far higher for large geographical areas such as government regions and local authorities/municipalities than for small areas such as neighbourhoods, wards and census tracts. This can impact the viability of GIS in social policy research if the objective is to monitor and evaluate the effect of policy interventions in a timely manner at small spatial scales such as within cities or neighbourhoods.

There can be complex privacy and ethical issues associated with mapping data relating to people of interest in social policy research, such as vulnerable children or people with mental health problems, which can either prevent the use of GIS or impede analysis. Maps can hide as well as reveal people and their relationships with places (Dorling and Fairbairn, 1997). Vulnerable or minority groups are either often hidden in the detail of the maps or missing altogether.

This is partly because these groups are missing from the data records (for example homeless persons) or they appear in numbers so small that they are redacted due to data disclosure issues or vanish when aggregated into larger populations. Mapping can be a disclosive act in itself – showing where a person or group of people live can often identify them and therefore the publication of a map may be restricted or the data obscured in some way.

Nevertheless, despite these technical and ethical challenges, arguably the largest barrier to the uptake of GIS in social policy research concerns the knowledge of what GIS can offer and the training and skills to undertake the research. GIS education and training tends to be focused within particular disciplines in universities (Harris et al., 2014) and not necessarily those disciplines associated with social policy research. Within government organisations, GIS tends to be a function of particular teams (for instance, in Planning) as oppose to being embedded throughout the organisation, and this is particularly true of smaller organisations. The result is that the people with the GIS knowledge and skills are not necessarily working within social policy research teams and this limits the application of GIS in this domain.

There are several developments in GIS and the social policy data landscape that could have positive impacts on the use of GIS in social policy research. The first is the emergence of Big Data and linked data especially around administrative datasets. Big Data not only refers to the enormous size of some social datasets that now exist, or their completeness in terms of population-level data, but also to the use of machine learning to undertake predictive analysis of user behaviour to find correlations between different socioeconomic processes in different geographical environments. In social policy this has been used for example to identify patterns in crime rates, disease prevention, and understanding how different types of people move around areas at different times of the day. Coupled to this is the new types of data becoming available gathered by cheap and numerous devices such as mobile devices (such as smart phones), wireless sensor networks (such as for capturing movement of people) and CCTV cameras, as well as social media outputs such as Twitter feeds, that can provide live or near-live information on people and places. These data can have an associated geographical reference enabling them to be mapped and analysed within GIS and have the potential to inform social policy research.

The second development is the Open Data movement which encourages organisations and agencies that collect and host data, including government, to make these more accessible to researchers.

In the UK, the Economic and Social Research Council (ESRC) have funded a series of Big Data Research Centres whose aim is to facilitate the promotion, access and use of data collected by government and other organisations by academic and policy researchers. Centres include the Administrative Data Research Centres in the four nations of the UK – which deal with data relating to health and social security records, benefits and tax records and crime and justice records – the Business and Local Government Data Research Centre and the Consumer Data Research Centre which allows access to government and commercial data. The centres provide facilities to link data from different datasets to individuals and provide safe settings in which to analyse the data. It is likely that the types of data made available via the Research Centres would be valuable for social policy research and may address some of the issues discussed earlier associated with ethics, privacy and disclosure as well as the currency and availability of data for small areas. Furthermore, accessing data geographically referenced to individuals and households may be one way to address MAUP as this allows data to be aggregated to bespoke areas that better reflect the underlying population and social processes being investigated.

The final development concerns the increasing pervasiveness of GIS technology and spatial data within social science and related research (partly reflecting the 'spatial turn' in the social sciences) and also within the policy and civil society spheres. As GIS, and in particular mapping technology, becomes more prevalent, social policy researchers and the groups they research may become more spatially literate and start to use maps and spatial analysis more in their research. A good example of this is the gradually increasing uptake of open source GIS software and the development of qualitative GIS which is slowly being adopted into new academic and policy areas that have previously viewed GIS as inaccessible, unfamiliar or even inappropriate. However, qualitative GIS is still emerging and it lacks the suite of analytical tools and processes available for traditional GIS applications. There remain challenges with geo-referencing qualitative data, particularly textual data where spatial references may be encoded using descriptions such as 'close to where I live' or 'in the neighbouring town' or 'far away from here' or use vernacular place names that may not exist in official gazetteers. Recent developments in natural language processing, fuzzy matching and querying, and crowd-sourced mapping products such as OSM are helping here though and GIS software packages are now better at handling qualitative data records.

To conclude, GIS and the socioeconomic data landscape are evolving, and increasingly the field has a lot to offer to social policy.

Innovations in qualitative GIS have allowed a more mixed-method approach, better suited to social policy research with its emphasis on understanding lived experiences and also evaluating the impact of policy interventions. New mapping techniques that emphasise flows of people, trade, ideas, and so on, allow maps to move away from the limited view of containerised Cartesian space whilst dynamic and interactive mapping challenges the static view of GIS and opens up temporal and well as spatial analysis of policy outcomes. Increasing access to micro-level and population-level data sources through open data and Big Data initiatives can start to address some of the concerns of sample size, data currency, MAUP and EF in relation to policy analysis whilst the increasing pervasiveness of maps and mapping in the social sciences and beyond means that geographical methods and ways of thinking are becoming more salient in the policy arena.

References

Alexander, B., Hubers, C., Schwanen, T., Dijst, M. and Ettema, D. (2011) Anything, anywhere, anytime? Developing indicators to assess the spatial and temporal fragmentation of activities. *Environment and Planning B: Planning and Design* 38: 678–705.

Andrienko, G., Andrienko, N., Dykes, J., Kraak, M.J., Robinson, A. and Schumann, H. (2016) GeoVisual analytics: interactivity, dynamics, and scale. *Cartography and Geographic Information Science* 43(1): 1–2.

Arampatzis, G., Kiranoudis, C., Scaloubacas, P. and Assimacopoulos, D. (2004) A GIS-based decision support system for planning urban transportation policies. *European Journal of Operational Research* 152(2): 465–475.

Ashby, D. and Longley, P. (2005) Geocomputation, geodemographics and resource allocation for local policing. *Transactions in GIS* 9(1): 53–72.

Bright, J., De Sabbata, S., Lee, S., Ganesh, B. and Humphreys, D.K. (2018) OpenStreetMap data for alcohol research: reliability assessment and quality indicators. *Health and Place* 50: 130–136.

Brown, A., Raynor, P., Benton, D. and Lee, M. (2010) Indices of Multiple Deprivation predict breastfeeding duration in England and Wales. *European Journal of Public Health* 20(2): 231–235.

Burgess, S. and Briggs, A. (2010) School assignment, school choice and social mobility. *Economics of Education Review* 29(4): 639–649.

Carver, S., Evans, A., Kingston, R. and Turton, I. (2001) Public participation, GIS, and cyberdemocracy: evaluating on-line spatial decision support systems. *Environment and Planning B: Planning and Design* 2001(28): 907–921.

Cheshire, P. and Sheppard, S. (2004) Capitalising the value of free schools: the impact of supply characteristics and uncertainty. *Economic Journal* 144: 397–424.

Cinderby, S. and Forrester, J. (2005) Facilitating the local governance of air pollution using GIS for participation, *Applied Geography* 25: 143–158.

Corbett, J. and Rambaldi, G. (2009) Geographic information technologies, local knowledge and change. In Elwood, S. and Cope, M. (eds) *Qualitative GIS*. London: Sage, 75–93.

Davoudi, S. and Strange, I. (eds) (2009) *Conceptions of Space and Place in Strategic Spatial Planning*. London: Routledge (RTPI Library Series).

Deas, I., Robson, B., Wong, C. and Bradford, M. (2003) Measuring neighbourhood deprivation: a critique of the index of multiple deprivation. *Environment and Planning C: Politics and Space* 21(6): 883–903.

Dennis, S. (2006) Prospects for qualitative GIS at the intersection of youth development and participatory urban planning. *Environment and Planning A* 38(11): 2039–2054.

Dorling, D. and Fairbairn, D. (1997) *Mapping Ways of Representing the World*. London: Longman.

Elwood, S. and Cope, M. (2009) *Qualitative GIS: A Mixed Method Approach*. London: Sage.

Fischer, M. and Nijkamp, P. (1993) *Geographic Information Systems, Spatial Modelling and Policy Evaluation*. Berlin: Springer-Verlag.

Fry, R., Rodgers, S., Morgan, J., Orford, S. and Fone, D. (2017) Using routinely collected administrative data in public health research: geocoding alcohol outlet data. *Applied Spatial Analysis and Policy* 10: 301–315.

Gartner, G. (2012) Putting emotions on maps – the wayfinding example. Mountain Cartography workshop in Taurewa, New Zealand, 1–5 September. http://www.mountaincartography.org/publications/papers/papers_taurewa_12/papers/mcw2012_sec3_ch08_p061-065_gartner.pdf

Geertman, S. and Stillwell, J. (2004) Planning support systems: an inventory of current practice. *Computers, Environment and Urban Systems* 28: 291–310.

Gilfoyle, I. and Wong. C. (1998) Computer applications in planning: twenty years' experience of Cheshire County Council. *Planning Practice and Research* 13(2): 191–197.

Glen, J. and Nellis, J.G. (2010) 'The price you pay': the impact of state-funded secondary school performance on residential property values in England. *Panoeconomicus* 4: 405–428.

Göçmen, Z.A. and Ventura, S.J. (2010) Barriers to GIS use in planning. *Journal of the American Planning Association* 76: 172–183.

Graymore, M., Wallis, A. and Richards, A. (2009) An index of regional sustainability: a GIS-based multiple criteria analysis decision support system for progressing sustainability. *Ecological Complexity* 6(4): 452–462.

Haklay, M., Singleton, A. and Parker, C. (2008) Web mapping 2.0: the neogeography of the GeoWeb. *Geography Compass* 2, 2011–2039.

Hamnett, C. and Butler, T. (2011) 'Geography matters': the role distance plays in reproducing educational inequality in East London. *Transactions Institute of British Geographers* 36: 479–500.

Harris, R., Sleight, P. and Webber, R. (2005) *Geodemographics, GIS and Neighbourhood Targeting*. Chichester: Wiley.

Harris, R., Tate, N., Souch, C., Singleton, A., Orford, S., Keylock, C., Jarvis, C. and Brunsdon C. (2014) Geographers count: a report on quantitative methods in geography. *Enhancing Learning in the Social Sciences* 6(2): 43–58.

Harris, R., Johnston, R. and Burgess, S. (2016) Tangled spaghetti: modelling the core catchment areas of London's secondary schools. *Environment and Planning A* 48(9): 1681–1683.

Higgs, G., Langford, M. and Norman, P. (2015) Accessibility to sports facilities in Wales: a GIS-based analysis of socio-economic variations in provision. *Geoforum* 62: 105–120.

Higgs, G., Zahnow, R., Corcoran, J., Langford, M. and Fry, R. (2017) Modelling spatial access to general practitioner surgeries: does public transport availability matter? *Journal of Transport and Health* 6: 143–154.

Hincks, S., Kingston, R., Webb, B. and Wong, C. (2018) A new geodemographic classification of commuting flows for England and Wales. *International Journal of Geographic Information Science* 32(4): 663–684.

Kingston, R., Carver, S., Evans, A. and Turton, I. (2000) Web-based public participation geographical information systems: an aid to local environmental decision-making. *Computers, Environment and Urban Systems* 24: 109–125.

Kwan, M-P. (2008) From oral histories to visual narratives: re-presenting the post-September 11 experiences of Muslim women in the United States. *Social and Cultural Geography* 9(6): 653–669.

Kwan M.-P. and Knigge, L. (2006) Doing qualitative research using GIS: an oxymoron endeavour? *Environment and Planning* A 38: 1999–2002.

Kwan, M.-P. and Ding, G. (2008) Geo-narrative: extending Geographic Information Systems for narrative analysis in qualitative and mixed-method research. *The Professional Geographer* 60(4): 443–465.

Langford, M., Higgs, G. and Fry, R. (2016) Multi-modal two-step floating catchment area analysis of primary health care accessibility. *Health and Place* 38: 70–81.

Longely, P.A., Goodchild, M.F., Maguire, D.J. and Rhind, W. (2015) *Geographic Information Science and Systems*, 4th edition. London: Wiley.

Mackenzie, I., Nelder, R., Maconachie, M. and Radford, G. (1998) 'My ward is more deprived than yours'. *Journal of Public Health Medicine* 20: 186–190.

Noble, M., Wright, G., Smith, G. and Dibben, C. (2006) Measuring multiple deprivation at the small-area level. *Environment and Planning A* 38: 169–185.

Orford, S. (2005) Cartography and visualization, in Castree, N. Rogers, A. and Sherman, D. (eds) *Questioning Geography: Fundamental Debates*. Oxford: Blackwell, 189–205.

Orford, S. (2018) The capitalisation of school choice into property prices in the UK: a case study of grammar and non-selective state schools in Buckinghamshire. *Geoforum* 97: 231–241.

Orford, S. and Leigh, C. (2014) The relationship between self-reported definitions of urban neighbourhood and respondent characteristics: a study of Cardiff, UK. *Urban Studies* 15(9): 1891–1908.

Orford, S. and Webb, B. (2018) Mapping the interview transcript: identifying spatial policy areas from daily working practices. *Area* 50(4): 529–541.

Orford, S. Rallings C., Thrasher M. and Borisyuk, G. (2011) Changes in the probability of voter turnout when re-siting polling stations: a case study in Brent, UK. *Environment and Planning C, Government and Policy* 29: 149–169.

Ortag, F. and Huang, H. (2011) Location-based emotions relevant for pedestrian navigation, in Ruas, A. (ed) *Proceedings of the 25th International Cartographic Conference*, 3–8 July, Paris, France, https://icaci.org/files/documents/ICC_proceedings/ICC2011/

Pain, R., MacFarlane, R., Turner, K. and Gill, S. (2006) 'When, where, if, and but': qualifying GIS and the effect of streetlighting on crime and fear. *Environment and Planning A* 38(11): 2055–2074.

Panek, J. (2016) From mental maps to GeoParticipation. *The Cartographic Journal* 53(4): 300–307.

Pavlovskaya, M. (2006) Theorizing with GIS: a tool for critical geographies? *Environment and Planning A*, 38(11): 2003–2020.

Pelzer, P., Geertman, S., van der Heijden, R. and Rouwette, E. (2014) The added value of planning support systems: a practitioner's perspective. *Computers, Environment and Urban Systems* 48: 16–27.

Perkins, C. (2007) Community mapping. *The Cartographic Journal* 44(2): 127–137.

Rae, A. (2017) The geography of travel to work in England and Wales from the 2011 Census. *Applied Spatial Analysis and Policy* 10(4): 457–473.

Ramsay, S.E., Morris, R.W., Whincup, P.H., Subramanian, S.V., Papacosta, A.O., Lennon, L. and Wannamethee, S.G. (2015) The influence of neighbourhood-level socioeconomic deprivation on cardiovascular disease mortality in older age: longitudinal multilevel analyses from a cohort of older British men. *Journal of Epidemiology and Community Health* 69: 1224–1231.

Rebel, M. (2007) Geographic information systems and spatial data processing in demography: a review. *Population Research and Policy Review* 26(5–6): 601–618.

RECLUS (1989) *Les Villes Europeénnes. DATAR.* Montpellier: RECLUS.

Saunders J, (1998) Weighted census-based deprivation indices: their use in small areas. *Journal of Public Health Medicine* 20: 253–260.

Singleton, A.D. and Spielman, S.E. (2014) The past, present and future of geodemographic research in the United States and United Kingdom. The Professional Geographer 66(4): 558–567.

Singleton, A., Longley, P., Allen, R. and O'Brien, O. (2011) Estimating secondary school catchment areas and spatial equity of access. *Computers, Environment and Urban Systems* 35: 241–249.

Smith, L.K., Manktelow, B.N., Draper, E.S., Boyle, E.M., Johnson, S.J., and Field, D.J. (2014) Trends in the incidence and mortality of multiple births by socioeconomic deprivation and maternal age in England: population-based cohort study. *BMJ Open* 4(4): 1–13, doi: 10.1136/bmjopen-2013-004514

Snow, J. (1855) *On the Mode of Communication of Cholera*, 2nd edition. London: J. Churchill.

Van der Horst, D. (2007) Assessing the efficiency gains of improved spatial targeting of policy interventions; the example of an agri-environmental scheme. *Journal of Environmental Management* 85(4): 1076–1087.

Vickers, D. and Rees, P. (2007) Creating the UK National Statistics 2001 output area classification. *Journal of the Royal Statistical Society A* 170: 379–403.

Vonk, G., Geertman, S. and Schot, P.P. (2005) Bottlenecks blocking widespread usage of planning support systems. *Environment and Planning A* 37(5): 909–924.

Wong, C. (2006) *Indicators for Urban and Regional Planning: The Interplay of Policy and Methods*. London: Routledge.

Wong, C., Baker, M., Webb, B., Hincks, S. and Schulze-Baing, A. (2015) Mapping policies and programmes: the use of GIS to communicate spatial relationships in England. *Environment and Planning B: Planning and Design* 42(3): 1020–1039.

Retrospective

10

Developing a spatial social policy: taking stock and looking to the future

John Clarke

This book brings about a long overdue, and much needed, encounter between social policy and geography. Now that it has finally arrived, we can see some of the possibilities and problems that might be at stake in developing the encounter into a more long-running dialogue. Here my aim is to reflect back on some of the issues and arguments that emerged in the preceding chapters and their implications for the study of social policy. Later, I try to pick out two or three themes that might add to the potential conversation between geography and social policy by thinking a little further about ways in which space, place and policy are entangled. The chapter is written from the perspective of an occasionally disaffected social policy scholar who had the good fortune to mix with geographers who taught him the benefits of 'taking geography seriously' (Massey and Allen, 1984).

One of the conditions underlying my social policy disaffection is shared with many of the authors in this collection, and with the position that underpins it. The book is inspired by a deafening silence about place and space in social policy, characterised by the assumption that place is a self-evident and unquestioned terrain where policy and its practices happen. It is treated as a backdrop, location or passive context rather than an active force in the organisation of social life. Whether analysis is directed to the nation state or the neighbourhood, social policy is shot through with geographical reference points that are rarely questioned. For me, the assumptions about the nation (and its accompanying state) have always been a stumbling block, with national borders taken for granted as the framework within which analysis could be conducted – or between which comparisons could be safely made. The presumption of what we might call spatial tidiness, the belief that there is a stable entity bounded by fixed borders, in which the people, the policy and culture form a coherent and harmonious whole, has dominated much of social policy – with unfortunate consequences.

It should not have taken the more recent troubles of different globalisations, the regional alignments (from the EU to ASEAN (Association of Southeast Asian Nations)), the transnational flows of people, capital and ideas (including policies), or even the varieties of emergent nation making (from the former Yugoslav republic to the struggles over Catalan independence) to suggest that the nation is a contingent entity, shaped by complex internal and external relations. Even starting with the UK, we might have noticed some problems with the container model of space that underpins methodological nationalism: the uncomfortable coupling of different countries into one more of less united place; the different legal systems, the varying governmental arrangements, and the different identities, cultures and languages. All of these spoke to some issues about the internal coherence or unity of the 'United' Kingdom. At the same time, the long history of colonialism might have pointed to questions about borders and bordering: from the varieties of colonial rule and the economic surpluses they generated; through differential decolonisations, the sifting of the white dominions from the non-white, and the subsequent layering of citizenship status and access. All of these phenomena interrupt the conception of the closed and bounded nation, its integral state and the associated conditions and practices of social welfare. We might have noticed such things but, in practice, social policy remained dominated by methodological nationalism (occasionally substituting a sort of methodological globalism). As a result, the encounter with geography and a dynamic understanding of the spatial is indeed long overdue – and welcome.

Making place matter

One of the most striking features of this collection is the discovery of the different geographies through which this encounter can be approached. Each chapter opens a different route to spatial thinking: from GIS to Foucault, or from the new localism to neuro-geography. They offer a rich array of resources through which to think about social policy geographically. Each of the chapters here illuminates one of those routes, indicating how taking geography seriously might sharpen our understanding not just of where, but how, policy works.

Chris Philo's argument for treating Foucault as an analyst of the spatial provides an unexpected and uplifting opening, adding a new persona to the many Foucaults who currently circulate in social analysis. The chapter does an impressive job of inviting us to think with Foucault about how power is spatialised and, indeed, how it has spatialising effects. As he notes, the chapter focuses on Foucault's earlier work, where the articulations of space, policy and power are embodied in 'institutional architecture from the classroom to the design of hospitals' (Foucault, 1980: 149). The organisation of power, policy and place shifts as this institutional architecture of disciplinary power gives way to, or perhaps more accurately is supplemented by, the threading of power and regulation through multiple social spaces en route to the self-surveillance of advanced liberal governmentality. The sites and settings of performance and scrutiny, of evaluation and judgement, multiplied, as did the policy knowledges – especially what Nikolas Rose (1985) called the 'psychological complex' – that were put to work.

Thereafter, the 'capillary' workings of power reorganised social space in dramatic ways before the latest governmental turn – what Jessica Pykett heralds as the emergence of 'neurogeography'. Her chapter traces the changing sites, scales and connections being forged as the neurological becomes a privileged object of intervention. In the process, she draws out the ways in which neurogeography involves new scalar dynamics of policy and intervention – from the transnational circuits through which this new knowledge circulates to the molecular scale of intervention, which imagines the individual differently from the classic individualist conceptions of social policy, especially that rational, calculating subject beloved of liberal political and economic theory. However, both these chapters point to another issue for policy studies (not only social policy): the danger of assuming that grand plans work as prescribed. Foucault is both an immensely productive resource and a slightly misleading guide. In *Discipline and Punish*, for example, he instructs us that, while tracing the institutional architecture of 'disciplinary power', he had never been interested in the 'witches' brew' of practices that went on inside prisons (1991: 81–82). But, for most policies, there remain important questions about how (and even if) they work in practice. Tania Li (2007), for example, has argued that it is precisely their limited effectivity that stimulates governmental innovation.

The issue of where and how one starts to think about policy and place is illuminated by the different strategy of Anna Minton's chapter on housing, locating the Grenfell Tower Fire of 2017 as a point of departure. The Grenfell Fire condenses a whole series of dynamics of public policy – about the place of social housing in a new housing 'market', in the management strategies of local government, in the regulatory practices of an 'anti-red tape' culture of government, and in the social devaluation of those occupying social housing. Housing is the focus of economic and political strategies for the organisation of social space and people's place within it. The rhetoric of choice has been accompanied by a deepening sense of powerlessness, the shrinking of social rights and deepening ontological insecurity. Minton argues that this confluence of dismal trends should be the condition for rethinking housing as an object of policy and as a focal point of how people understand and inhabit place.

The question of people's sense of place arises in a different way in Adam Whitworth's chapter on local activation services. His exploration of how dioramas can productively map people's sense, and use, of space highlights important issues about the shape and structuring of the local (a point to which I return later). In particular, he draws on Hägerstrand to emphasise the 'daily rhythms' that give a shape to everyday life. He makes dynamic use of David Harvey's three versions of space – absolute, relative and relational – to animate the discussion of the relationships between people, place and service provision. I confess that I find Harvey's conception of relational space thinner and less productive than Doreen Massey's relational view of space and place. I regularly go back to an interview she did with Andrew Stephens in which she expressed this nugget of relational thinking:

> For me, places are articulations of 'natural' and social relations, relations that are not fully contained within the place itself. So, first, places are not closed or bounded – which, politically, lays the ground for critiques of exclusivity. Second, places are not 'given' – they are always in open-ended process. They are in that sense 'events'. Third, they and their identity will always be contested (we could almost talk about local-level struggles for hegemony). (Massey, no date)

Later, I will come back to what this view does to questions of social, political and economic distance that bear on the making of the local: for example, how the distances between the 'central' and the 'local' aspects of the state; or where the decision-making powers that shape local employment possibilities are located. Reading Adam Whitworth's chapter, I was reminded about some of the strange ways in which policy makers and policy scholars use spatial concepts such as distance. I was once at a conference listening to a set of papers about employment activation policies and stumbled over the idea that services were graduated according to 'people's distance from the labour market'. So I asked a (sadly) naïve question about the significance of geography in policy and received a careful explanation that distance here referred to the individual's attitudinal and developmental 'distance' from the labour market. Sometimes, spatial metaphors are merely metaphorical, but I thought it provided a striking example of how to legitimate the stratification of social assistance.

The local appears in other guises in the book, for example in Richard Harris' chapter on spatialising social statistics. He offers a compelling critique of the sorts of a-spatial or spatially naïve statistical methods that are commonplace within social policy. He argues that they treat geography as a 'nuisance' rather than as a constitutive feature of social life. Taking a typical policy problem, the causes of differential pupil attainment, he offers two alternative approaches – object and field – to taking place seriously as a formative influence on pupil outcomes. For me, his chapter also raised characteristic problems about how we think about the 'local' because in exploring the two approaches he engages with conceptual and methodological challenges about how we locate the local, how we identify its boundaries and how we think about proximate or 'neighbouring' places. Such discussions remind me of other contemporary debates about borders and bordering which engage with processual conceptions of how lines are drawn, who gets to draw them and with what consequences (for example, Rajaram and Grundy-Warr, 2007; Kramsch, 2010; Green, 2012). So who gets to define the local and with what consequences? The question is posed in a different way in Martin Jones's chapter on the return or revival of 'localism' in policy making, which explores both geographical and policy debates about the nature of the local and makes a subtle argument for 'locality' as a focal point for critical policy analysis, one that should enable us to attend to the 'combined and uneven development' of policy impacts. The chapter makes a strong case for rescuing 'locality' from the previous conceptual disputes and tangles in which it became enmeshed in the 1980s and 1990s (and it is useful to be reminded of disciplinary histories in this way).

Scott Orford and Brian Webb explore the complex possibilities of GIS for considering the spatial dynamics of social policy. They are attentive to the ways in which the organisation of spaces for GIS purposes reflects older histories and purposes, while considering emerging approaches to mapping that are more open and enable a more relational understanding of places – and how they are imagined and inhabited. These emerging possibilities include participatory processes that enable user-generated mappings and they are attentive to the ways in which GIS approaches may exclude or render invisible some categories of people (such as those who are homeless). They also cast an eye on the possibilities of 'Geodemographics' – an approach that is underpinned by the view that 'where you are says something about who you are' (Harris et al., 2005: 2). Like other demographic categorisation approaches, this has problems of both categorisation and generalisation (see the interesting discussion of place and politics against categorisation in McQuarrie, 2017). As recent arguments around the use of AI (artificial intelligence) in policing policy have indicated, the value of such predictive approaches depends heavily on both the reliability and validity of the base data: if current crime and policing data is racially structured, then it will produce racially profiled approaches to policing (see Sharkey, 2018).

Finally, Jay Wiggan's examination of Social Investment Bonds explores a neglected set of spatial dynamics in what has become a much-feted approach to funding policy interventions. His discussion of the 'intensive financialisation' of welfare policy draws out the complex spatial restructuring of social policy that this device brings into play. Such policies are directed at localised (and often profoundly immobilised) populations which thereby become the object of deterritorialised financial risk and reward, a process that connects (albeit not reciprocally) local populations to global financial markets. This analysis intersects with other spatially dislocating dynamics of welfare policy and government, not least the uneven impacts of what Jamie Peck (2012) has called 'austerity urbanism'. As Sarah Phinney (2018) has recently argued in relation to Detroit, both the (projected) causes of austerity policies and their effects are profoundly racialised. Places and policies can form toxic combinations.

The analyses collected here also point to how questions of space are closely coupled to questions of scale in relation to social policy, ranging from the global to the neuromolecular. Scale is not exactly the same as space, even though scalar logics are often underpinned and reinforced by spatial imaginaries – the bounded nation, the intimate neighbourhood or even the household. Here, too, social policy makers and scholars have tended to take scales as simple facts, the levels at which policy is made, enacted and experienced. Even if it is sometimes necessary to attend to multilevel analysis, the levels are understood as pre-existing conditions. In her critique of such scalar conceptions, Doreen Massey (2004: 9) notably described this logic as treating scales as 'a nested set of Russian dolls'. Instead, policy studies might benefit from an understanding of scales as relationally constituted, open to contestation and changing constructions that are geographically variable. As Jones reminds us, the local is not the same everywhere. In a recent book on education policy, Natalie Papanastasiou (2019) has explored how a 'politics of scale' both shapes – and is shaped by – education policies and practices, from inventing the 'European level' and its differences from national spaces to the new localism in education policy. Scale, in this sense, is critically important for studying policy because forms and sites of governing are typically, and common-sensically, thought of in scalar terms (Ferguson and Gupta, 2002).

The chapters collected here make a substantial contribution to demonstrating both the necessity and the value of that encounter between social policy and geography. Even so, I want to sketch two further aspects of what might be at stake in putting policy in its place. The first concerns social policy; the second geography.

The problem of social policy

As a long-term inhabitant in the field of social policy, I live with many problems, but here I want to focus on one in particular: its shape-shifting character. The mutability of social policy has two important implications for trying to construct conversations. The first is that social policy designates both an object of study (a sub-set of policies to be distinguished from economic, foreign or public policy) and a field of study (Social Policy, or what used to be Social Policy and Administration, as the study of social policies). This is a banal, but consequential, distinction: the doubling of the name demands some care about which social policy might benefit from a geographical encounter. Social policy as a more or less loosely bounded set of policies takes us to the business of governing. Here the problem of social policy demands that we think about the relationships between governing and the social. Do we accept a story of social progress and improvement, in which social policy contributes to and enhances the greater good? Or do we take a more sceptical view of social policy as a means of managing the social, through which divisions are reproduced, inequalities are secured and the reproduction of systems and hierarchies of power is maintained?

If we accept the former, then improving the quality of knowledge – not least geographical knowledge – is an important way in which social scientists can contribute both to the improvement of policy and the enhancement of social life. The more sceptical view, however, raises questions not just about the improvement of knowledge but political contention about the purpose and direction of policy (for example in arguments about the purposes and effects of austerity policies; see McKee et al, 2012 and Cooper and Whyte, 2017).

Geographical knowledge also matters here, albeit in a different way, in tracing the flows of policy making (such as the spread of austerity as the new transnational governmental wisdom after 2008) and in terms of the uneven social and spatial distribution of its consequences. The chapters here range across these possibilities, from seeking to generate better knowledge for policy making, through generating alternative knowledges (through participatory mapping practices) to critical deconstructions of the social and spatial effects of policy. But I suspect the issue is worth a more explicit place in the conversations between geography and social policy.

The second aspect of the mutable character of social policy is linked to this first problem. As a field of study, social policy does not have a single, coherent intellectual disposition. It certainly has its roots in a Fabian belief in combining social knowledge and social improvement, but it has fractured as many of the wider debates, arguments and controversies in the social sciences have found a foothold in the field. These include the arrival of Marxist analyses of social policy and welfare states, feminist expansions of the horizons of social policy to questions of gender, labour and care, anti- and post-colonial approaches to the imperial foundations of national welfare systems and the reproduction of racialised hierarchies through welfare – and more (see, for example, Williams, 1995). Just as there are many geographies that might bring their voices to this conversation, so too are there different social policy voices, including some that have begun to worry about the spatial and scalar assumptions that underpin so much social policy and so much social policy scholarship.

This is not just an argument that 'it's more complicated than that'. Rather, I am suggesting that 'conversation' is a difficult practice and that identifying likely and potentially productive interlocutors is part of the process of mutual exchange. The diversity of voices both makes this a more difficult challenge (how to find a friend?) and potentially more productive as lines of intersection flow across disciplinary borders. Certainly, I feel fortunate to have found geographers who were willing to both tell me about why geography matters but, perhaps more importantly, to talk about what's at stake in the encounter between social policy and geography. This leads me to my next set of concerns about social policy as place making.

Social policy as place making

For me, one of the critical issues at stake in the encounter between geography and social policy is not just that social policies *take place* (that is, they have a distinct spatial character) but that they also help to *make place*. By this, I mean something more than the now recognised interest of local and regional governments in 'place making' (my local authority has a 'Director of Place'). Rather I am interested in the questions of how space and places are imagined, are folded into policy, are governed through and materialised in policies and practices (echoing some of Jones's concerns about the making of the local). Policies help to reconfigure places – both their internal elements, relationships and processes and the external relationships through which particular places are located. Entangled in such processes are the dynamics of political economy and what Eugene McCann (2002), in the context of local economic development, nicely calls 'cultural politics' (or the contested meaning making that surrounds places). But there are also varieties of governing institutions, actors and practices that translate, mediate and manage these complex dynamics.

Here we encounter what Neil Brenner (2004) called 'new state spaces' as states were reconfigured, rescaled and re-tooled for the challenges of managing neoliberalism's contradictory and crisis-ridden trajectories. As Brenner's stress on urban governance indicated, the urban became a privileged site and scale in these remakings – the beneficiary/victim of decentralising strategies; the local embodiment of the 'competition state' (competing for grants as well as investment); feted as the new location of compulsory partnership models of governing; and, eventually, the fiscal conduit through which 'austerity' could be delivered (Peck, 2012). In particular, these urban/local sites were imagined as repositories of resources (assets, skills, dispositions) that could be competitively mobilised. These new spaces and scales also became the setting for the new localism in welfare, as states sought to make 'welfare' (most obviously in the form of 'workfare') responsive to local needs and conditions. As Allan Cochrane and David Etherington (2007: 2972) argued:

> Within the new policy landscape, a range of relationships is being configured across traditional levels of governance, generating hybrid state and quasi-state forms and producing distinctive welfare spaces. It is perhaps no surprise that where you live makes a difference to how you live; but it also makes a significant difference to the forms of support that will be available and the ways these are managed, whether they appear to come through the working of the market (in the form of employment), through community-based schemes, or directly through state institutions. The nature

of the governance arrangements may be summarised in terms such as public–private partnership that identify shared features and point to their hybrid form; but terms like these can mask very different sets of social and governing relationships.

Significant though these spaces and scales are, they do not exhaust the changes in the state as a nexus of policy and governance. Nation states were remade in other scalar terms (as part of the unevenly developing dynamics of globalisation and the emergence of supranational alliances, agencies and apparatuses). They were subjected to contradictory pressures, not least those of emerging nationalisms that disrupted the apparent coherence of the nation space. In the context of deepening transnational relations of competition (and the increasing circulation of 'league tables' and 'best practice' learning), states were invited/ incited to take up new devices, techniques and technologies to govern in a 'modern' way. Such innovations involved the cultivation of the 'self-directing' responsible subject (and the disciplining of those who failed to self-direct in the required directions). They also involved the expansion of the repertoire of governing strategies, for example the rise of practices of emotional or affective governance (Jupp et al., 2017). In the midst of all this, states were experimenting with new ways to govern (sometimes called the shift from government to governance) in which they sought new organisational forms through which to manage different domains, involving the dispersion of state power through new relationships. Such changes are well documented, but it harder to think about their spatial character given the coincidence of so many different, if not divergent, dynamics. It is the challenges of conceptualising this complexity that has driven some geographers to argue for a topological rather than topographical understanding of spatial relationships. For example, writing about emerging forms of regional governance, John Allen and Allan Cochrane (2010: 1072– 1073) have argued that:

> We start from a topological account of state spatiality, one that draws attention to the spatial reconfiguration of the state's institutional hierarchies and the ways in which a more transverse set of political interactions holds that hierarchy in place, but not in ways conventionally understood through a topographical lens. In contrast to a vertical or horizontal imagery of the geography of state power, what states possess, we suggest, is reach, not height. Topological thinking

suggests that the powers of the state are not so much 'above us' as more or less present through mediated and realtime connections, some direct, others more distanciated.

This approach refuses some well-established figures through which we think about the state, not least that of 'height' in which the state rises above society. This view of the state, which James Ferguson and Akhil Gupta (2002) describe as resting on the images of verticality and encompassment, has been central to the treatment of the state across the social sciences (a significant exception being Philip Abrams' essay on the idea of the state, 1988). Topological approaches, by contrast, change our understanding of proximity and distance in important ways, enabling attention to how certain forms of reach mobilise power across space, bringing apparently 'distant' agents and agencies into close contact. Thus, global organisations and their governing logics, such as the OECD PISA (Organization for Economic Cooperation and Development Programme for International Student Assessment) tables of educational performance, come to be folded into both nation states and the workings of individual schools. As Glenn Savage (2019: 10) has recently put it:

> The OECD, therefore, serves as an exemplar of Prince's (2017) argument that the 'technocracy' – that is, 'the technical experts who produce ostensibly neutral and objective knowledge of objects like the economy in the form of universal measures of economic performance' (p. 338) – is an increasingly powerful force in bringing nations into new topological assemblages, 'often in the form of a ladder with the "best" at the top and the "worst" at the bottom' (p. 339).

Like Allen and Cochrane, Savage approaches these policy questions through the concept of assemblage (derived, often through circuitous routes, from the works of Deleuze and Guattari as a translation of their concept of *agencement*, see also Clarke et al., 2015). For me, this combination of topological thinking and assemblage enables us to think again (and think better) about persistent problems within social policy. Let me note three such issues here. First, they offer a way of thinking about the local which does not fix it in a scalar hierarchy, but allows an approach which foregrounds the relationships and dynamics through which particular locals are constituted and remade, for example though the decision-making 'reach' of global corporations that can calculate and enact factory closures, the levels of service provision that they offer (for example in commercial and financial services), or their engagement in 'partnerships' to provide (or fail to provide) public services – all with profound local consequences. This topological view offers a route to grasping what Massey (2004) described as 'geographies of responsibility'.

Second, for these authors, as for many others, the concept of assemblage is productive because it highlights the *contingent* quality of particular assemblages (rather than reified and singular conceptions of the state or government). This contingent quality has two linked dimensions. On the one hand, it points to the complex internal composition of assemblage – the linking together of diverse and heterogeneous elements to make up a temporary unity – a formation that exists in a condition of 'unstable equilibrium' (to borrow from Gramsci). These diverse elements always have the potential to revert to their separated condition – to disassemble – or to be realigned in new or emergent assemblages through processes of borrowing, bending and blending (or what Lévi-Strauss called *bricolage*). Savage (2019: 7) nicely poses the centrality of contingency:

> Assemblages are heterogeneous, comprised of a multiplicity of component parts that have been arranged together towards particular strategic ends. Given the aforementioned commitments to relations of exteriority, anti-reductionism and the rejection of 'coherent wholes', the heterogeneous component parts that constitute an assemblage are also understood to have a contingent rather than necessary relationship, brought together into particular relational configurations which have mutable rather than fixed forms. This means an assemblage approach emphasizes the always moving and evolving nature of social formations. The complex relationships between heterogeneity, relationality and flux – and how these features can inform an assemblage approach to policy analysis – require careful unpacking.

The other dimension of contingency is not shared by all who use assemblage but feels vitally important to me. Assemblages require the labour of assembling: they are the product of contextually specific agents and agencies, working in forms of relationship (from conflict to collaboration) with the intention of bringing about a new ordering of things (things including problems, people, places, policies, practices and forms of power). Consequently, assemblages are vulnerable to mobilisations (organisational, political, ideological and more) that seek to disassemble them: in this sense, policy and governance are marked by continual efforts to remove, reform, improve or supersede existing assemblages. Assemblages are, in short, *contestable*.

Finally, the shift to assemblage thinking raises an interesting question about temporality. To what extent do we understand the concept of assemblage as marking a historical shift in the organisation of power from old (state-centric) forms to new forms (diverse assemblages)? There is clearly a temptation to see this as a shift from what were formerly integrated institutions – the state, especially the *nation* state – towards more complex disaggregated and dispersed formations (for example, Slaughter, 2004) or as the shift from government to governance. I think this is a temptation to be resisted, resting as it does on a common ahistorical distinction between old and new (what Janet Fink and I once referred to as 'sociological time' as a way of capturing the binary juxtaposition of past and present, 2008). We might be better served by looking back at older formations and wondering whether their apparently integral/integrated character was, in fact, the effect of sets of state-making practices that produced an assemblage with the appearance of being integrated, or what might be called the performance of integration. For example, we might look behind the assumptions about the closed and bordered territorial space of the British nation (and its accompanying state) and treat them (nation and state) instead as topological assemblages of colonial power. Those assemblages organised multiple relationships (including racialised and gendered divisions of labour). They ordered flows (of people, power and profit) in which metropoles and colonies were intimately entangled. And they enabled the surpluses through which the metropoles were able to craft welfare settlements from the late nineteenth century. Such a view of past assemblages might also enable us to better grasp the complex relations of proximity and distance – and of denial and intimacy – that characterise the post-colonial period. From that standpoint, we might have a new understanding of the current rise of 'nativist' sentiments about who is entitled to welfare in the global north. Such possibilities might be part of a committed attempt to put place into policy – and to put policy in its place.

References

Abrams, P. (1988) Notes on the difficulty of studying the state (1977). *Journal of Historical Sociology* 1(1): 58–89.

Allen, J. and Cochrane, A. (2010) Assemblages of state power: topological shifts in the organization of government and politics. *Antipode* 42(5): 1071–1089.

Brenner, N. (2004) *New State Spaces: Urban Governance and the Rescaling of Statehood.* Oxford: Oxford University Press.

Clarke, J. and Fink, J. (2008) Unsettled attachments: national identity, citizenship and welfare. In van Oorschot, W., Opielka, M. and Pfau-Effinger, B. (eds) *Culture and Welfare State: Values and Social Policy in Comparative Perspective.* Cheltenham: Edward Elgar.

Clarke, J., Bainton, D., Lendvai, N. and Stubbs, P. (2015) *Making Policy Move: Towards a Politics of Assemblage and Translation.* Bristol: Policy Press.

Cochrane, A. and Etherington, D. (2007) Managing local labour markets and making up new spaces of welfare. *Environment and Planning A* 39: 2958–2974.

Cooper, V. and Whyte, D. (eds) (2017) *The Violence of Austerity.* London: Pluto Press.

Ferguson, J. and Gupta, A. (2002) Spatializing states: towards an ethnography of neo-liberal governmentality. *American Ethnologist* 29(4): 981–1002.

Foucault, M. (1980) The eye of power [trans]. In Gordon, C. (ed) *Michel Foucault – Power/Knowledge: Selected Interviews and Other Writings, 1972–1977, by Michel Foucault.* Brighton: Harvester Press, 146–165.

Foucault, M. (1991) *Discipline and Punish: The Birth of the Prison* (translated by A. Sheridan). London: Penguin Books.

Green, S. (2012) A sense of border: the story so far. In Wilson, T.M. and Donnan, H. (eds) *A Companion to Border Studies.* Blackwell Companions to Anthropology; vol. 19. Chichester: Wiley Blackwell, 573-592.

Harris, R., Sleight, P. and Webber, R. (2005) *Geodemographics, GIS and Neighbourhood Targeting.* Chichester: Wiley.

Jupp, E., Pykett, J. and Smith, F. (eds) (2017) *Emotional States: Sites and Spaces of Affective Governance.* London: Routledge.

Kramsch, O. (2010) Regulating European borders: a cultural perspective, in Veggeland, N. (ed.) *Innovative Regulatory Approaches: Coping with Scandinavian and European Policies.* New York: Nova Science Publishers.

Li, T. (2007) *The Will to Improve.* Durham, NC: Duke University Press.

Massey, D. (2004) Geographies of responsibility. *Geografiska Annaler* 86 B(1): 5–18.

Massey, D. (2005) *For Space*. Cambridge: Policy.

Massey, D. (no date) The future of landscape: Doreen Massey: an interview by Andrew Stevens. *3:AM Magazine*. www.3ammagazine. com/3am/the-future-of-landscape-doreen-massey/

Massey, D. and Allen, J. (eds) (1984) *Geography Matters: A Reader*. Cambridge: Cambridge University Press.

McCann, E.J. (2002) The cultural politics of local economic development: meaning-making, place-making, and the urban policy process. *Geoforum* 33(3): 385–398.

McKee, M., Karanikolos, M., Belcher, P. and Stuckler, D. (2012) Austerity: a failed experiment on the people of Europe. *Clinical Medicine* 12(4): 346–350. http://citeseerx.ist.psu.edu/viewdoc/dow nload?doi=10.1.1.658.5696&rep=rep1&type=pdf

McQuarrie, M. (2017) The revolt of the Rust Belt: place and politics in the age of anger. *British Journal of Sociology* 68(S1): S120–S152.

Papanastasiou, N. (2019) *The Politics of Scale in Policy: Scalecraft and Education Governance*. Bristol: Policy Press.

Peck, J. (2012) Austerity urbanism. *City: Analysis of Urban Trends, Culture, Theory, Policy, Action* 16(6): 626–655.

Phinney, S. (2018) Detroit's municipal bankruptcy: racialised geographies of austerity. *New Political Economy* 23(5): 609–626.

Prince, R. (2017) Local or global policy? Thinking about policy mobility with assemblage and topology. *Area* 49(3): 335–341.

Rajaram, P.K. and Grundy-Warr, C. (eds) (2007) *Borderscapes: Hidden Geographies and Politics at Territory's Edge*. Minneapolis: University of Minnesota Press.

Rose, N. (1985) *The Psychological Complex: Psychology, Politics and Society in England, 1869–1939*. London: Routledge and Kegan Paul.

Savage, G. (2019) What is policy assemblage? *Territory, Politics, Governance*. https://doi.org/10.1080/21622671.2018.1559760

Sharkey, N. (2018) The impact of gender and race bias in AI. *Humanitarian Law and Policy*. https://blogs.icrc.org/law-and-policy/2018/08/28/impact-gender-race-bias-ai/

Slaughter, A. (2004) *A New World Order*. Princeton, NJ: Princeton University Press.

Williams, F. (1995) Race, ethnicity, gender and class in welfare states. *Social Politics: International Studies in Gender, State and Society* 2(1): 127–159.

Index

Page numbers for figures appear in *italics*.